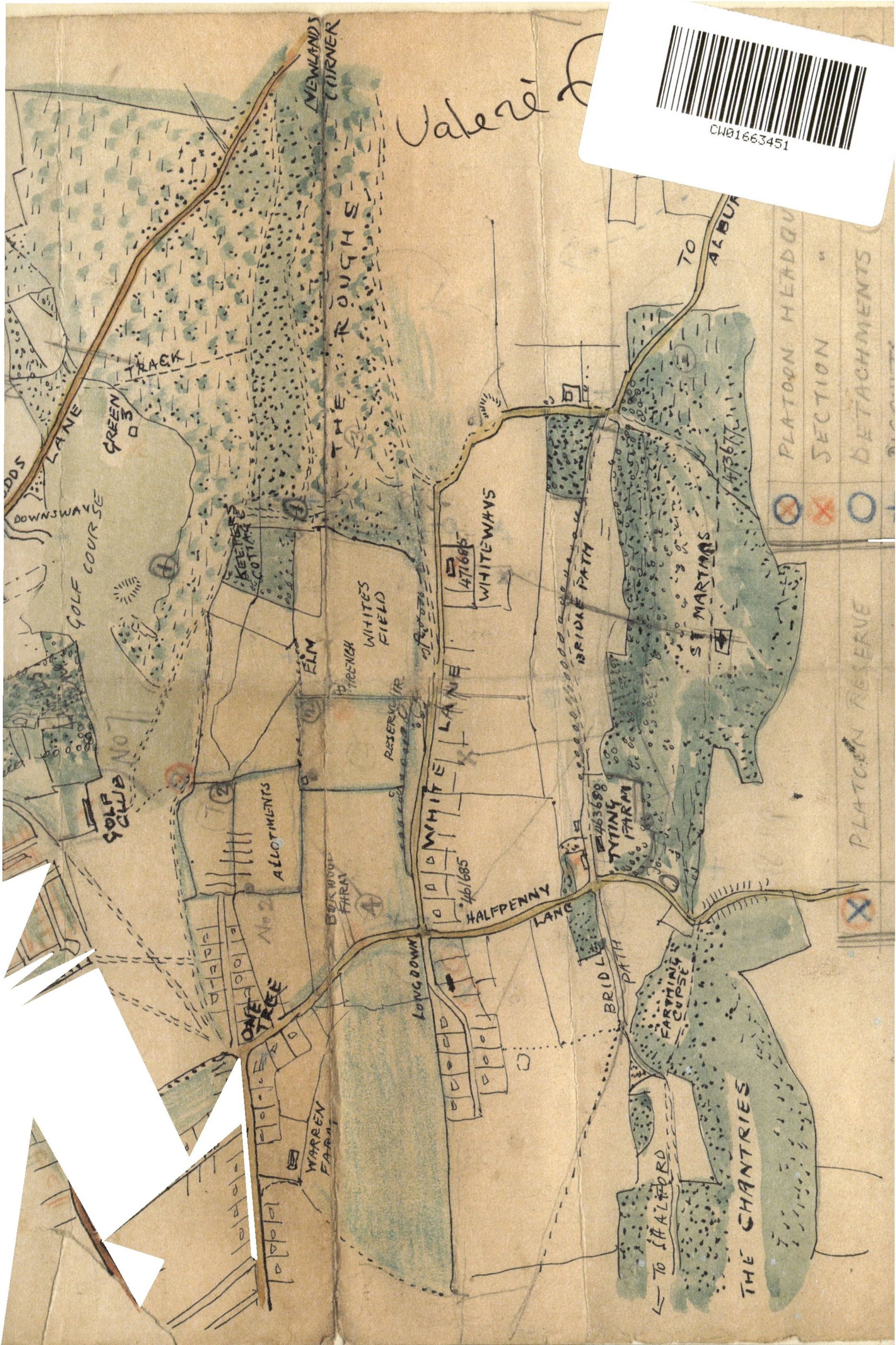
NEWLANDS CORNER
THE ROUGHS
Valerie
TO ALBURY
PLATOON HEADQU
SECTION
DETACHMENTS
PLATOON RESERVE
LANE
GREEN 3
TRACK
DOWNSWAYS
GOLF COURSE
KEEPERS COTTAGE
WHITEWAYS
471685
WHITES FIELD
TRENCH
ELM
RESERVOIR
WHITE LANE
BRIDLE PATH
ST MARTHAS
473677
TYTING FARM
463688
No 1
GOLF CLUB
ALLOTMENTS
No 2
BURROWS FARM
461685
HALFPENNY LANE
LONGDOWN
ONE TREE
WARREN FARM
BRIDLE PATH
FARMING COPSE
TO SHALFORD
THE CHANTRIES

The Story of

E H Shepard

THE MAN WHO DREW POOH

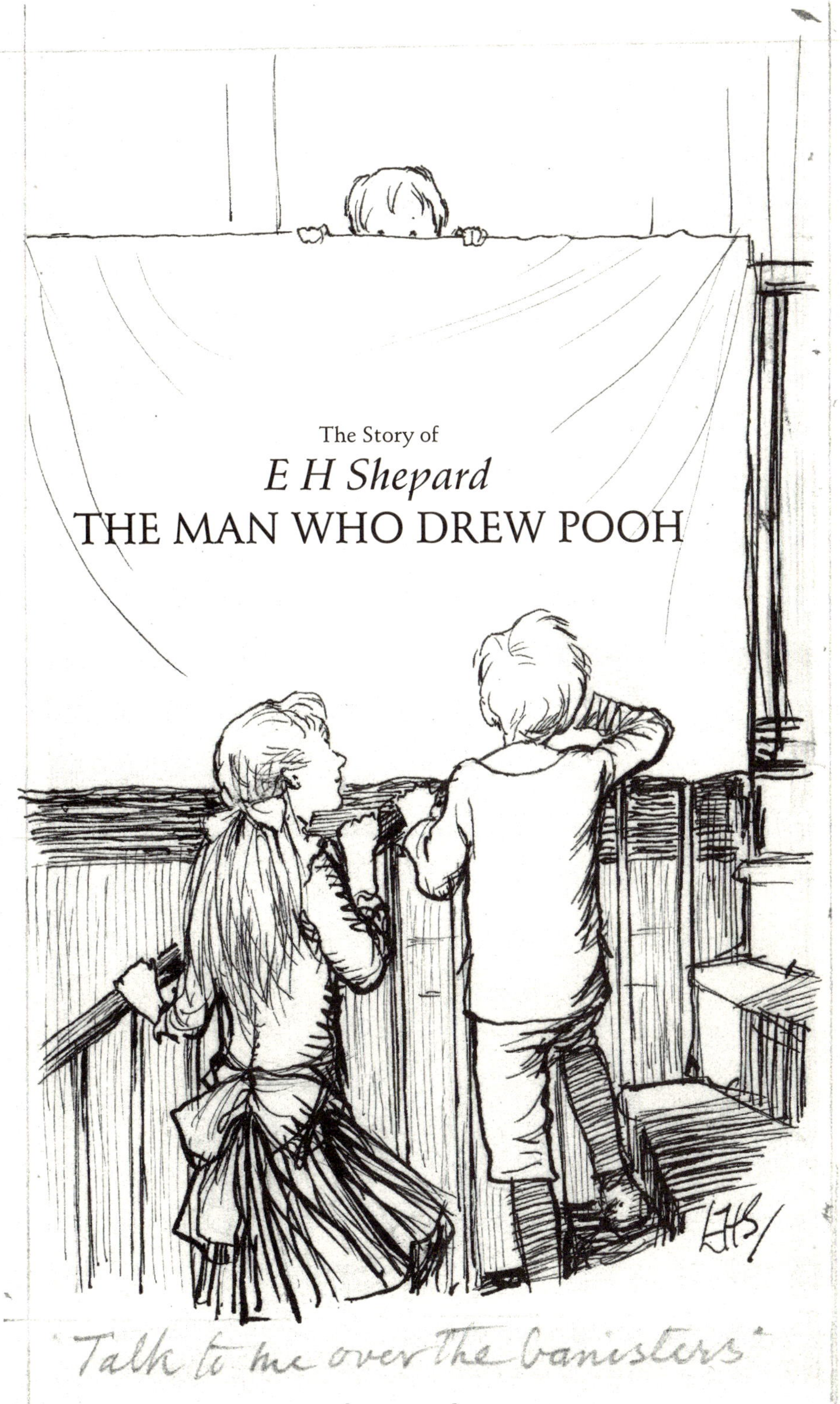

THE OFFICE OF TRH THE DUKE AND DUCHESS OF KENT
ST. JAMES'S PALACE
LONDON SW1A 1BQ

TELEPHONE: (0171) 930 4872
FACSIMILE: (0171) 930 1223
E-MAIL: kent.office@btinternet.com

Foreword

Ernest Shepard, one of the greatest book illustrators, moved to Guildford upon his marriage and lived there for fifty-one years. He felt, therefore, that his papers should be deposited in the local university and placed them there personally four years before his death.

The University of Surrey is privileged to hold this unique collection which is available to students and researchers. This book will enable the archive to be brought to life and for the information, normally restricted to a few, to be shared by others throughout the world.

Edward

H.R.H. The Duke of Kent, KG

'Through the Shepard Archive'

The Story of

E H Shepard
'THE MAN WHO DREW POOH'

Arthur R Chandler

Jaydem Books
Winkinswood Farm
West Sussex
RH14 OPQ

First published in Great Britain in 2000 by Jaydem Books
Winkinswood Farm
West Sussex
RH14 OPQ

A catalogue record for this book is available from the British Library.

ISBN 1903368022

Designed by Geoffrey A.J.Butcher FCSD
Printed by Eurolitho, Milan

To

Minette Hunt,

the only grandchild of Ernest Shepard,

and her family

The Author's thanks are recorded to:
The Vice Chancellor of the University of Surrey for his support
Terry Shand for supporting this special publication
Angela Rossetti for her research work
Jennifer Ferguson for technical assistance
Caroline Sherlock for genealogy research
Valerie Lewis Chandler for the index.

All Royalties donated to the Shepard Archive Fund

Contents

Chapter 1
Through the Shepard Archive

In his will, Ernest Howard Shepard asked that no biography should be written until thirty years after his death. Therefore this book does not attempt to tell his life story but takes a look 'through the Shepard Archive' at the University of Surrey.

The Collection arrived in April 1974 when Ernest Shepard visited the University and presented to the Vice Chancellor the residue of his drawings, manuscripts, papers, diaries and memorabilia. The gift was carefully stored and made available to research students.

Nineteen years later the University Archivist was handed this unique collection and he immediately set about finding its true content (and incidentally its true value). Nobody had realised the amount of unknown material that was stored in the boxes and filing cabinet drawers and it soon became obvious that such a special and valuable Collection needed rehousing in its own section of the University Archive.

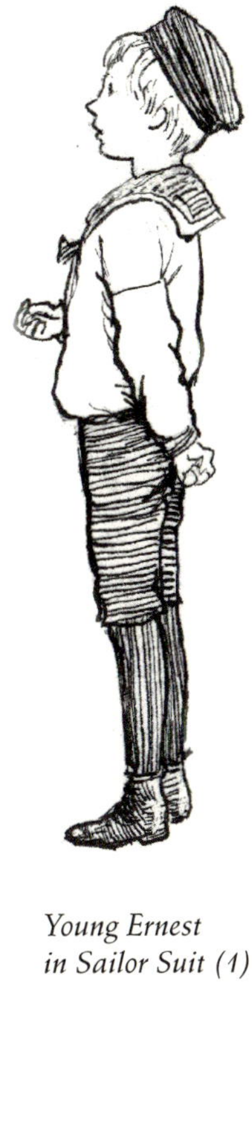

Young Ernest in Sailor Suit (1)

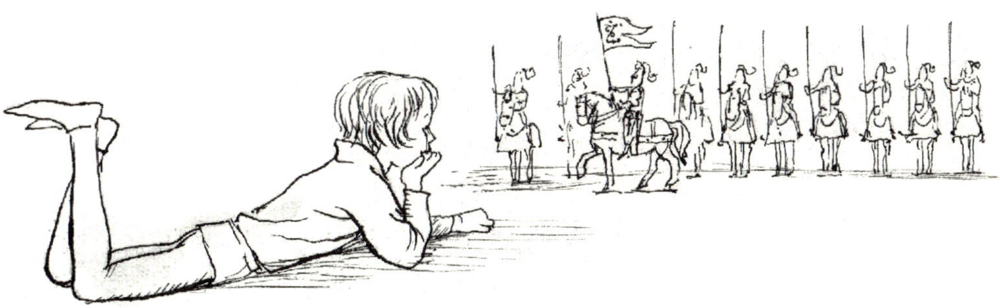

In Shining Ranks across the Nursery Floor from 'Royal Reflections' (2)

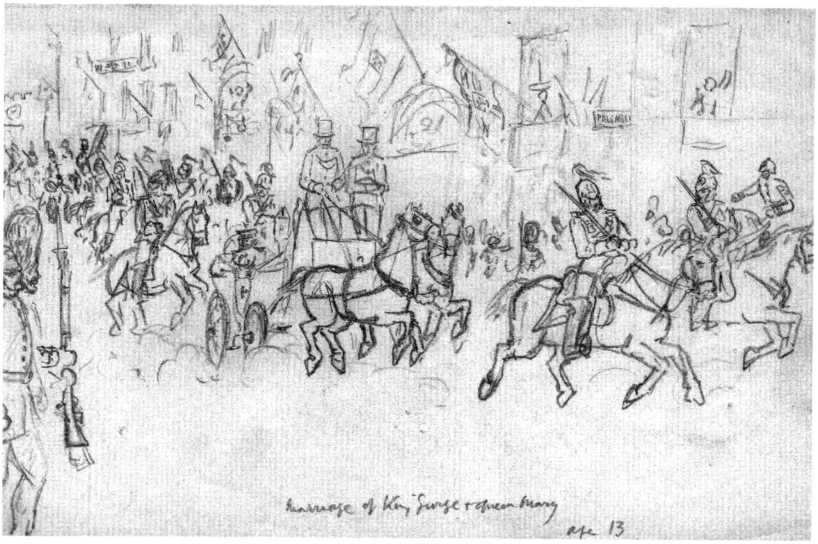

Marriage procession of Duke and Duchess of York, later King George V and Queen Mary drawn by Ernest when aged 13 (3)

At University expense, such an area was created into which the Shepard Archive was able to move in April 1998.

The Shepard Archive consists of :

- Fifty-three hand-written diaries.
- Manuscripts for *Drawn from Life, Drawn from Memory, Betsy and Joe, Lamb* and various minor works.
- School exercise books, notebooks and sketchbooks showing his comments and sketches covering seventy-nine years.
- Over three thousand letters are held: i) 1914-1918, ii) private letters, iii) thirteen folders of business transactions.
- Photographs of his family and his war service in Italy.

- *Punch* drawings including three hundred and sixty-seven headings for Charivari twenty cartoons to do with wartime and special events, and thirty-nine others.
- Pencil sketches being fifty-six early drawings, thirteen war drawings, thirty for *Little One's Log*, forty-nine for *Let's Pretend*, and one hundred and five for *Drawn from Life*.
- Pen and ink drawings include eighty for *Ben and Brock*, fifty for *Betsy and Joe*, forty-four for *Drawn from Memory* and sixty-five for *Drawn from Life*.

The vast majority of drawings for *Winnie-the-Pooh* and *The House at Pooh Corner* are in other collections. The Shepard Archive holds fourteen of these pencil sketches, the coloured cover design for *The Pooh Cook Book* and two coloured paintings, dated 1970, of Piglet and Eeyore playing instruments for a Pooh Orchestra.

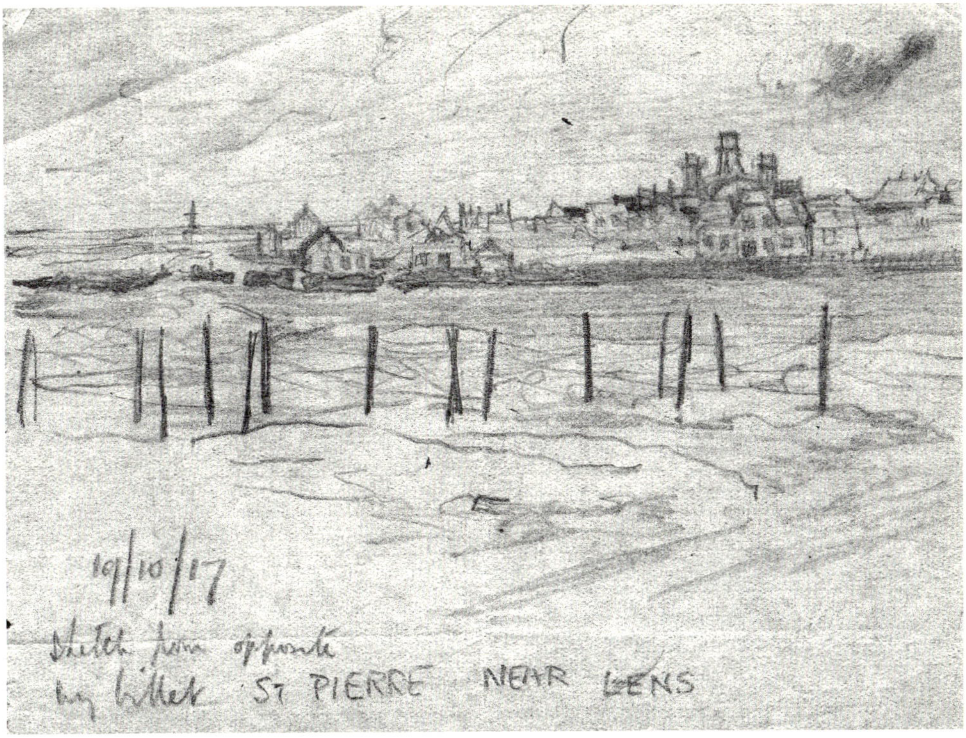

Sketch from Opposite Shepard's Billet at St Pierre, near Lens (4)

The Archive must be one of the most important resources on E H Shepard in the world. This book covers a span of ninety years and enables us to see pictures, the originals of which are held by the University, and to delve into written information that he presented to us during his lifetime. All research material has been taken directly from the Shepard Archive. Some of the pictures have not been published before and it is hoped that the text will act as notes to put the time of their drawing into their social context and tell the reader something of the artistry and talent of this great illustrator

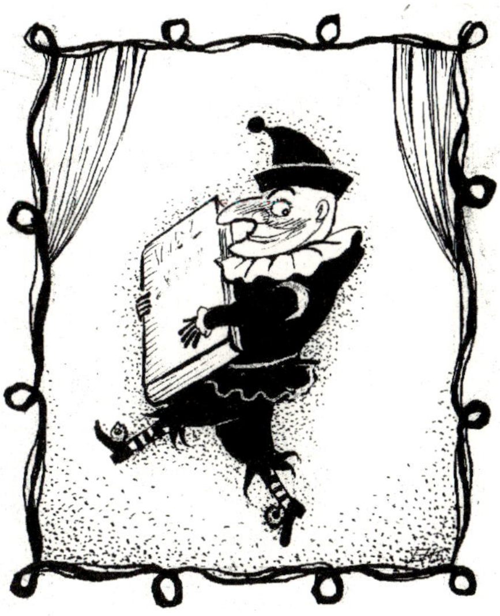

Mr Punch (5)

SHEPARD FAMILY TREE

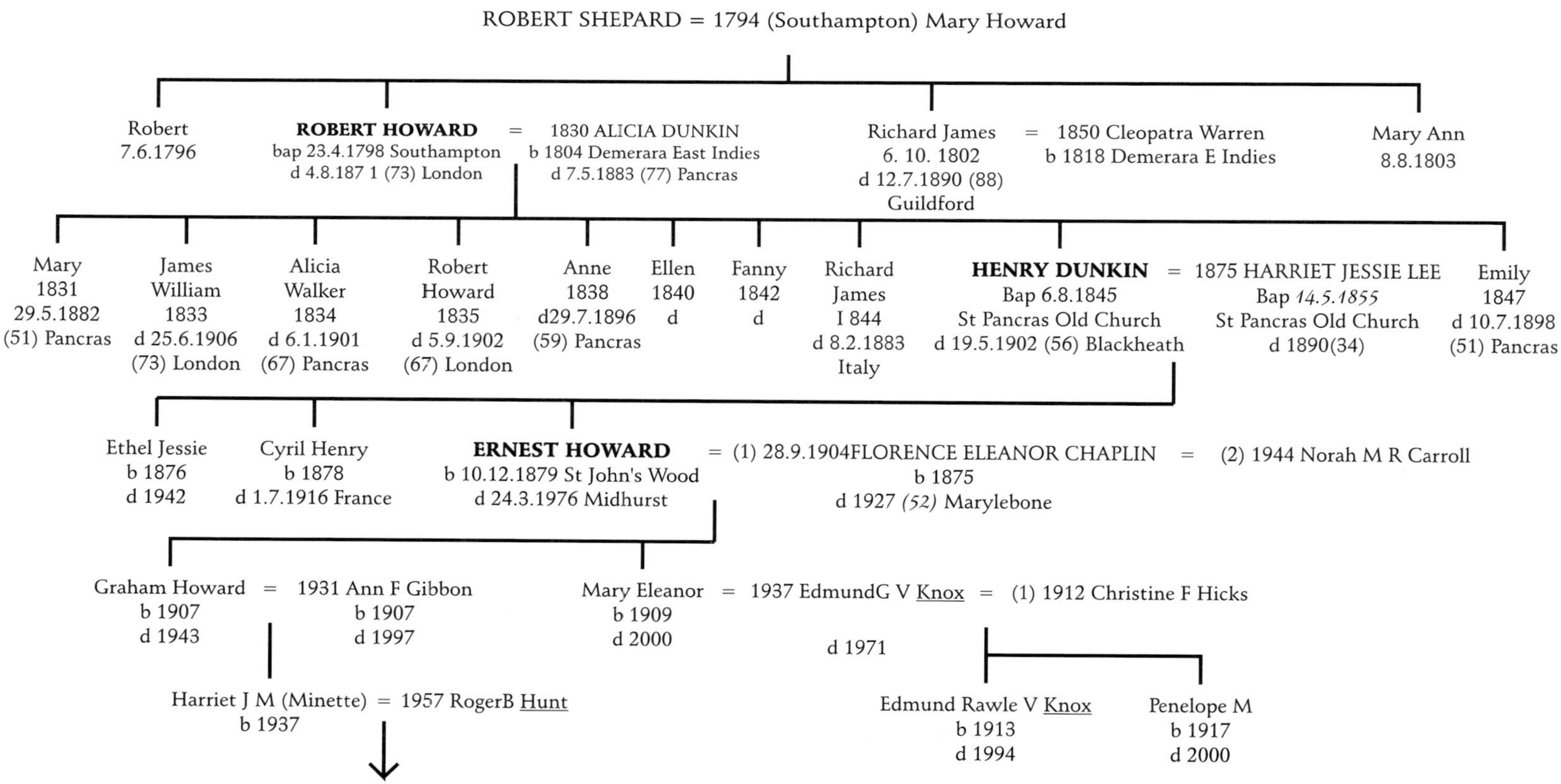

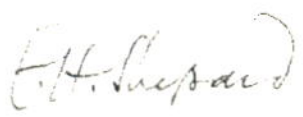

Chapter 2

The Shepard Family 1798 - 1890

To most people the name E H Shepard is synonymous with Winnie-the-Pooh. To some the name conjures up the cartoons in *Punch*. To the art historian Ernest Shepard is not only a master of line drawing but is also one of the great illustrators of the early twentieth century.

In order to see what made this man we have been able to look through his personal archive at the University of Surrey and find the ingredients that created the artist.

No person is immune to the inheritance of the genes of his ancestors or to the various influences of the many people around him throughout his life. Before studying the story of Ernest Shepard we need to look into the mid-nineteenth century family which preceded him.

His paternal grandfather was Robert Howard Shepard who was born in 1798. Robert's younger brother, Richard James, was born in 1802 in Southampton. In those days this was a great trading port on the south coast and may well have had some influence on the lives of the two brothers for they married women who were born eight years apart at Demerara in the East Indies, islands with which Southampton had considerable trade in the nineteenth century.

In 1830 at St George's Church, Bloomsbury, Robert, the elder brother, married twenty-four year old Alicia Dunkin. Twenty years later the younger brother, Richard, married Cleopatra Warren at Holy Trinity Church, Brompton. She was then aged thirty-two. Robert had built a family home at Guildown in 1844 and when Richard was married six years later he also became attracted to the area and set up a home in Guildford. He lived there throughout his married life and served as a founder member of the Surrey Royal County Hospital where he died in his eighty-ninth year.

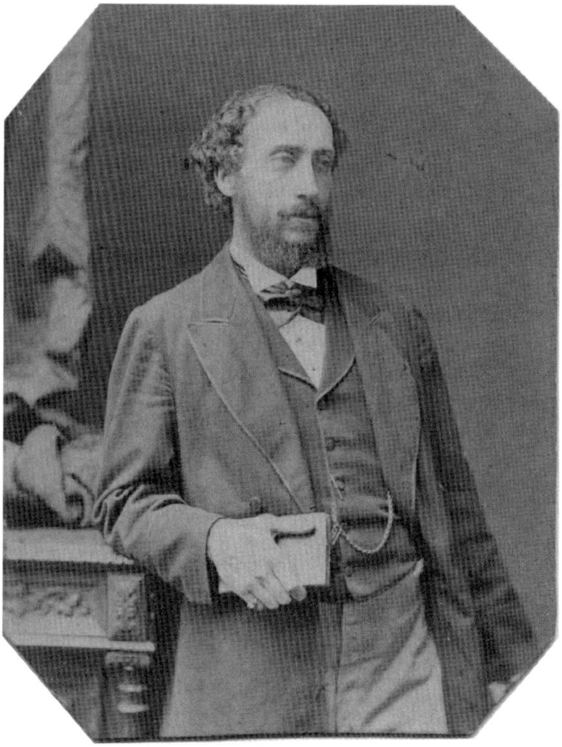

Henry Dunkin Shepard, 1845-1902
Photograph taken just
before his marriage in 1875 (7)

Guildford is to loom large in the Shepard story that is to unfold.

Robert had a family of ten children, four sons and six daughters. Of the four sons, James was ordained in the Church of England, married and became Senior Master of St Paul's School in London. Robert Junior also married and became a member of Lloyds. The third son, Richard, went to Italy and died there at the age of thirty-eight. The youngest son was Henry Dunkin Shepard (7) who was born in 1845 and lived to the age of fifty-six. Henry became an architect and acted as advisor to the University College Hospital in London. He married Harriet Jessie Lee (8) at St Pancras Church, London in 1875. She was the daughter of William Lee, a well-known watercolour artist at the time. They had three children, Ethel born in 1876, Cyril in 1878 and the youngest, Ernest Howard Shepard who was born at St John's Wood in the year 1879.

A highly respected architect, Henry would have been proficient in the use of both pen and pencil. As the daughter of a painter, and possibly with ability herself, Harriet knew the importance of encouraging her offspring to use their inherited talents.

In their house in Kent Terrace situated in St John's Wood in North West London, Henry and Harriet instilled in their younger son the idea that he should always have a pencil in his hand, always have paper nearby, and always be ready to draw anything that interested him.

This advice was readily accepted by the young Ernest and was diligently acted on. It remained with him as a guiding light throughout the whole of his life. He would draw anything, anywhere, at any time, as can be seen from many of Shepard's notebooks that have survived. He would draw on the back of not only his own work, but also on the back of his brother's Latin translations. This passion continued as he grew older and he would include drawings in many of his personal letters.

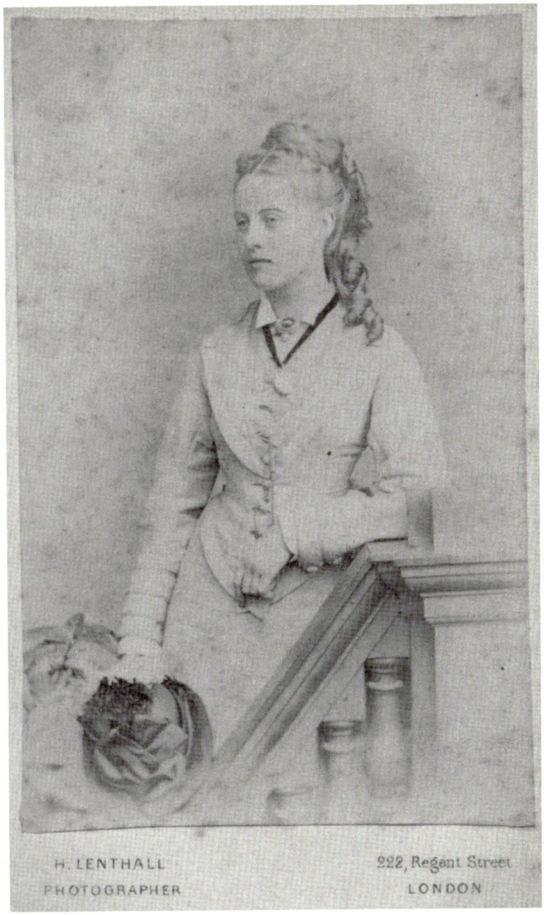

Harriet Jessie Lee,
taken when aged 17 (8)

He had a photographic memory and could reproduce any scene that he had witnessed, even one from an event that had taken place years earlier, with uncanny accuracy. Sometimes a page in his notebook would show a few lines and a few words describing colours and textures. From that one page of scrappy notes he was able to produce a complete painting or drawing.

As a young child he thoroughly enjoyed going to school and spent four happy years at the Church of England School in Baker Street (9). On his seventh birthday his godmother gave him a wooden horse on wheels (10). This magnificent toy was christened 'Septimus' and became one of Ernest's most treasured possessions. The horse stood outside their house in St John's Wood 'with eyes dilated and distended nostrils pawing the air with his two forelegs as though yearning to discard his three wooden wheels'. He later went to the Prep School of St Paul's where began the internal tug of war between the academic subjects which he studied reluctantly and the sketching which he naturally and thoroughly enjoyed.

When the young family was at home, the three children Ethel, Cyril and Ernest would sing together with Ethel playing the piano. Later in life she became a very good pianist and Ernest painted portraits of her, one of which was shown in a Royal Academy Summer Exhibition.

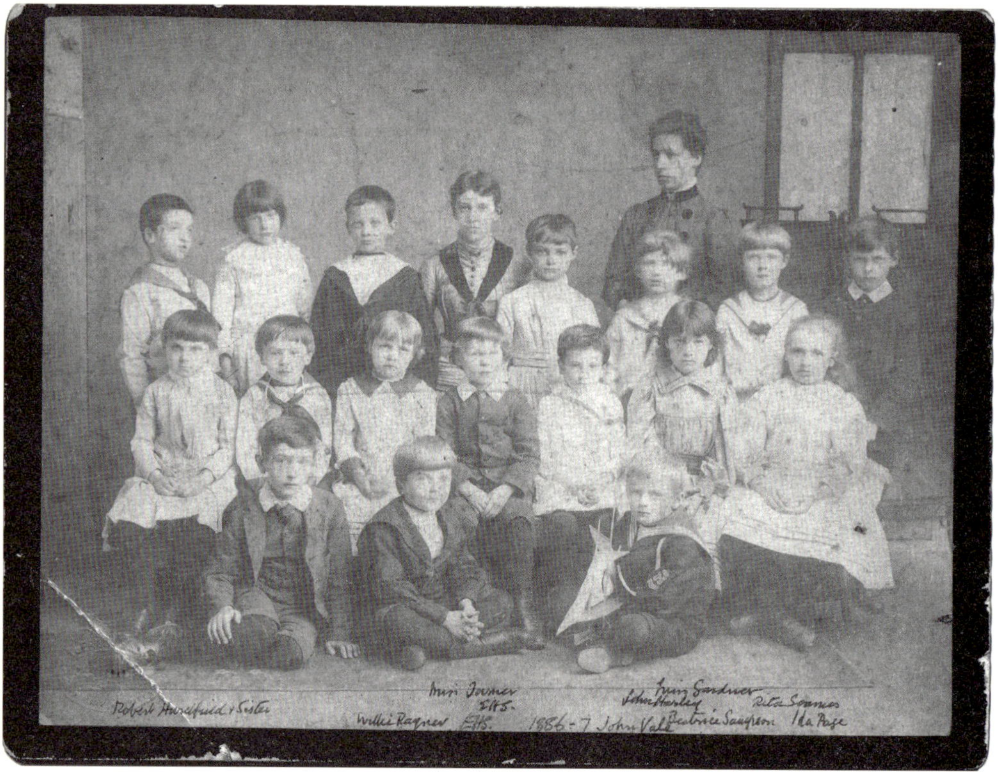

Infants School Baker Street, 1886-1887.
Ernest in the middle of his class (9)

Ernest was able to express himself not only with his drawings and paintings, but he was also able to show his powers of observation by the written word. While on holiday in London with his father in June 1888, he wrote a very descriptive letter to his mother (15).

In 1889 the happy family atmosphere in the Shepard household changed considerably as Harriet first became ill and then became bedridden. She was only able to go out of doors when pushed in a wheelchair. It seems, however, that the three children accepted her illness as a natural part, and even a progression, of their life style and willingly carried trays up to their mother's bedroom as a normal daily task.

In April of the following year, 1890, the family life in Kent Terrace was completely shattered at a stroke when Henry suddenly sent his three children to live at the home of his sisters at 53 Gordon Square, Bloomsbury. Ernest was only eleven years old, his brother Cyril was 12 and his sister Ethel was 14. Their mother died soon afterwards.

The Gordon Square house was the London home of the Shepards, having been built by Robert Howard Shepard for his family. After his death, in 1871, his widow and ten children lived there together with a variety of servants. By the time the three motherless Shepards arrived at Gordon Square in 1890, the household had been reduced to four unmarried daughters: Alicia, Annie, Fanny and Emily. In addition there were members of a now reduced household staff consisting of five maids, a charwoman and an odd job man.

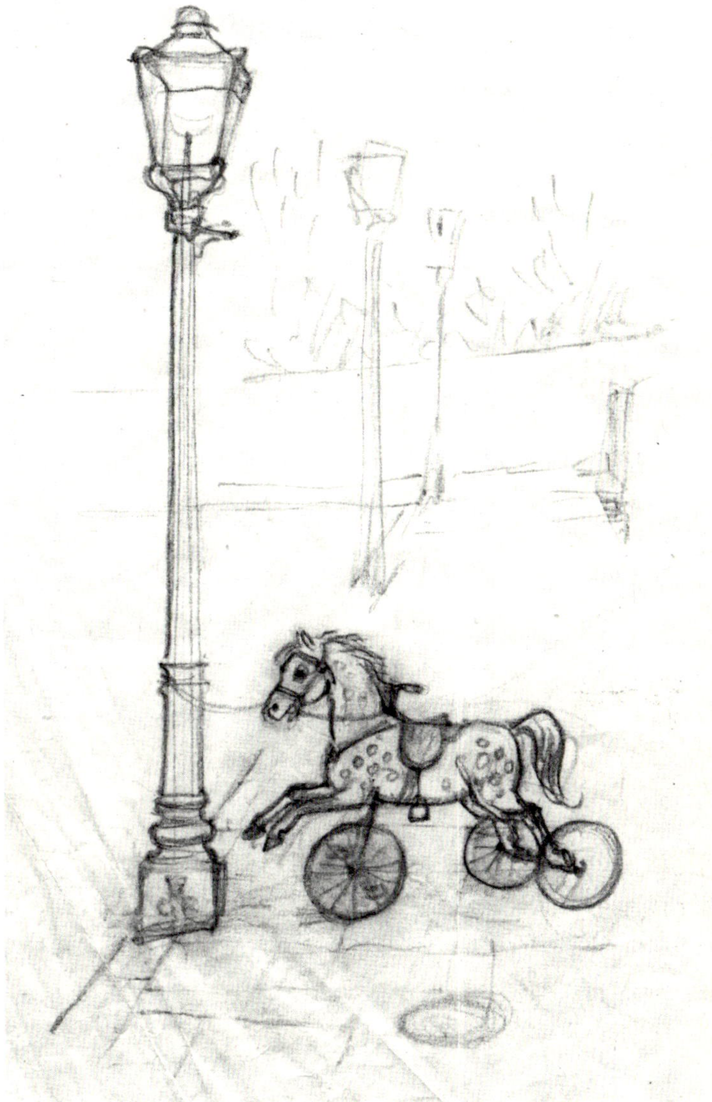

Septimus (10)

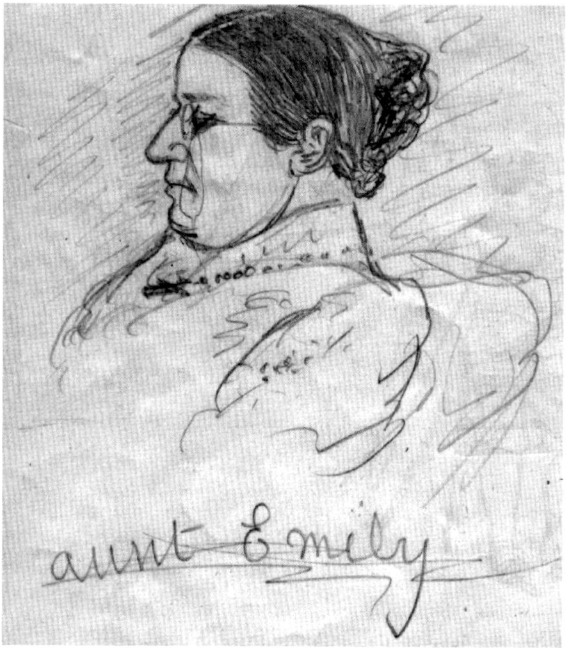

Aunt Emily (11)

The four maiden aunts (11, 12,13,14) must have proved a formidable team for the young Ernest and his siblings. As one can read in *Drawn from Life,* Shepard's autobiography, the influence of these aunts was considerable and seemingly to the benefit of all concerned. In general, the three children respected and loved their aunts. They very quickly became a coherent family that had its own set of rules although these were often very different from those that had been followed at St John's Wood.

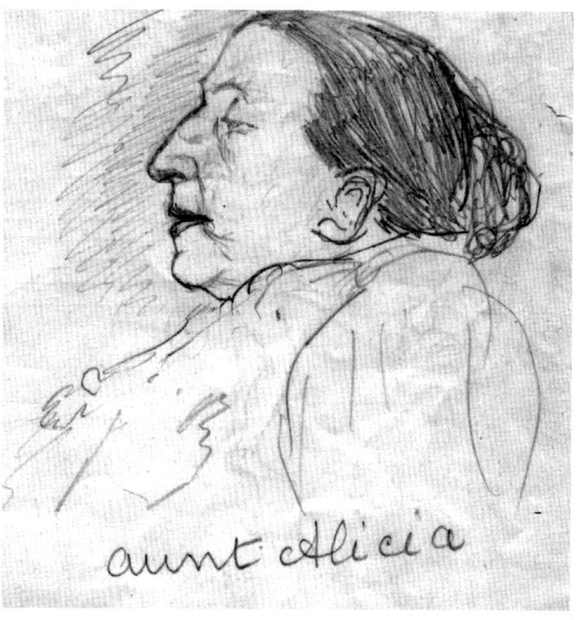

Aunt Alicia, (my godmother) (12)

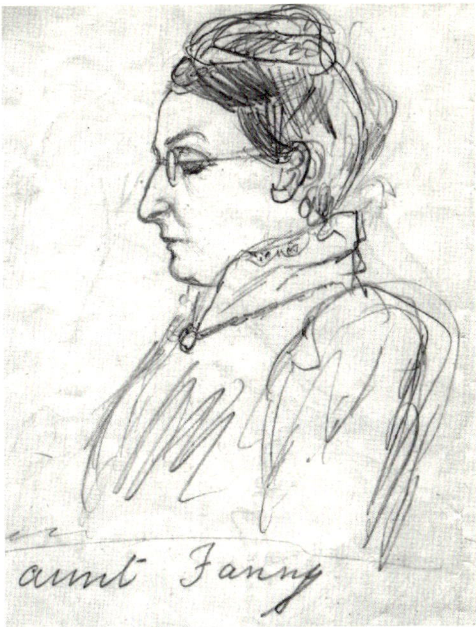

Aunt Fanny,
"the energetic one" (13)

However, some days were obviously better than others for the children. Sunday was the worst day of the week. That day had little to offer. That day the rules were those of a purely adult household.

As a complete family they would go to St Pancras Church but upon returning to the house at Gordon Square they would find that the servants had put away all their toys, and all secular reading was forbidden. The publications that were normally around, *The Illustrated London News* and *Punch* were nowhere to be seen.

Aunt Annie (14)

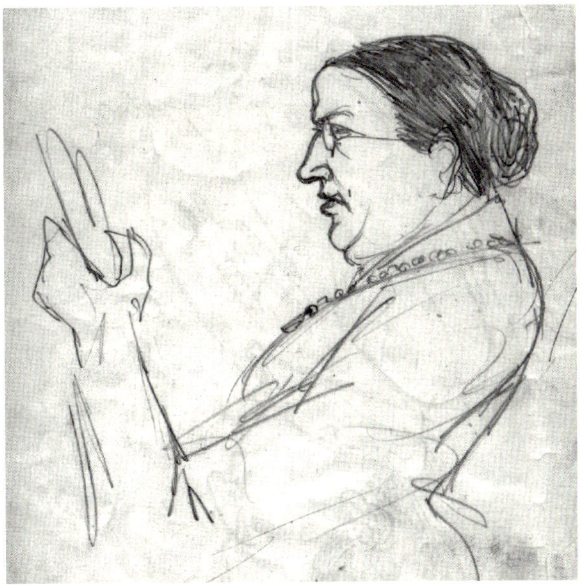

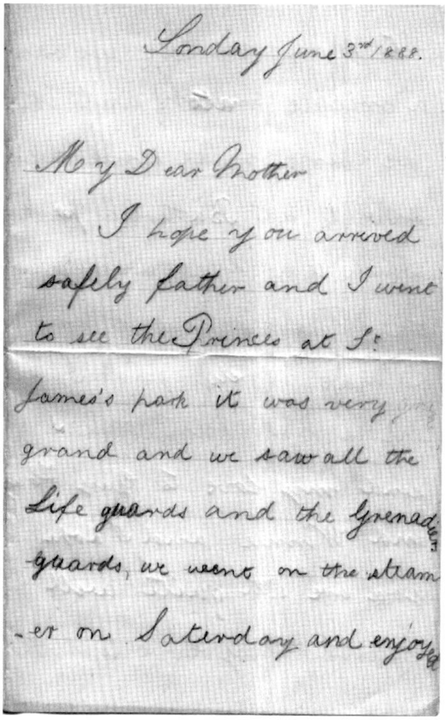
London June 3rd 1888.

My Dear Mother

I hope you arrived safely father and I went to see the Princes at St James's park it was very grand and we saw all the Life guards and the Grenadier guards, we went on the steam -er on Saturday and enjoyed

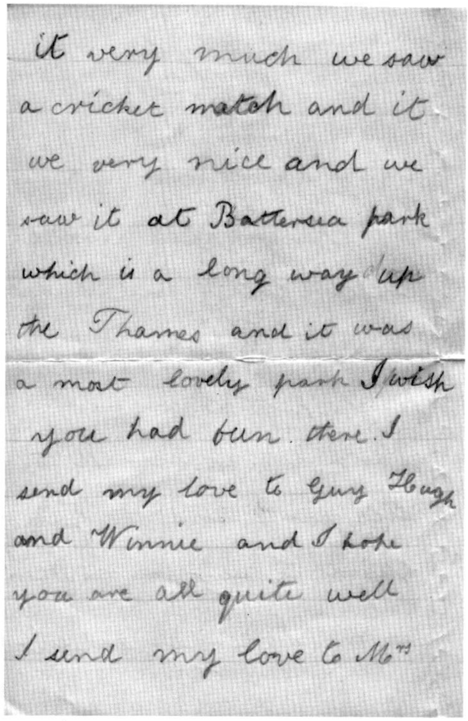
it very much we saw a cricket match and it we very nice and we saw it at Battersea park which is a long way up the Thames and it was a most lovely park I wish you had fun there. I send my love to Guy Hugh and Winnie and I hope you are all quite well I send my love to Mrs

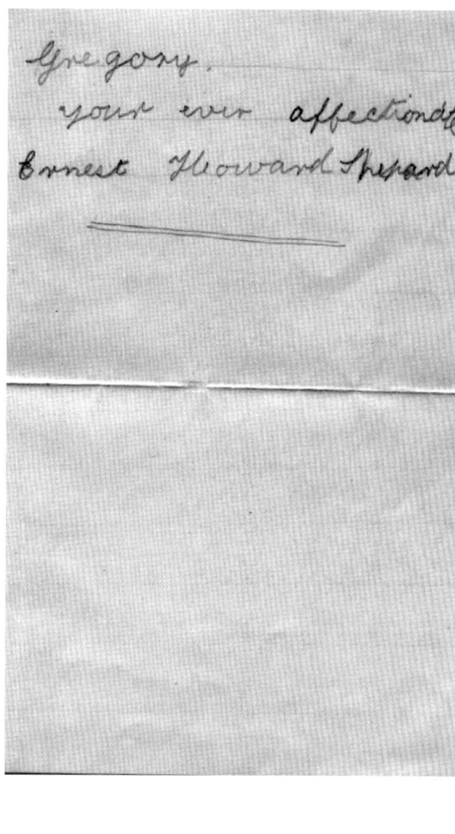
Gregory,

your ever affectionate

Ernest Howard Shepard.

Letter to his mother, from Ernest, aged nine (15)

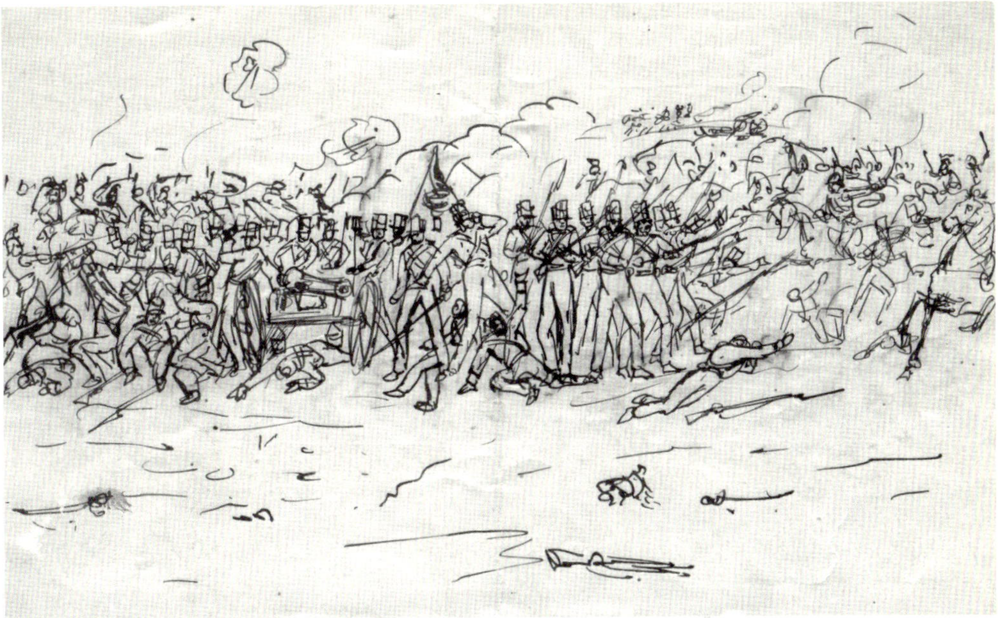

Soldiers in Battle
Pen and ink childhood drawing (16)

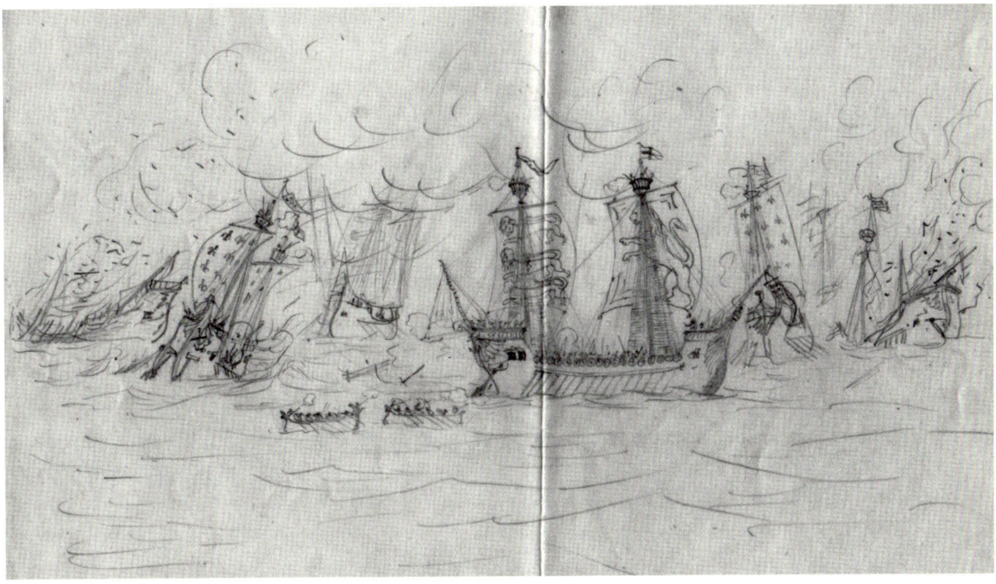

A Naval Battle
Pencil childhood drawing (17)

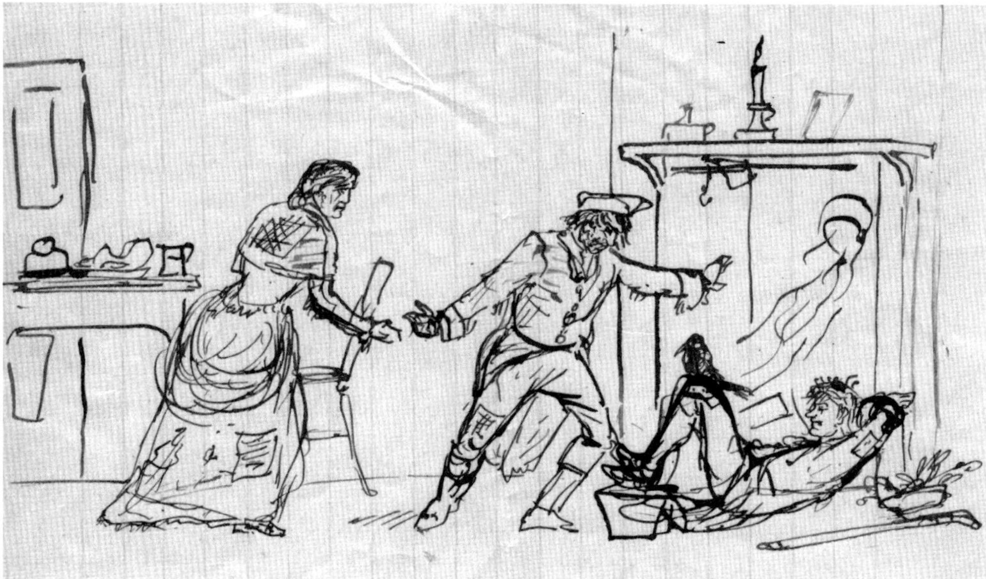

Illustration to Barnaby Rudge, *aged 12 (18)*

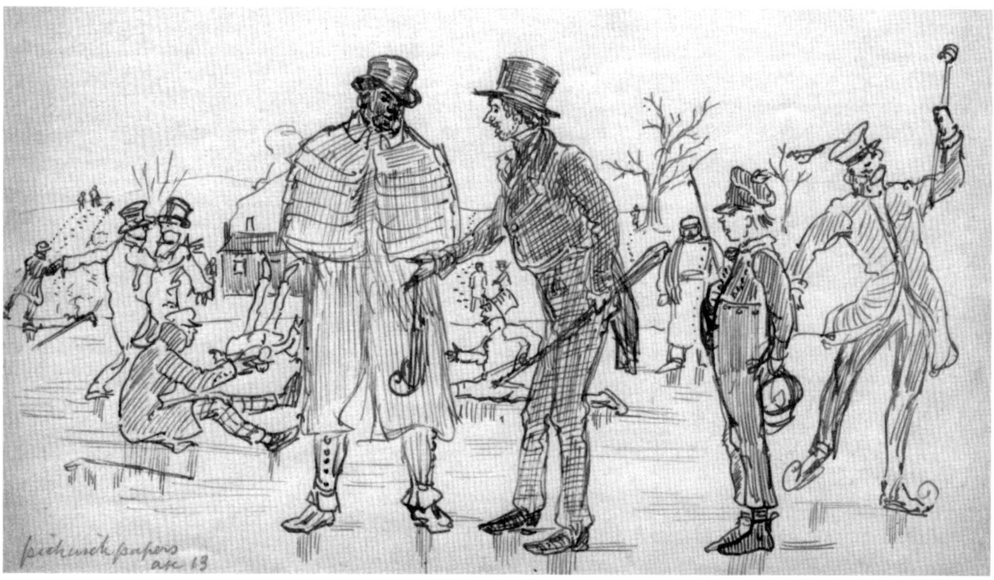

Illustration to Pickwick Papers, *aged 13 (19)*

Chapter 3
The Young Artist 1890 - 1896

Ernest was brought up in a house full of books. When his father moved into Gordon Square with the aunts soon after Harriet's funeral he took every opportunity to read aloud to his children although most of the reading was actually directed towards Ernest the youngest, then aged twelve.

At one time in his life, before setting up as an architect, Henry Shepard had had experience on the stage and often found himself acting the parts that he was reading. He was a friend of Henry Irving the great melodramatic actor and Henry Shepard with his friends founded 'The Irving Amateur Dramatic Club', one of its productions being 'Henry IV'. The Shepard children spent many hours painting and decorating flags and banners for this production which was staged at St George's Hall in West London. This interest in drama was to be further encouraged in the children when they were taken to the theatre by their father to watch performances of pantomimes and other appropriate plays.

Books in the house would have included the Dickens' favourites: *David Copperfield, Martin Chuzzlewit, Dombey and Son, The Old Curiosity Shop, Pickwick Papers* and *Barnaby Rudge*.. At the age of thirteen Ernest happily turned his attention to drawing illustrations for Dickens' stories, often on the pages of exercise books (18) (19). He also illustrated other books that he had read in the house such as *Robinson Crusoe.*

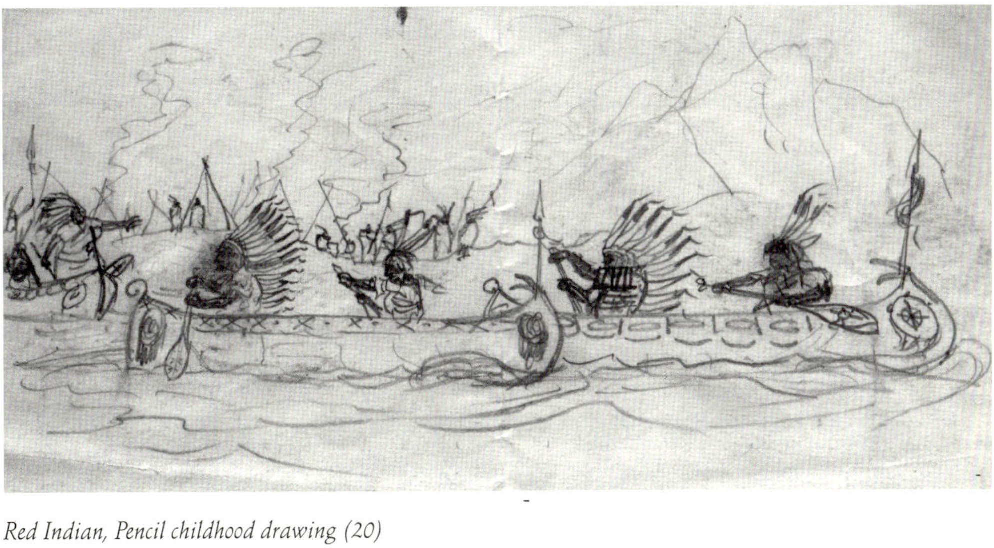

Red Indian, Pencil childhood drawing (20)

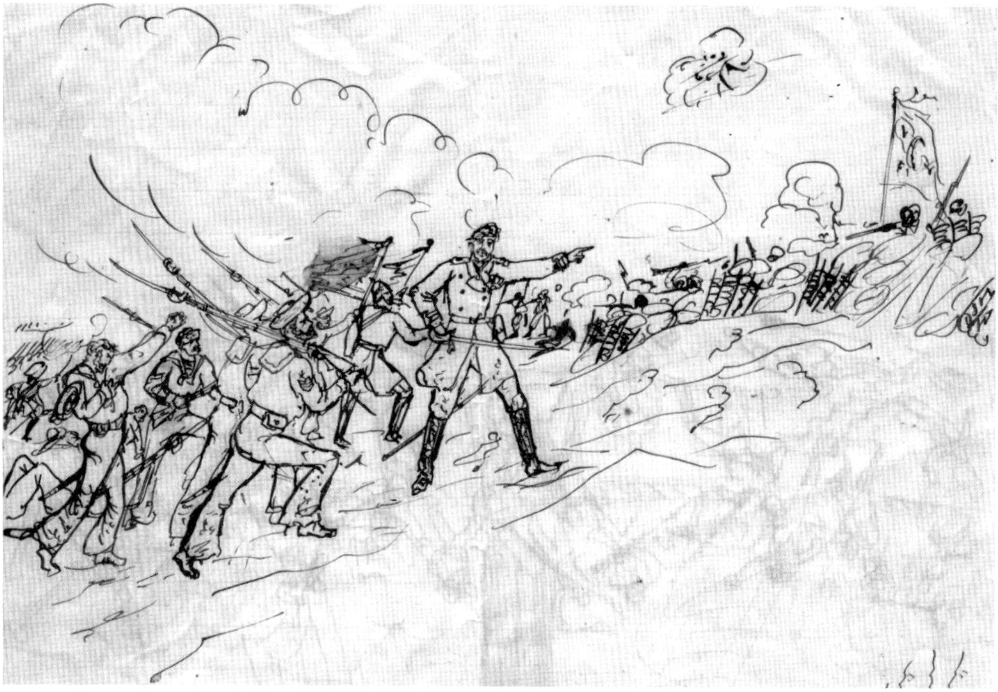

Naval Troops on Land
Pen and ink childhood drawing probably illustrating The World of Adventure *(21)*

At the time of the move to Gordon Square, possibly to help overcome his tragic loss, Ernest was given a book called *The World of Adventure*, which had just been published by Cassell. It was full of supposedly true stories and was very well illustrated. Subjects in the book included shipwrecks, fires, avalanches, and battles in India and Zululand and proved to be a mine of information. The young artist was intrigued with battles whether on land or sea, ancient or modern. It seems he was drawing about them almost every day. Ernest and his brother Cyril were both extremely keen on soldiers. They had quite an extensive toy army between them and fought many battles on the school room floor.

Ernest's father had the foresight to collect some of these drawings and decided to keep them carefully in a box which he presented to his son later in life when it was obvious that the boy was going to study art. These sketches show that he was gifted with a somewhat lively imagination although, at this time, it was mostly concerned with battle scenes! (20) (21)

His father's collection of pictures tells an incredible story of the artistic ability of a boy in his early teens. To the literary illustrations and historic battle scenes, he added contemporary sketches of events that were going on around him as he had done since the Golden Jubilee and before.

In later life he records that he and his brother had been to every pantomime at the Drury Lane Theatre for several years and after each visit he sat down and drew a scene or two from the production that had obviously impressed him. His practice of using paper sparingly is shown, as has already been seen with the drawings of his aunts, by sketching two drawings on opposite sides of the same sheet. He used this 'both sides of the paper' technique to record the performance of Harlequinade which took place at the end of the pantomime in 1892, which he had visited with his father and brother (22).

In 1887 Whiteley's, a department store in West London, caught fire. A large number of fire engines was called out to fight a fire that was not in their locality. He was taken to see the fire and, although he was only seven years old, he returned home to produce an amazing watercolour of the historic event (P.1a). On the back of this painting, circa 1891, he produced a pencil drawing of an Indian procession that included a most beautiful elephant (23).

Drury Lane Pantomime
Pen and ink drawing, aged 13 (22)

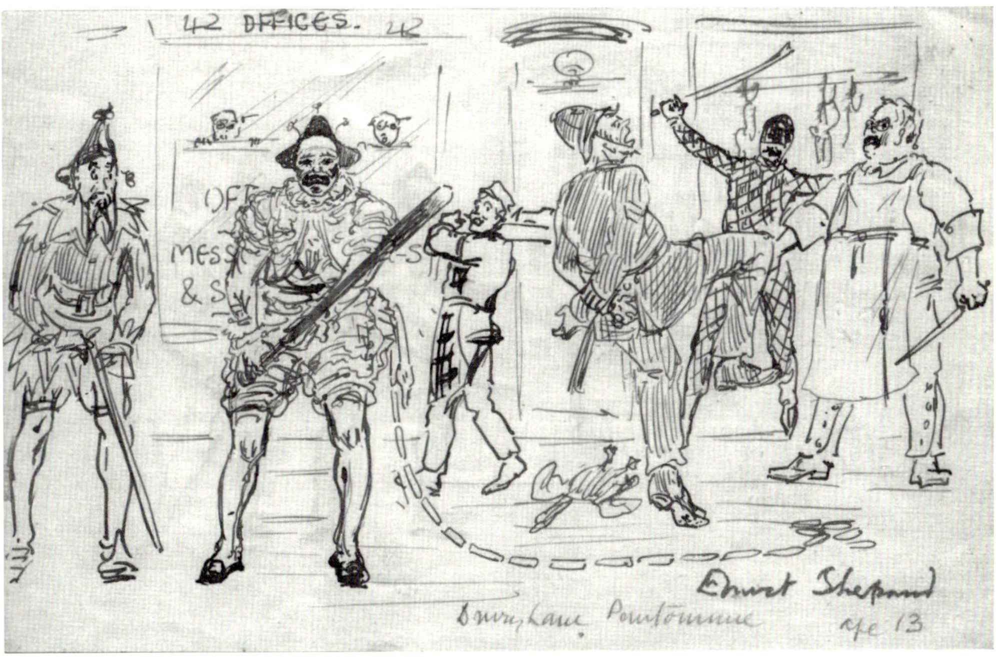

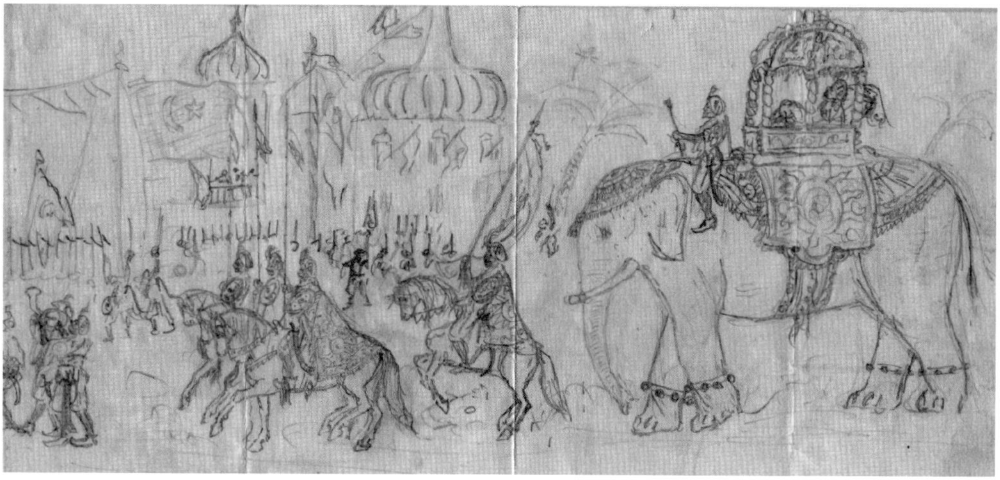

Indian Procession,
Pencil drawing, circa 1891, on the back of the painting of Whiteley's fire (23)

The year of Whiteley's fire made a great impression upon young Ernest. He chose it as the year that he was to describe in detail in one of his autobiographies. It was the Jubilee Year of Queen Victoria and one would suspect it was the year that he subconsciously, or more likely consciously, realised that he had a great gift and should record for posterity whatever he fancied. He would copy a window display that had been created to honour the Queen's Golden Jubilee. After a visit to Hampton Court he was inspired to draw a pencil sketch of 'Queen Elizabeth herself in an elaborately jewelled dress' . During the same year he travelled with his mother from London Bridge by boat to Ramsgate where to his great joy he saw the Fleet at anchor in the mouth of the Thames (27).

His ability to record history in the making is remarkable. He obviously was present at the procession of the marriage of Prince George and Princess Mary of Teck (later to be George V and Queen Mary). He drew two different aspects of this procession. One in pen and ink was drawn on the back of one of his Latin translations (24) (25). The other, on a piece of paper measuring eighteen by eleven centimetres, is of the carriage procession of the bridal pair (26). On the reverse of this he has a drawing of a detachment of the Yeomen of the Guard going to Westminster Abbey . When he was in his nineties Ernest Shepard wrote on this historical drawing 'Marriage of King George and Queen Mary, age 13'.

Ernest entered St Paul's School, where his uncle was Senior Master, at the beginning of 1892, having then attained the age of thirteen years. He left eight terms later and the High Master wrote of him "after making creditable progress for two years in his general studies he gave his time mainly to drawing and art. Experts speak well of his promise as an artist. His conduct and class notes have been excellent".

One of Ernest's friends at St. Paul's School was a boy called William Temple who, fifty years later, was to become Archbishop of Canterbury. Other contemporary pupils included G K Chesterton, the short story writer, Compton McKenzie, the novelist, and R O Schwartz, the cricketer, who had the nickname of 'Beautiful Reggie'.

While at St. Paul's his drawing ability developed. He not only used it to illustrate his school subjects such as a history essay on the Civil War (28) but also produced what probably started out as 'doodles' drawn during academic lessons but finished up as detailed figures of people and animals (29).

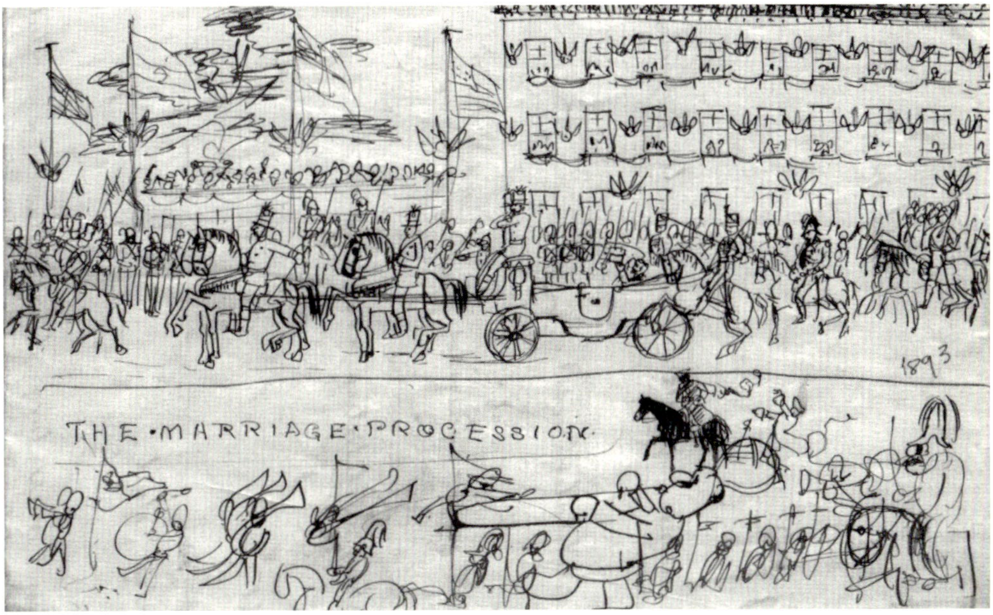

A Royal Marriage Procession Pen and ink, dated 1893
when George, Duke of York, married Princess Mary of Teck Later to be George V and Queen Mary (24)

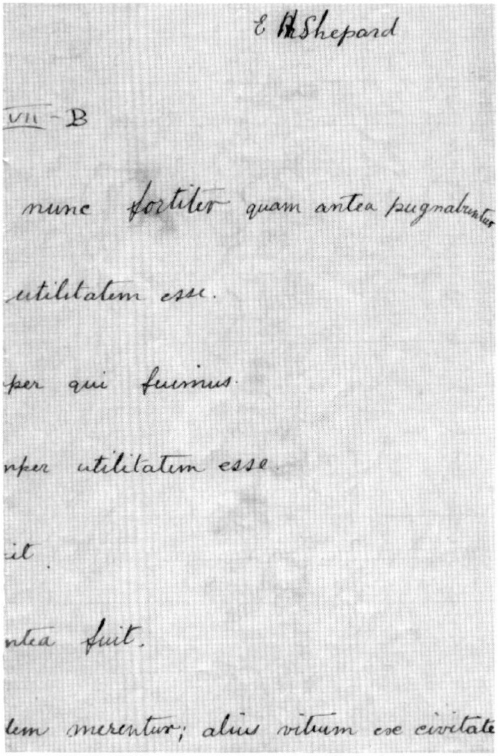

E H Shepard

VII – B

nunc fortiter quam antea pugnabantur

utilitatem esse.

per qui fuimus.

nper utilitatem esse.

it.

ntea fuit.

lem merentur; alius vitium esse civitate

Latin translation,
on the back of which was drawn
the previous picture (25)

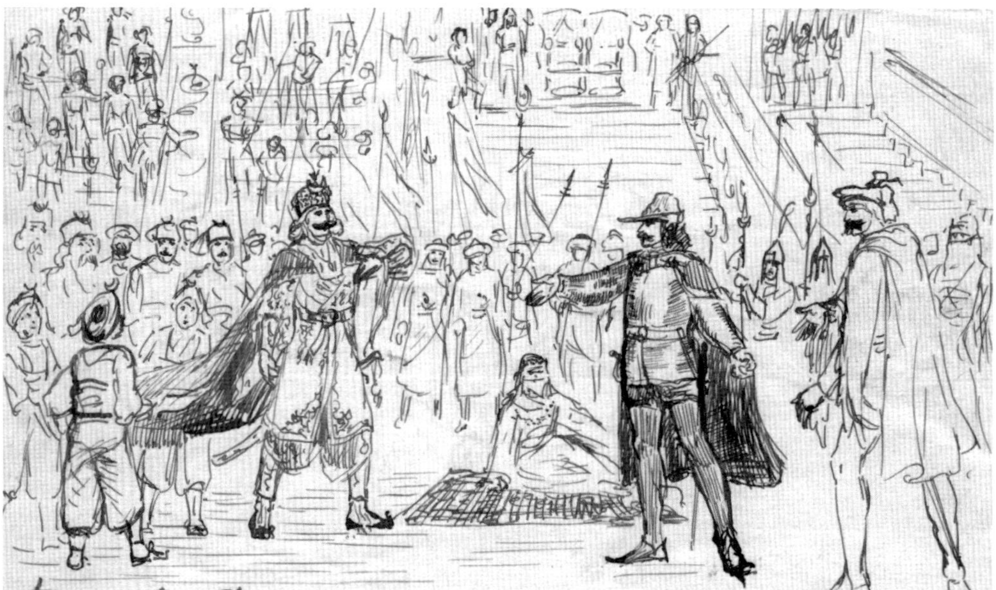

Middle East Interior Scene
Childhood drawing, signed later (26)

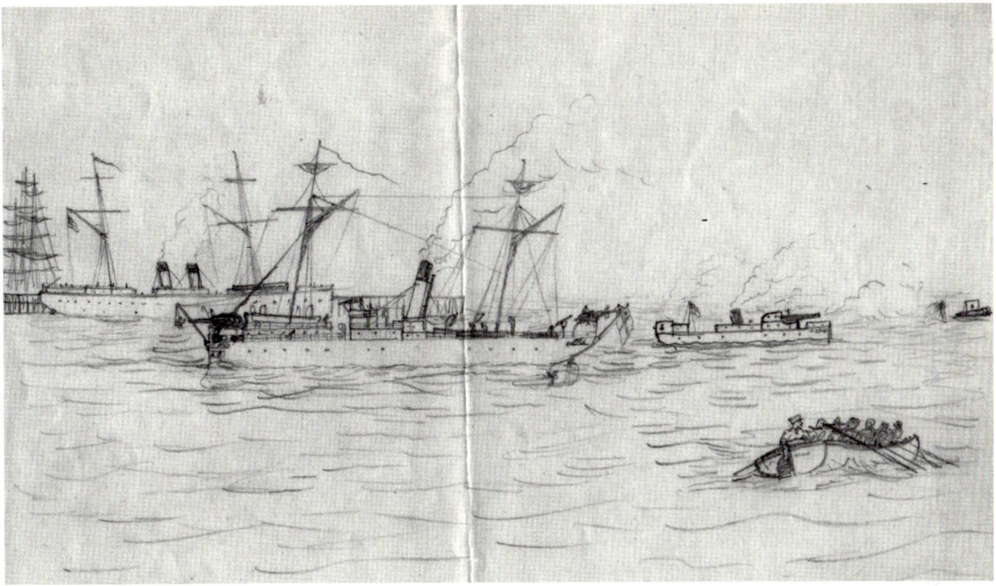

The Fleet at Anchor
Drawn by Ernest when he had travelled with his mother from London Bridge to Ramsgate by Boat (27)

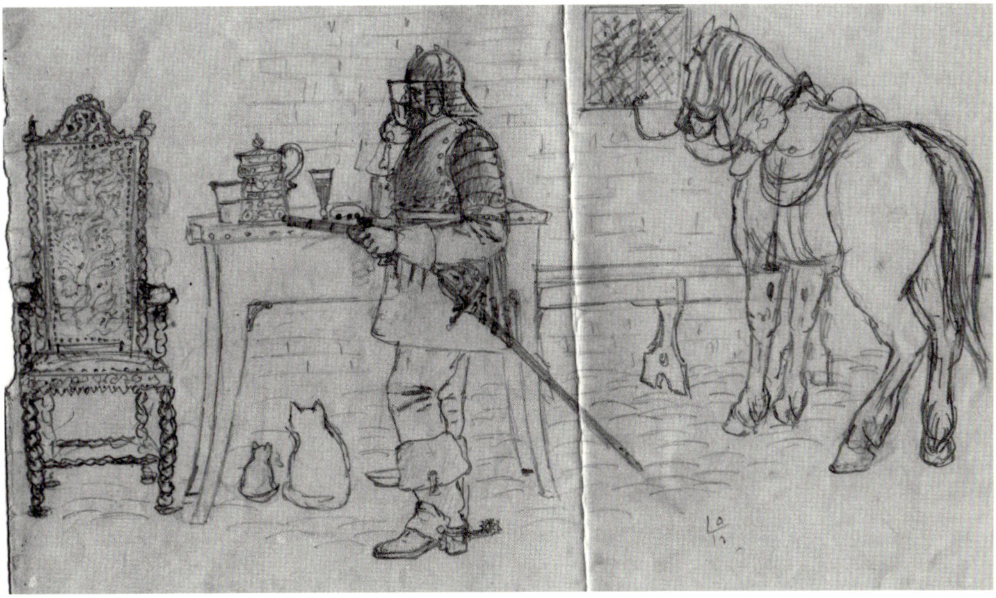

A Parliamentary Trooper and his Mount
Pencil childhood drawing (28)

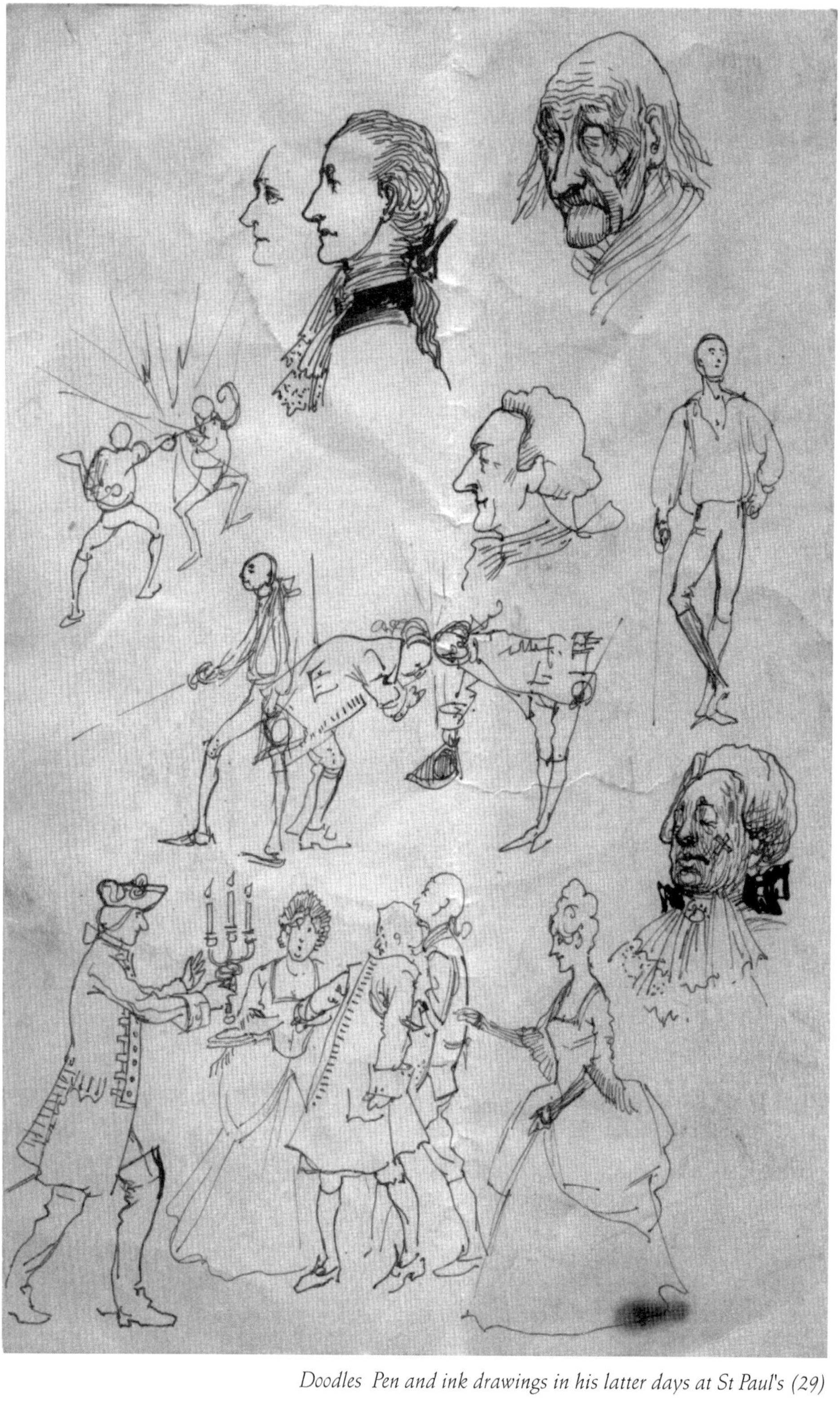

Doodles Pen and ink drawings in his latter days at St Paul's (29)

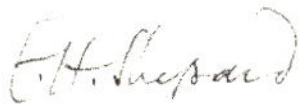

Chapter 4
Student Years 1896 - 1904

On leaving St Paul's he went on to Heatherleys School of Fine Art where he started a one-year course in 1896. While a student there, for reasons unknown, Ernest was given the nickname of 'Kipper' by which he was to be known for the rest of his life.

The school's principal at this time was John Compton. He was a man who had an imposing presence and whose criticisms were always conducted in the plural. Shepard records that while standing before one of his drawings he would say: "If we look at our legs, Mister Shepard, I think we will find them a trifle on the heavy side". Nothing seemed to upset John Compton. He never 'forgot his dignity' and was rarely seen to smile.

In his year at Heatherleys Ernest found it 'a queer old place'. He spent a lot of his time stippling antique pictures but he and his fellow students found recreation in the latter part of each day. 'Elderly' ladies came in on most days to paint from a costume model but after they had gone home the students played hockey among the casts with a paint rag rolled up for a ball.

Soldier in the Desert
Drawn in his first year as an art student (30)

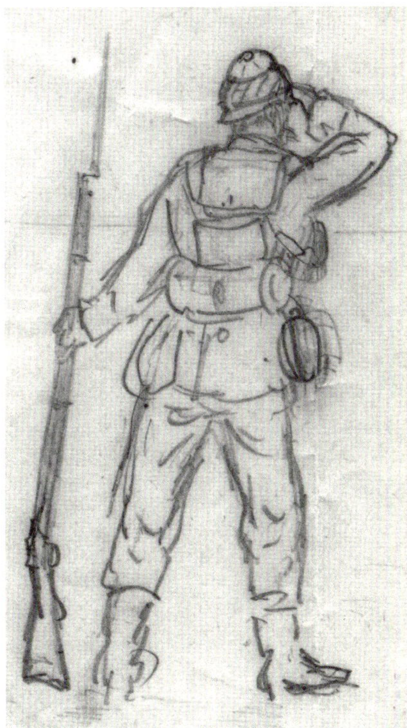

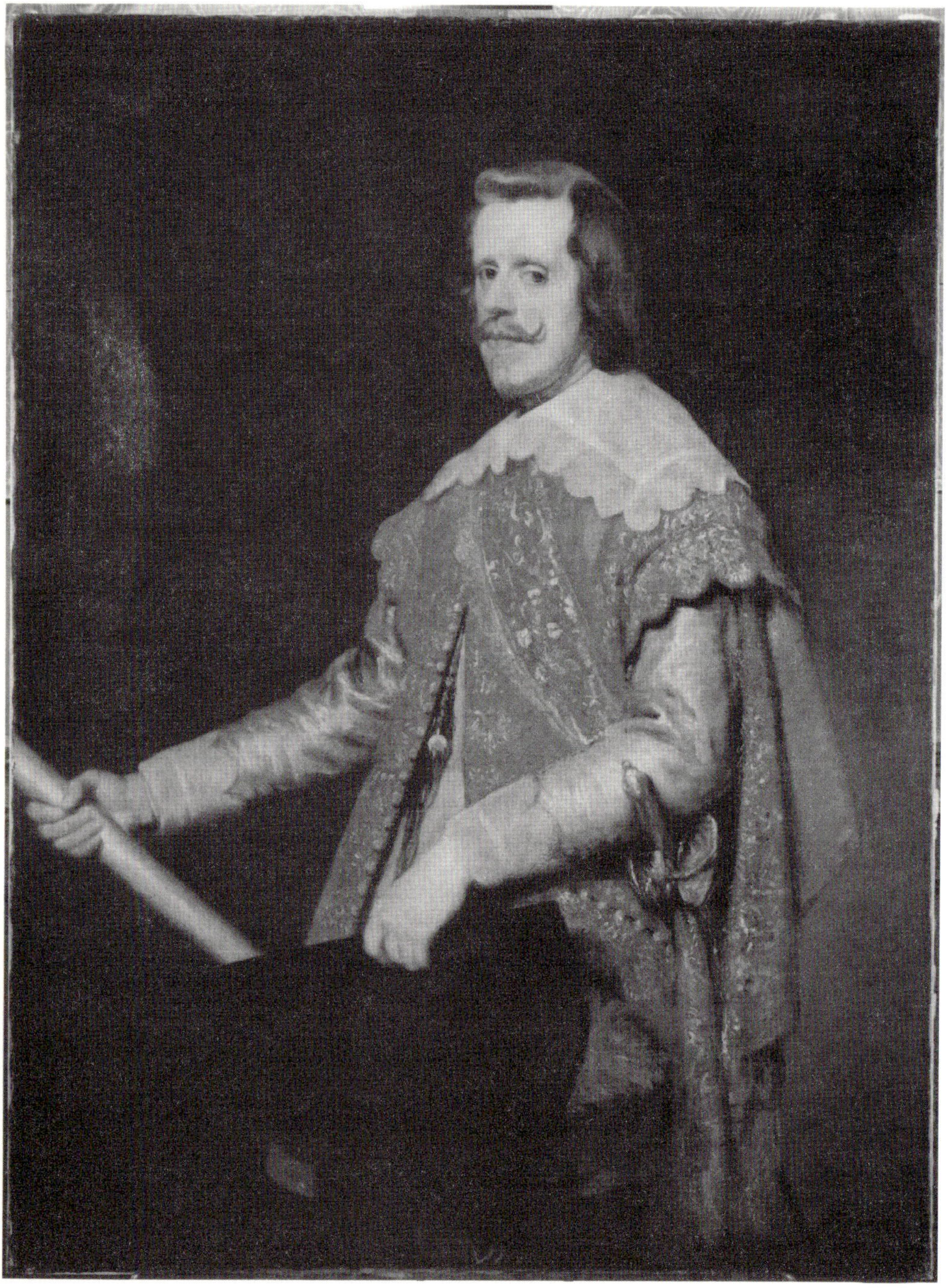

Philip IV of Spain
From the studio of Velazquez the original of which is held at The Dulwich Picture Gallery (31)

Reproduced by permission of the Gallery

Following in the style of his drawings of war that he produced in his younger days, the sketch 'Soldier in the Desert' (30) drawn in his first year as an art student shows a mature finish. He obviously enjoyed being at Heatherleys and made sufficient progress to win a scholarship to the Royal Academy Schools which meant five years of free tuition starting in 1897, when he was one of eight candidates who passed into the Schools 'on probation' (37). All passed their probationary period and moved on to start work in the Lower School. There Shepard worked on antiques and copied an Old Master, 'Philip IV of Spain', from the Studio of Velazquez, the original of which came from The Dulwich Picture Gallery (31).

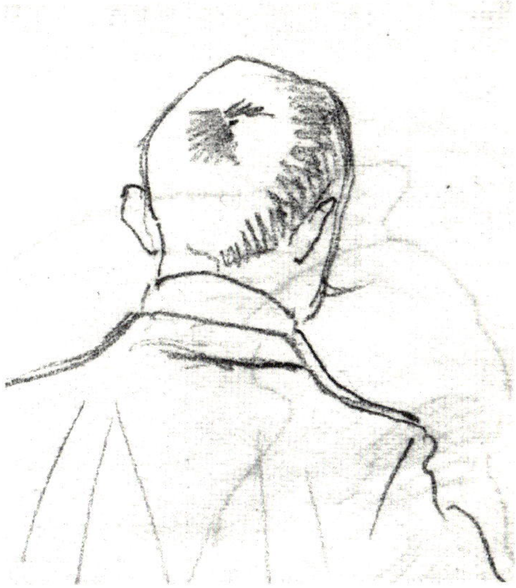

A Man's Balding Head
from his Student Notebook (32)

The students all enjoyed life there. They "were a cheerful lot and sang hymns in the washhouse while cleaning up after work". By now he was using a student notebook as a necessitous prop. At this period, although he was still using any piece of paper at hand, he conscientiously carried a student notebook at all times (32, 33, 34, 35, 36).

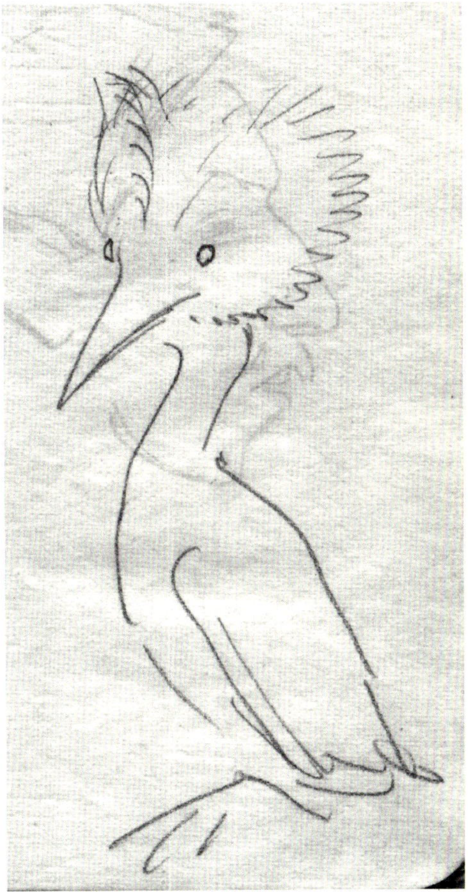

A Bird
from his Student Notebook (33)

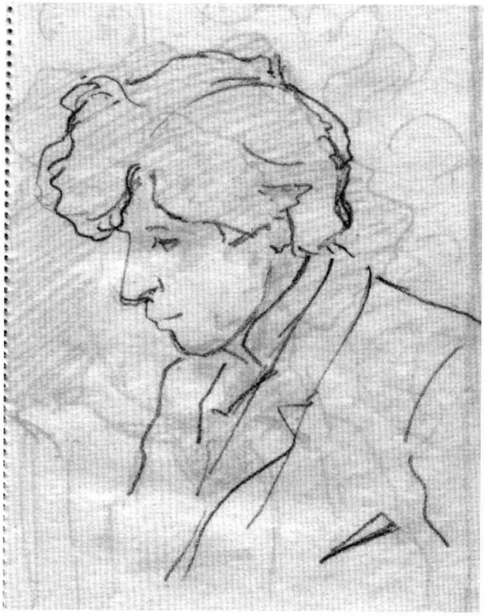

A Young Man's Head (34)

My Weight (36)

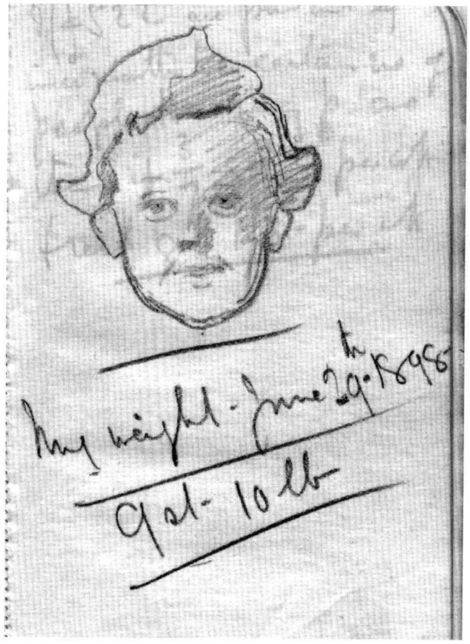

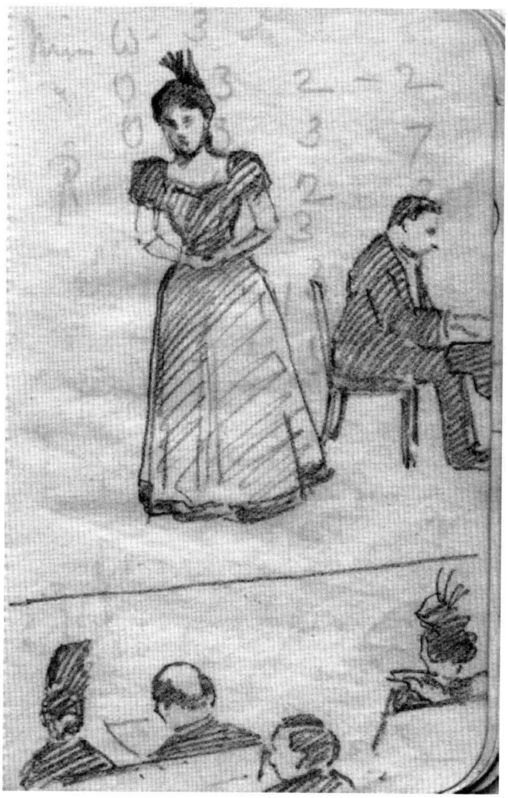

A Private Concert (35)

*A Selection of sketches
from his student notebook, 1897-1898*

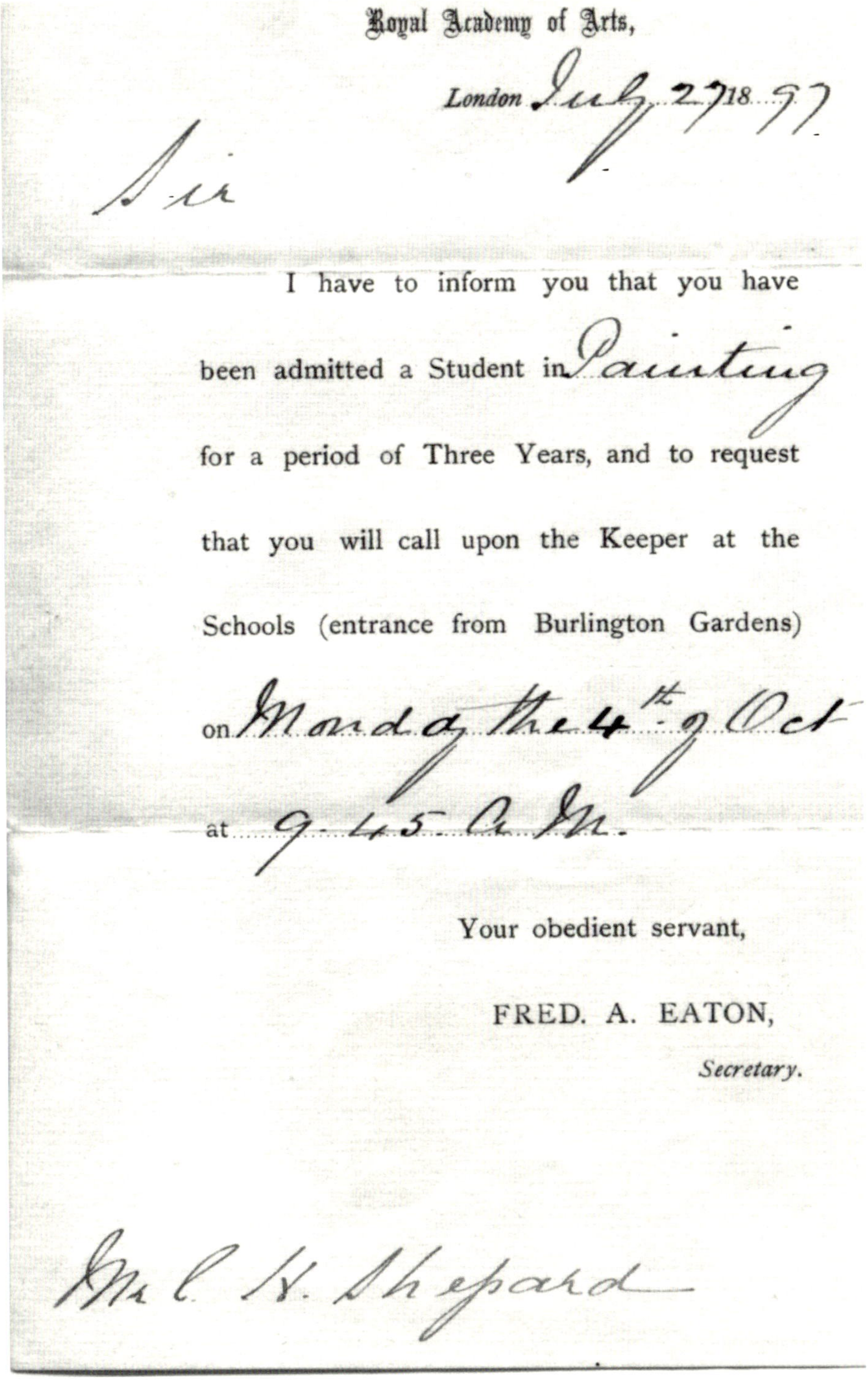

Royal Academy of Arts,

London July 27 1897

Sir

I have to inform you that you have been admitted a Student in Painting for a period of Three Years, and to request that you will call upon the Keeper at the Schools (entrance from Burlington Gardens) on Monday the 4th of Oct at 9-45 A M.

Your obedient servant,

FRED. A. EATON,

Secretary.

Mr C. H. Shepard

Admittance letter to The Royal Academy Schools (37)

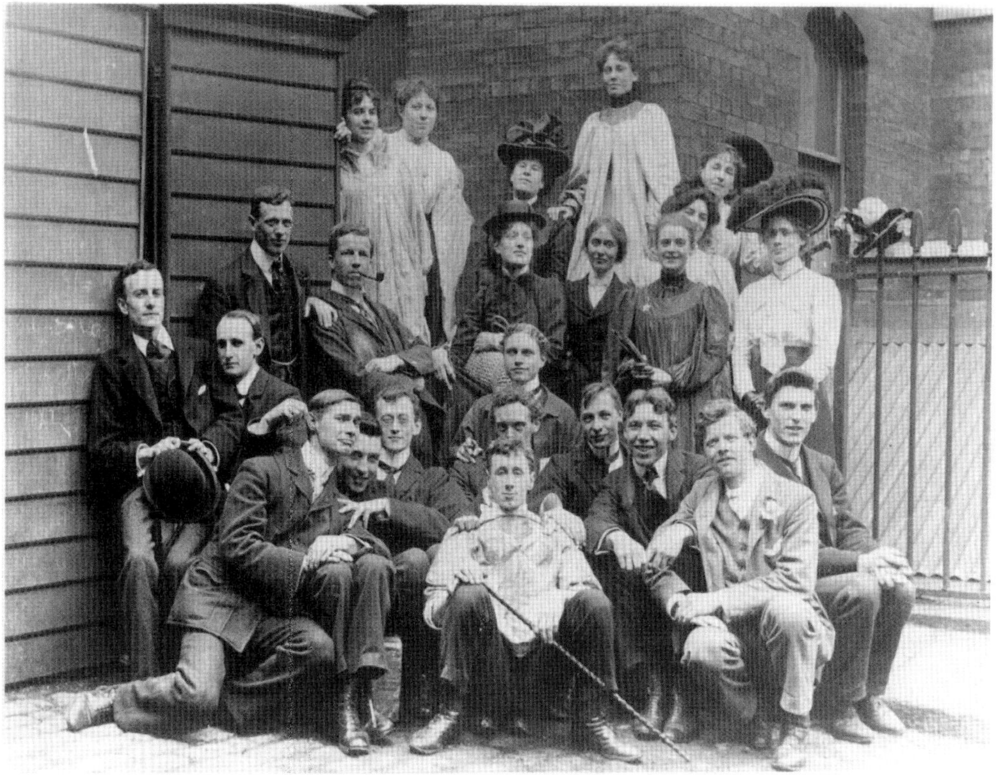

Students at The Royal Academy Schools, 1899-1900
Ernest Shepard, fourth from the right, Florence Chaplin, second from the right, partly hidden (38)

When he entered the Upper School a new class was added to the training programme. In the evening starting at five o'clock there was a two hour life class which was restricted to men students as the rules clearly stated that no lady student should ever be called upon to face the nude.

After two years at the Academy Schools he won both the Landseer and British Institution Scholarships which put him in the top rank of student artists. In 1900 he was awarded a silver medal for figure painting and also obtained the third prize for figure drawing. He had by now established himself as an artist and was already supplementing his scholarship money by selling his drawings and illustrations to magazines.

One of the most popular of the visiting Academicians was the great American artist, John Singer Sargent. Although tongue-tied and almost inarticulate, his personality was dynamic and he managed to inspire all the students, sometimes by taking over the palette and brushes in order to work on the student's study. On these occasions most of the students, including Shepard, thought they had a future as oil painters.

Another Academician, described as 'a grand teacher', was Edwin Abbey, also an American. He would attend an evening class complete with top hat, which he continued to wear even after removing his jacket. Abbey was a brilliant draughtsman and took a personal interest in all his students, helping many of them to obtain professional jobs. It was he who arranged for Shepard to have an introduction to *Punch* by buttonholing Linley Sambourne on Varnishing Day at the Academy. Abbey introduced Shepard to Sambourne and then left them together.

Some years later when speaking to the Reynolds Club Shepard stated that he was eternally grateful to the Royal Academy Schools not only for the training that he had been given but also for the lifelong friendships that he made there as a student.

At the turn of the century there were twenty-four ladies and gentlemen in his group at the Royal Academy Schools (38). It was within this group that he met another gifted student, Florence Eleanor Chaplin. When he first became attracted to her she was known as 'Eleanor' but she was soon to be given the nickname of 'Pie'. The friendship between 'Kipper' and 'Pie' was to develop into the love story that was to last for a quarter of a century until she tragically died while undergoing an operation.

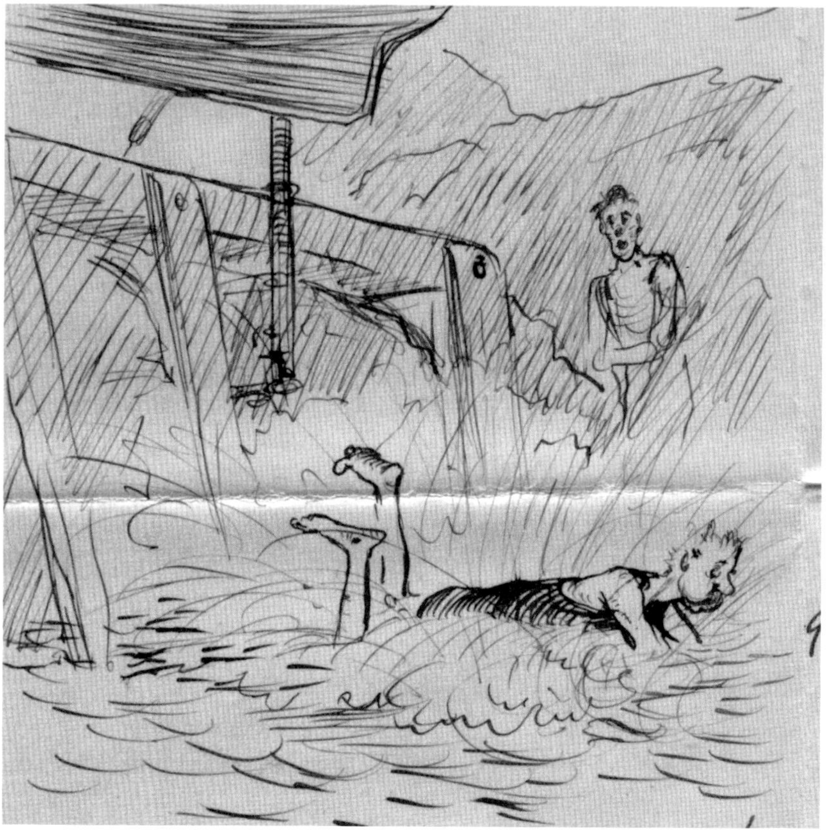

Swimming at Kingswear
At this period of his life, Ernest went for holidays to Kingswear in Devon.
He usually went with a friend, either Streatfield or Swaish, whose nickname was 'Swish' (39)

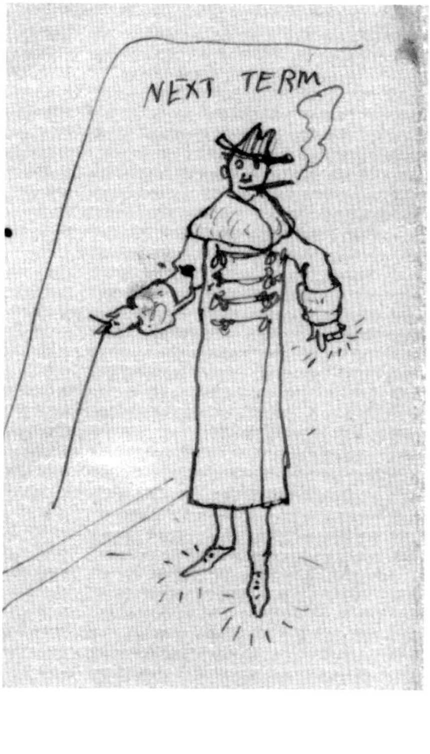

Next Term
Part of a letter showing what he thought he might look like in the coming term (40)

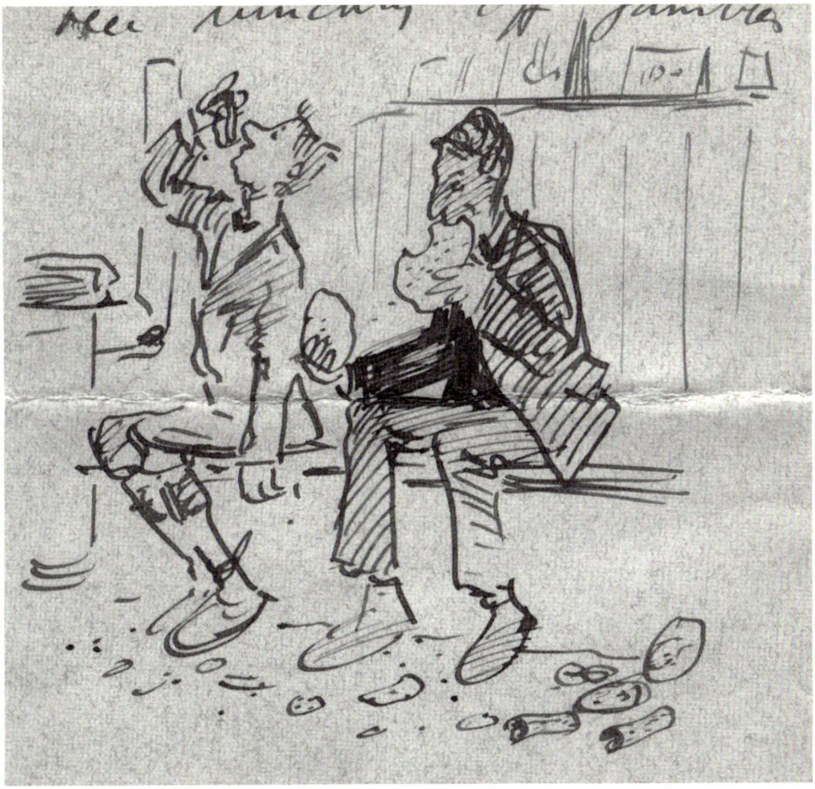

Lunching off jumbles
Letter to Pie (Florence) 10th March 1901 (41)

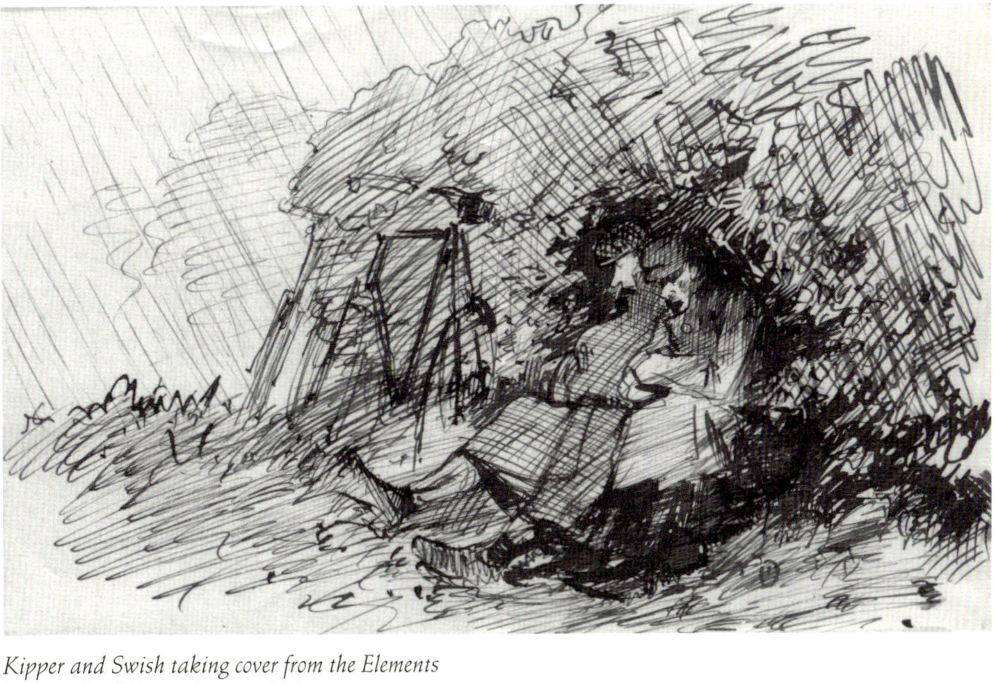

Kipper and Swish taking cover from the Elements
Letter to Pie (Florence), 1901 (42)

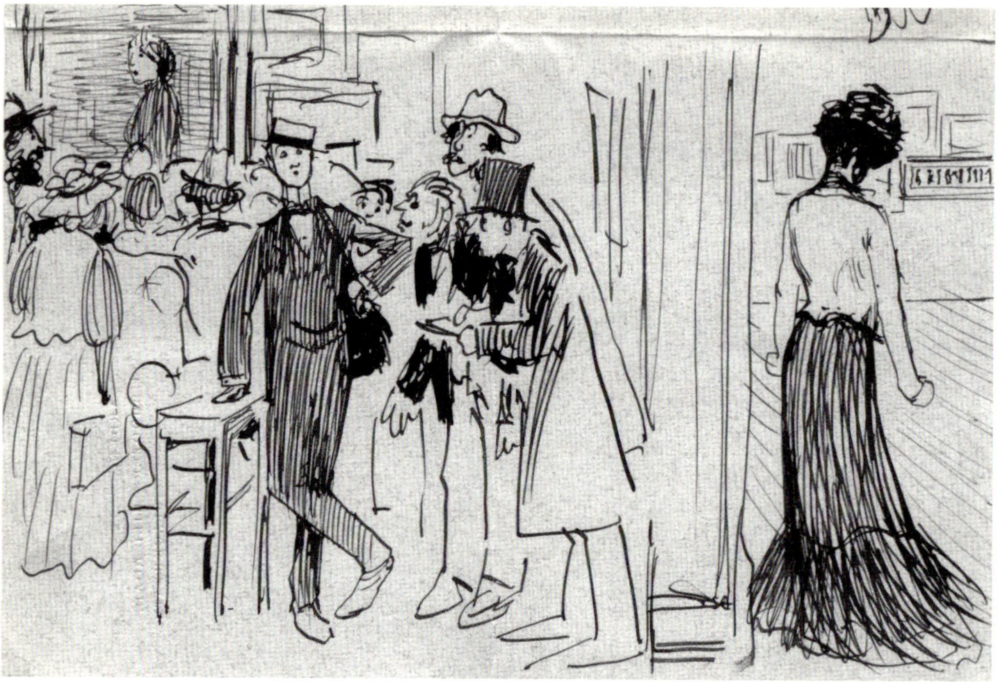

Varnishing Day at the Royal Academy Schools, 5th April 1901
Cartoon aimed at Florence who was left outside (43)

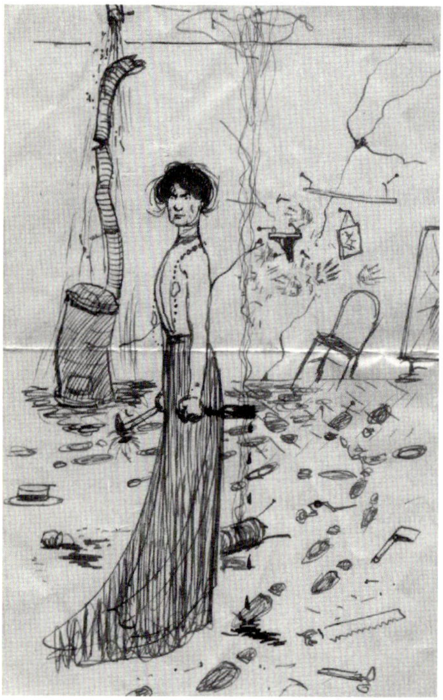

Pie trying to Hang a Picture,
24th May 1901 (44)

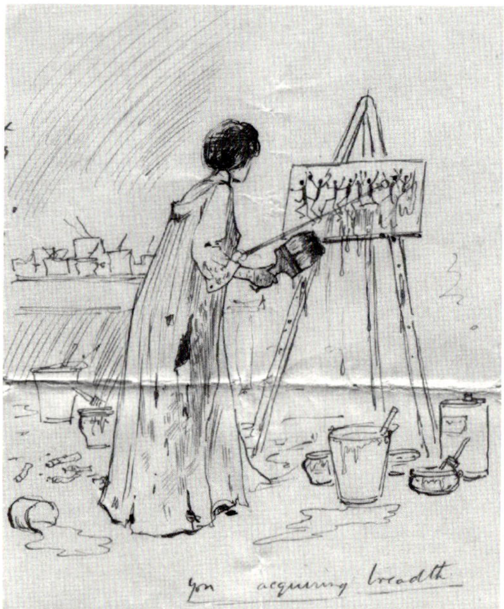

'You Acquiring Breadth'
Cartoon for Pie, May 1901 (45)

Vacations from the Academy presented opportunities for Ernest and colleagues to have holidays with friends and to visit other parts of the country. For some of these holidays he went to Kingswear in Devon usually accompanied by either Streatfield or Swaish, whose nickname was Swish (39). The visits enabled him to sketch to his heart's content but also, as he was a prolific letter writer, to tell others what he was doing. His letters normally contained illustrations to his text which were often cartoons against himself, such as the caricature, drawn in September 1900, dressed in the clothes that he intended to wear at the start of the following term (40), when he hoped to be able to 'show off' his new apparel.

His holidays in the spring of 1901 produced his normal daily letters to Pie. One of these referred to his 'lunching off jumbles' (41) and another showed him and Swish taking cover from the elements (42).

In his letter to Pie on Varnishing Day held on 5th April 1901, his drawing of the event seemed to suggest that either Pie was unable to be present or that she was cross in some way. He loved making fun of her in such drawings (43). As was stated earlier it was on this occasion that Shepard was introduced to a member of the *Punch* Table to which he was to be elected later in life.

On leaving Ernest obviously put the Academy behind him and set out to enjoy himself living life to the full. Shepard had an inner fount of wit and we are able to obtain a great deal of information about his character from the comments he makes on the cartoons that he put into his letters. His pictures would contain great detail enabling one to pinpoint the day they were drawn and, at times, the events to which they refer. On Tuesday 9th May 1901 Ernest wrote to Florence (Pie) asking her "will it get done¿". This shows her struggling in the throws of dressmaking for a costume that should be worn at a dance on Saturday 13th May. Two weeks later he again has a direct hit at Florence when she is trying to hang a picture on a wall (44). She was an excellent artist but not good with a hammer and nails. In his letter to her Shepard writes "n.b. in the cartoon on the last page please observe the hair on the hammer in your hand that is not ink on the chisel in your other hand.' Presumably Florence was getting her hair caught up in the hammer and hitting her own fingers!

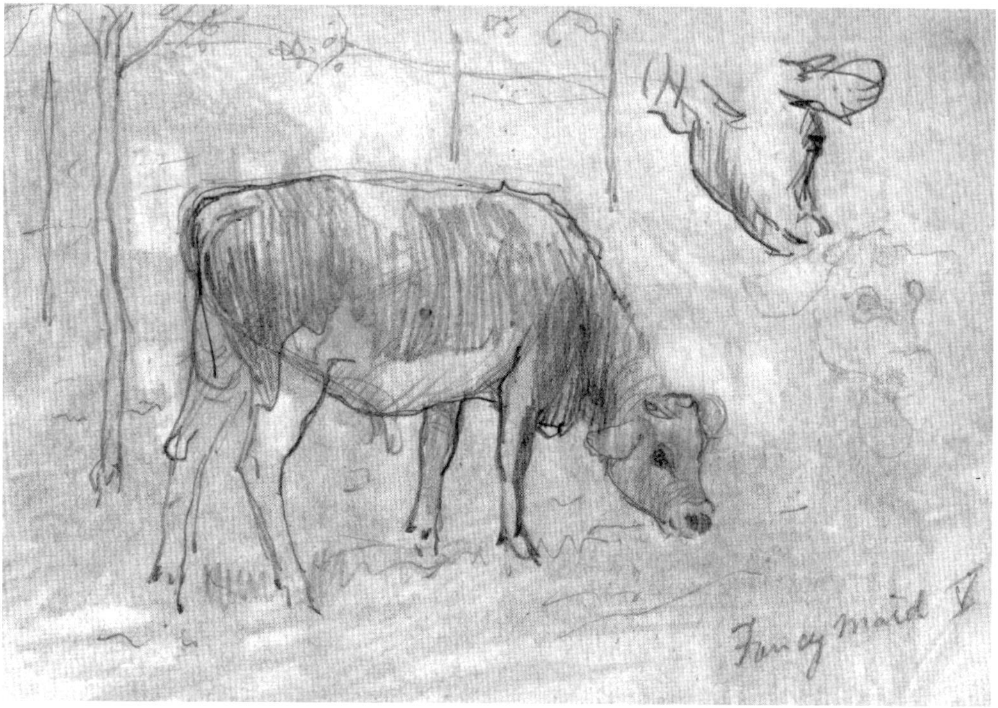

Fancy Maid V
from Student Notebook, 1901 (46)

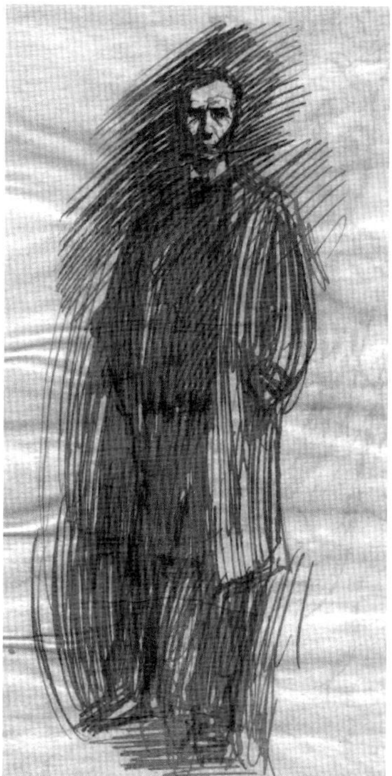

Man Emerging from
a Series of Lines
from Student Notebook (47)

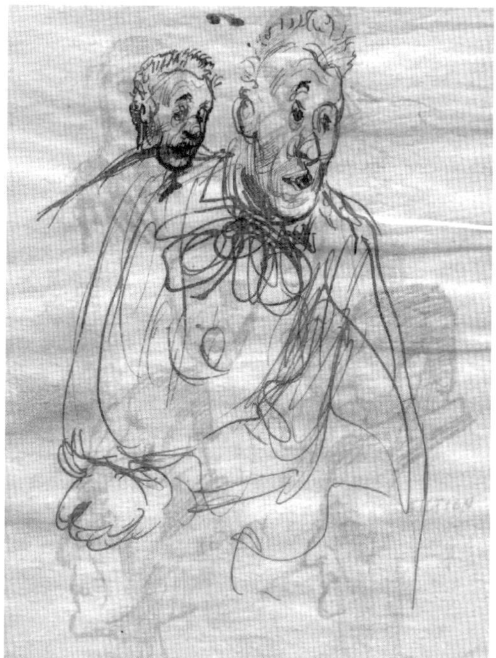

Two faces
from Student Notebook, 1901 (48)

At the time he entered the Academy Schools the family moved to Shooters Hill Road, Blackheath. The house was named 'Arden'. He must have been content and had many happy memories for he was attracted to a house of the same name in Shamley Green when trying to find somewhere to live near Guildford.

His sense of humour shone through his drawings. He again made great fun of Pie by putting her into one of his private cartoons in his letter of May 1901 when he referred to her 'acquiring breadth' in her paintings. He did this by showing her using an eight inch whitewash ceiling brush on her canvas when he possibly knew that she had been using a similar brush to distemper a wall (45).

Many drawings from his notebooks lay dormant for years before being brought to light for a specific topic. In his notebook of 1901, his sketch of Fancy Maid V reappears twenty-three years later in *The King's Breakfast*, in *When We Were Very Young (46).*

His letters of the following year show various aspects of his personal life including reference to his dog called Dan named after Dan Leno, the comic actor (49). Kipper tells of how this dog loved rousting about in the straw and came dashing out in the morning with bits of straw sticking to him.

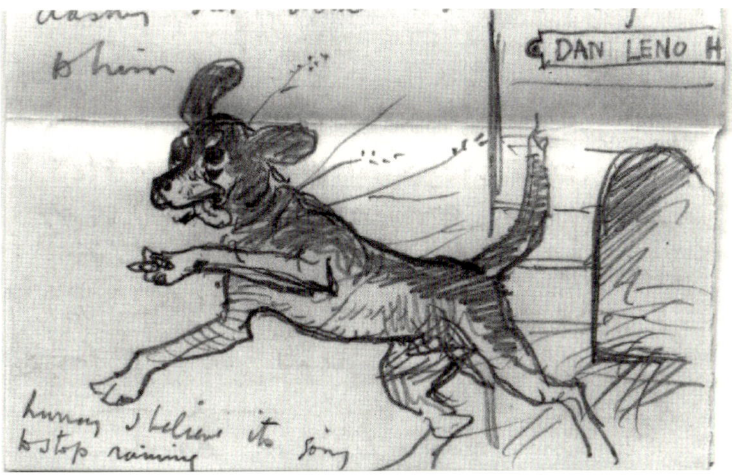

Dan Slept in his New Kennel (49)

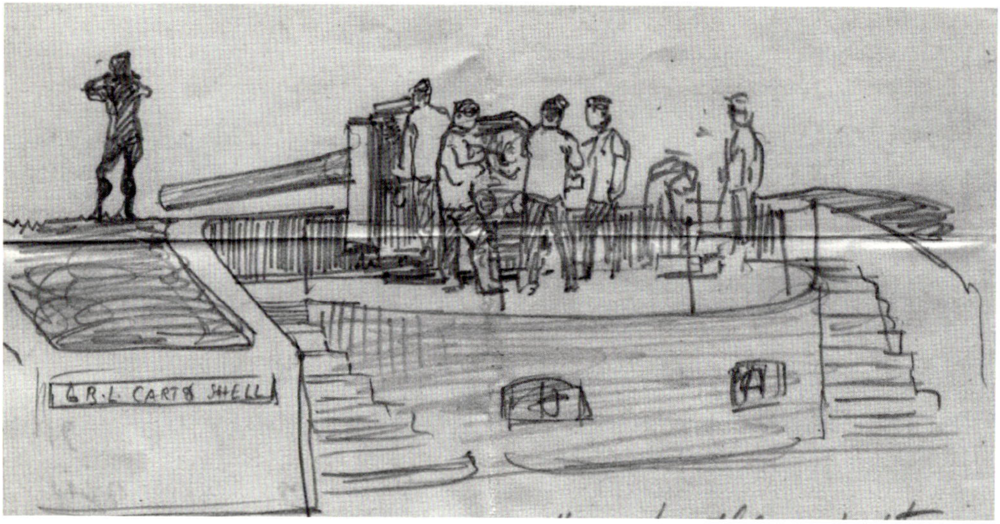

Gun Emplacement at Dover Castle
Letter when visiting Dover, April 1902 (50)

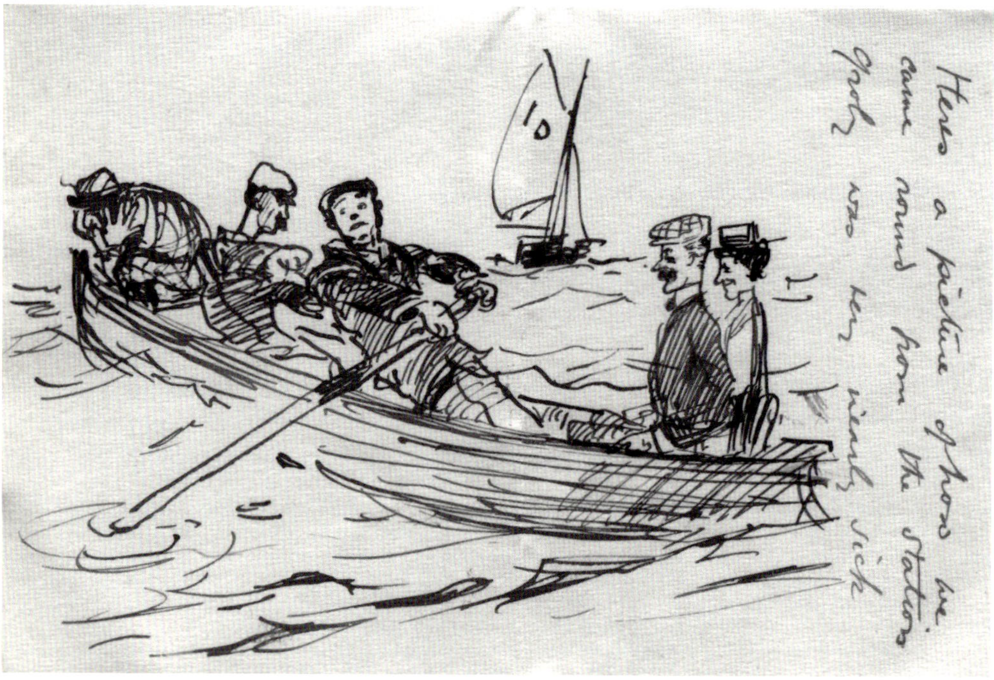

Groby was Very Nearly Sick,
Letter while on holiday with his sister Ethel, 1902 (51)

Old Man at Morden College, August 1902 (52)

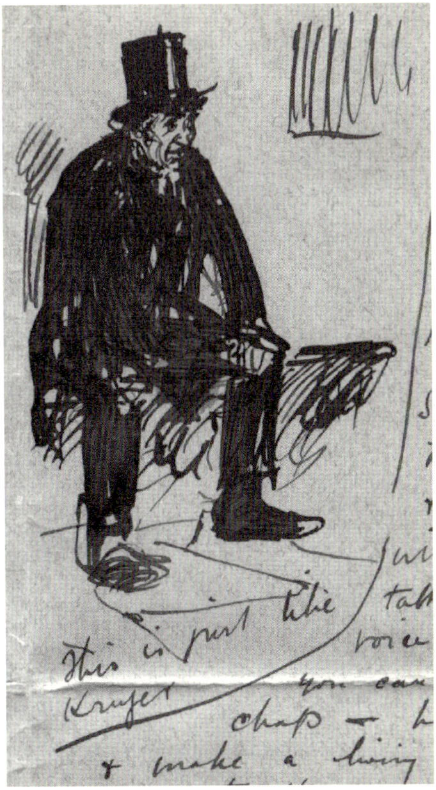

The spring of 1902 found him travelling around, needless to say with his notebook. In April he visited Dover Castle (50). While on holiday with his sister Ethel he included a cartoon about his friend Groby in his letter to Pie (51).

Later that summer he was working on a commission at Morden College, an almshouse. He became friendly with one of the almsmen and sketched him (52). Another character at the College was 'The Probationer' (53).

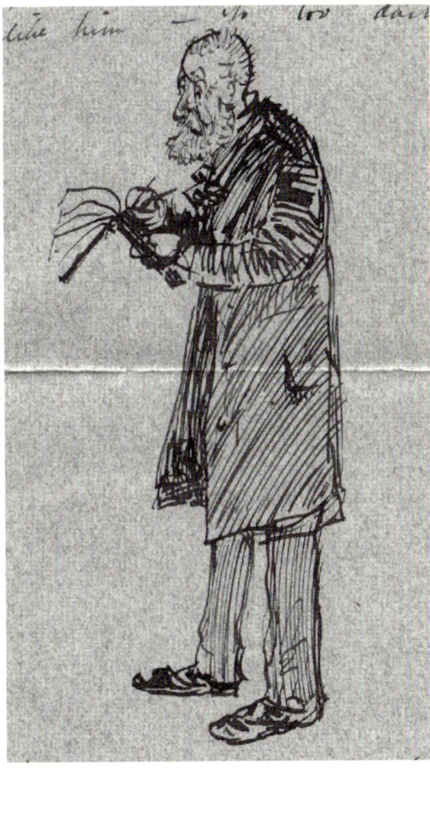

Probationer at Morden College, June 1902 (53)

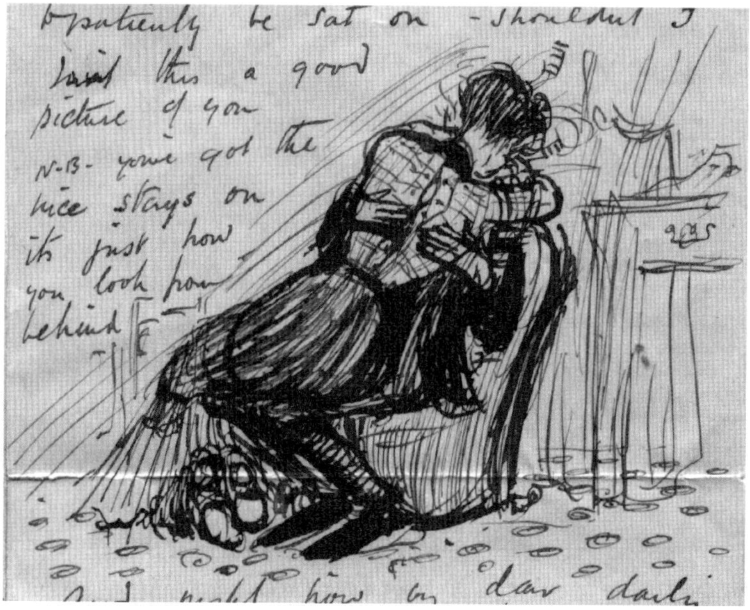

Pie and Kipper Engaged (54)

Ernest and Florence became engaged in 1903 when his letters and references become more intimate. His letter to Pie on 27th March has a drawing of her sitting on his knee with a note "N.B. you've got the nice stays on, it's just how you look from behind" (54).

A month before the wedding he arranged to have a bed re-painted for them and drew a picture of how he imagined his 'little girl' would look in the bed (55).

In 1904 he exhibited his first painting, a portrait of his sister Ethel, at the Royal Academy and also sold a picture called 'The Followers' to the Durban Art Gallery in South Africa (56) on the proceeds of which, one hundred pounds, they got married.

'My Little Girl-in-Bed'
Letter 19th August, 1904 (55)

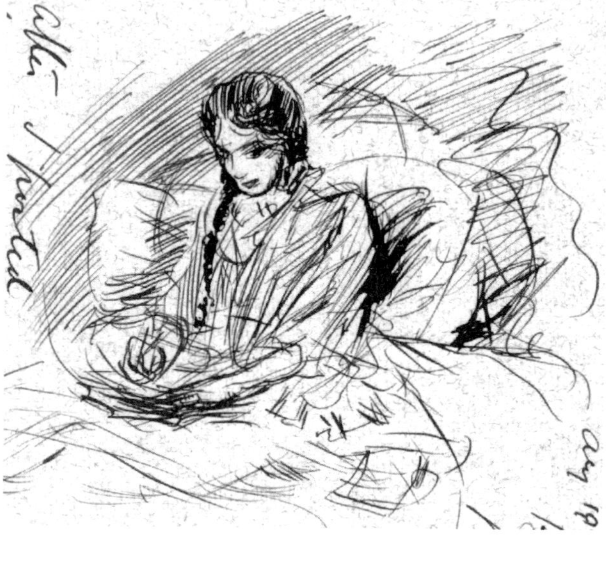

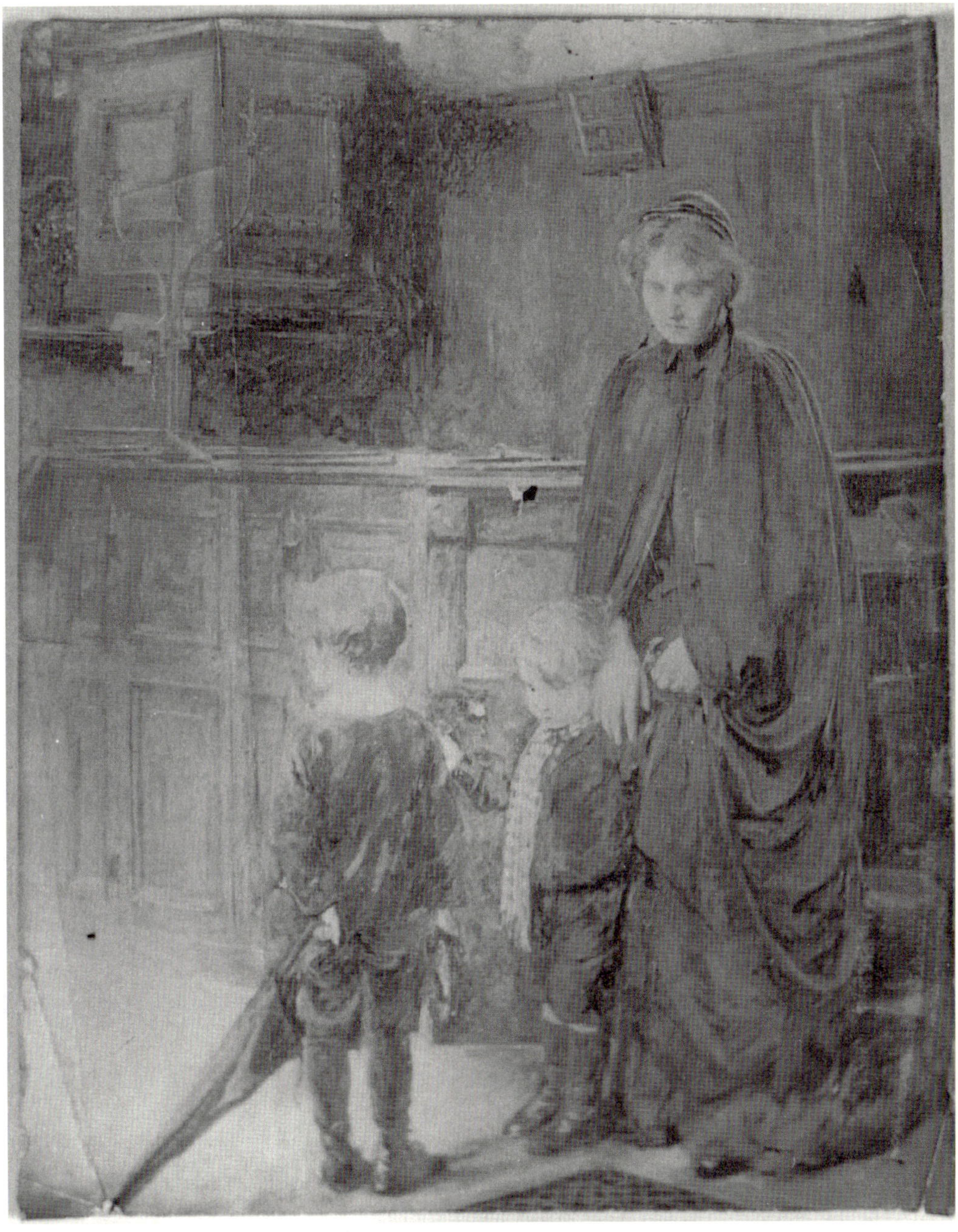

The Followers (56)

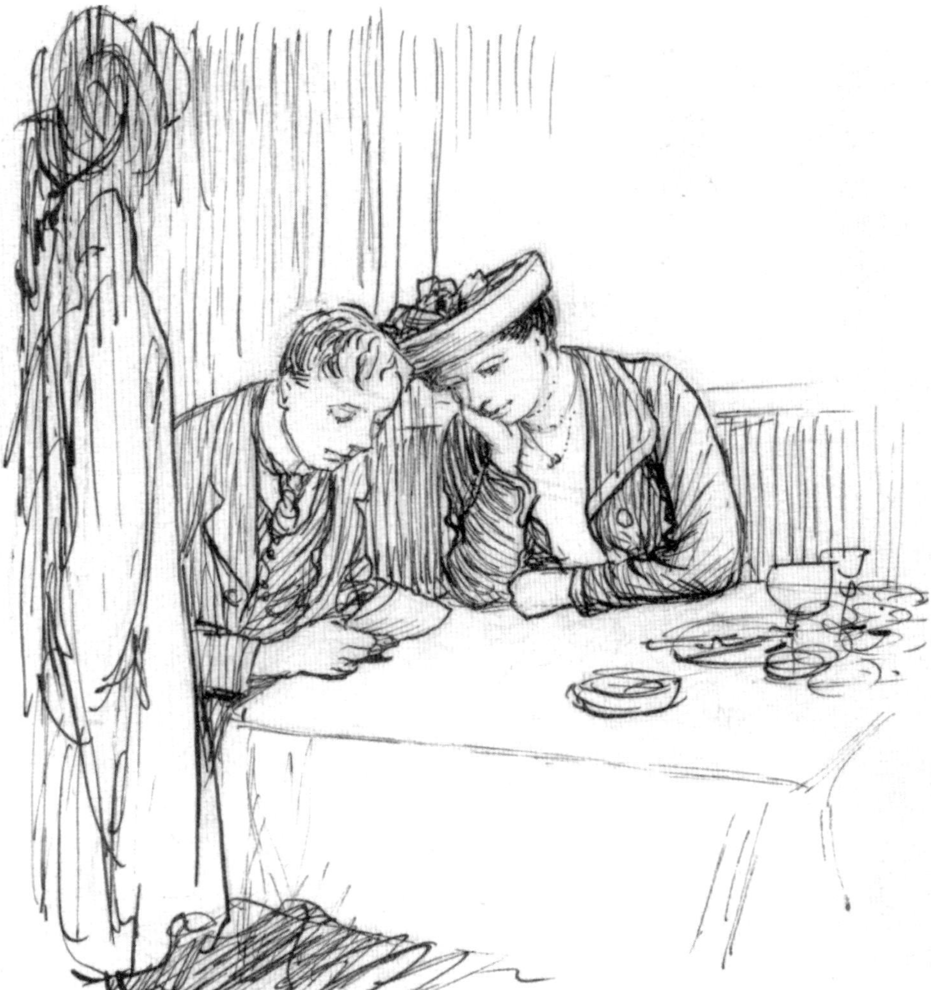

Totting up what we should Spend on Rent and Food
From Drawn from Life *(57)*

E.H. Shepard

Chapter 5
Shamley Green 1904 - 1914

On 28th September 1904 Ernest Howard Shepard married Florence Eleanor Chaplin at St Andrew's Church, Streatham. At the time Florence's mother was living in Deal but friends offered their house at Norbury, near Streatham, for the wedding reception and suggested that the couple should be married in their Parish Church. The Officiant was The Revd James William Shepard, Ernest's uncle. Florence was twenty-eight years old with Ernest being four years younger. In addition to the bride and groom, four Chaplins and four Shepards signed the Marriage Register.

In preparation for their married life, Ernest had rented a small house at Shamley Green near Guildford in Surrey. This was an early nineteenth century dwelling called 'Arden Cottage'. He fell in love with this cottage once he saw it mainly because of its name. It should be remembered that the family home in which he lived with his sister and brother at Blackheath, and of which he had such happy memories, was called 'Arden'.

As has been seen, the Shepard family had had connections with the Guildford area since Ernest's grandfather built a family home there sixty years earlier. The young married couple found that they would not be able to afford to live in London and therefore decided to move into Surrey near places that they already knew. Rent for the cottage in Shamley Green was two shillings and six pence per week and they found that they could live comfortably on one guinea (now one pound and ten pence) per week (57).

It should be borne in mind that, in those days, to live in the country and travel to London on business was rather a dashing thing to do. In some levels of London life it was looked upon as being 'not altogether respectable' and verging upon the Bohemian!

To make the house ready had not been an easy task. It took weeks of preparation with many visits to 'Arden' by Ernest and much help from his sister, Ethel. Builders, brought in from Cranleigh, had trouble with the soakaways that were thought to be drains before they were inspected (58). A local legend claimed that the cottage was haunted (59) and his sister suggested that the ghost should be called in to help with the curtains (60).

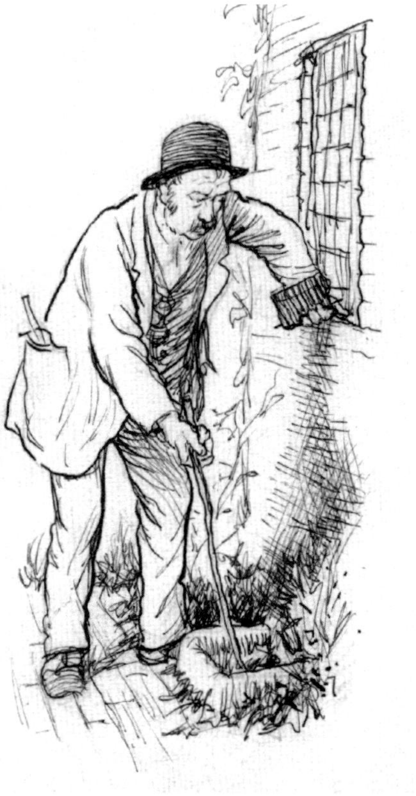

You'll have trouble with that!
From Drawn from Life *(58)*

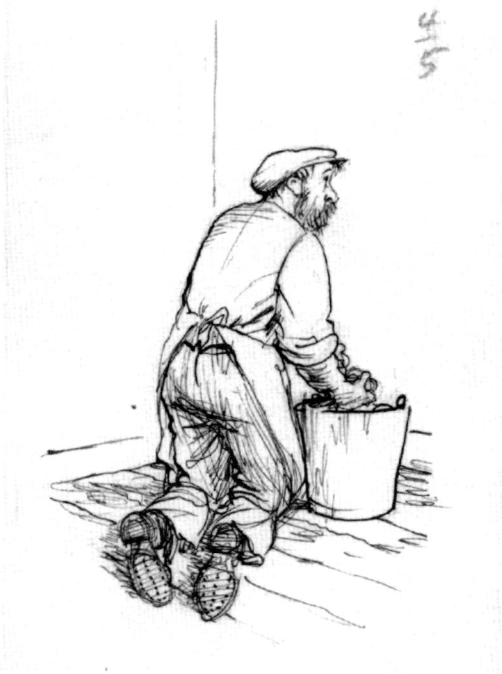

I suppose you know the place is haunted?
From Drawn from Life *(59)*

Shepard records their first night at 'Arden Cottage'. "Before we went to bed we looked out the special treasures we had brought with us.... Pie's enamel patch box and her tiny china mouse (61)." The following morning their dinner service was delivered by a local carrier and, not being used to dealing with deliveries, Ernest had no idea how much the tip should be (62).

The cottage had two rooms upstairs and two rooms downstairs. In addition there was a scullery at the rear of the property with a tiny room above. There was no gas, no electricity and water came from a well in the garden. Both cooking and warmth for the whole cottage came from the kitchen range. The cottage remained like this until after the Second World War when many additions were made to the structure. The restructured 'Red Cottage' which they moved into later and which has since been renamed, would be unrecognisable to Shepard today although his original studio remains.

They were both keen gardeners who enjoyed the outdoor exercise and watching the flowers grow but first they had to tackle the wilderness that they had taken on. It was not just a task for shears but one for a very sharp billhook. They needed a tidy garden as they both frequently used it as an outdoor studio.

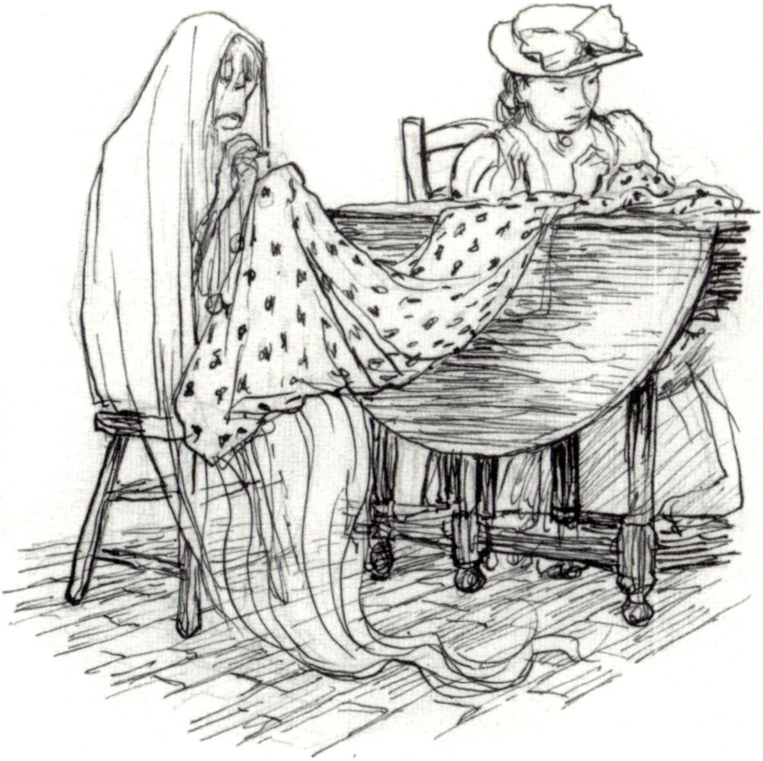

Making the Curtains
From Drawn from Life *(60)*
With reference to the 'ghost' Ernest's sister, Ethel, said "Get it to help me with the curtains!"

Pie's China Mouse
From
Drawn from Life *(61)*

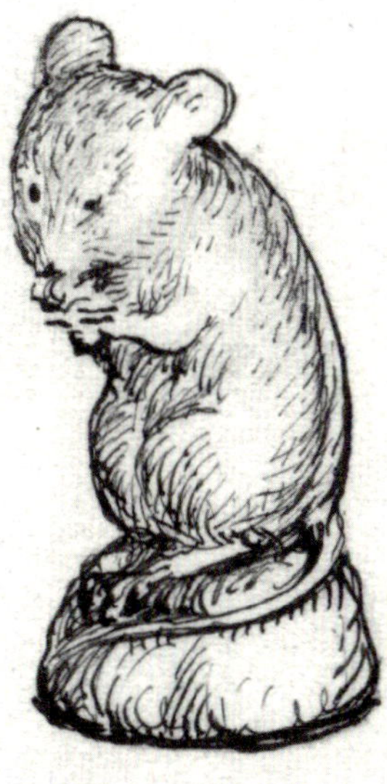

Letter writing continued whenever they were separated and he obviously was very distressed when they were apart, especially when Pie had to go into hospital (63).

It was while living here that Shepard really set himself up as an illustrator. By 1906 he had already had many illustrations accepted by publishers including those for three books. These books were already well known in the literary field but he was invited by the publishers to produce sketches for illustrated editions of such books as *David Copperfield, Tom Brown's School Days* and *Aesop's Fables*. It was at this time, two years into his marriage, that his career took off when his first illustration for *Punch* was accepted and published.

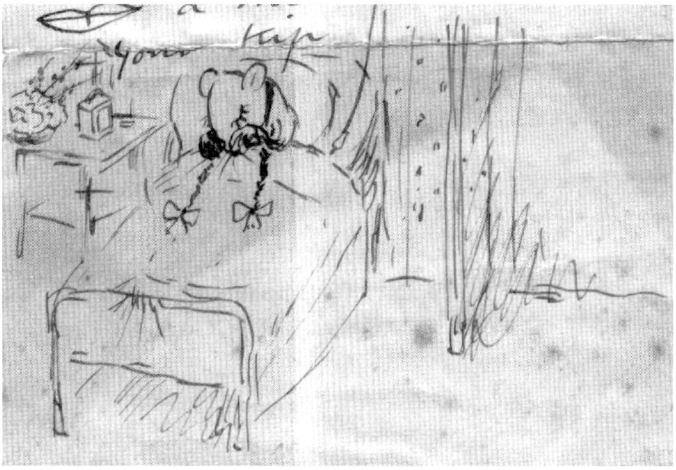

My little mouse in bed
Sent to Pie when she was in hospital
(63)

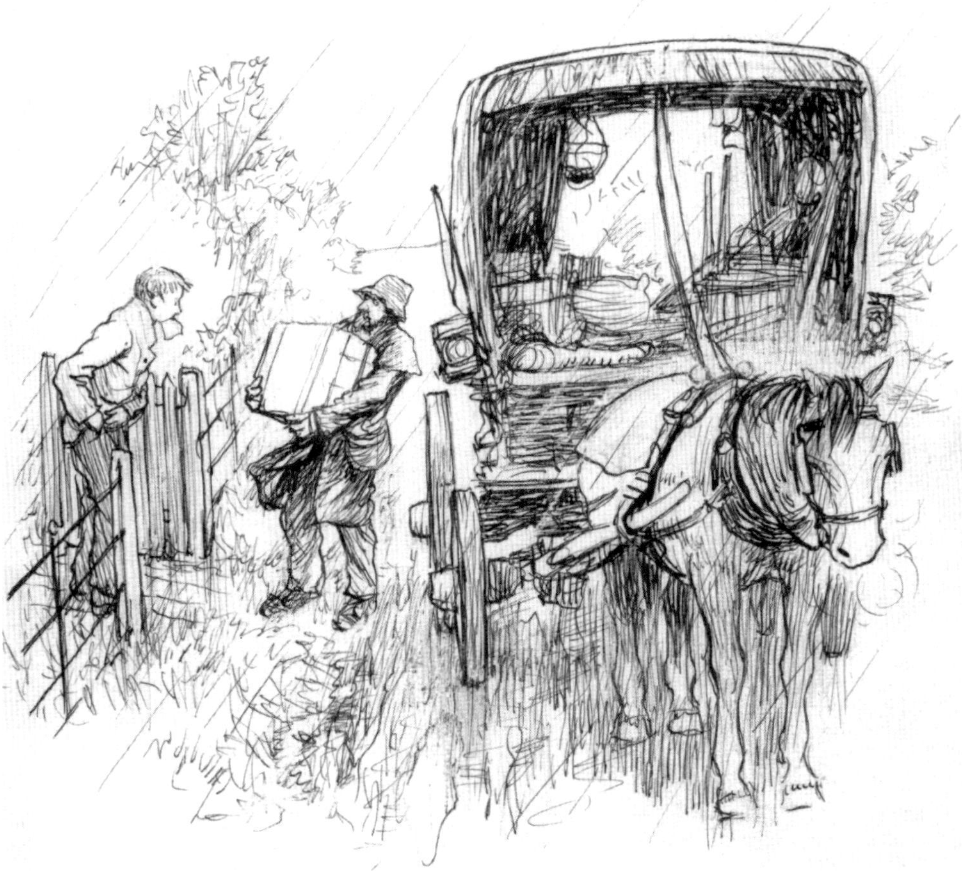

Our dinner service arrived the next morning
From Drawn from Life *(62)*

Both Kipper and Pie acted as models for each other, both drew and painted constantly. He learnt to cycle around the area (64) as well as to and from the station, for Ernest travelled to London regularly while Florence became the perfect hostess. There were many visitors to their cottage and they were known as a very sociable couple. Obviously Ernest was a happy man. A major cause of this is seen in the considerable evidence in his letters that Pie, four years his senior, was a 'mother' figure to him as well as a wife.

Cycling through Guildford floods
Letter 3rd November 1907 (64)
In a letter to his friend George, Ernest describes his dreadful journey through the flooded roads

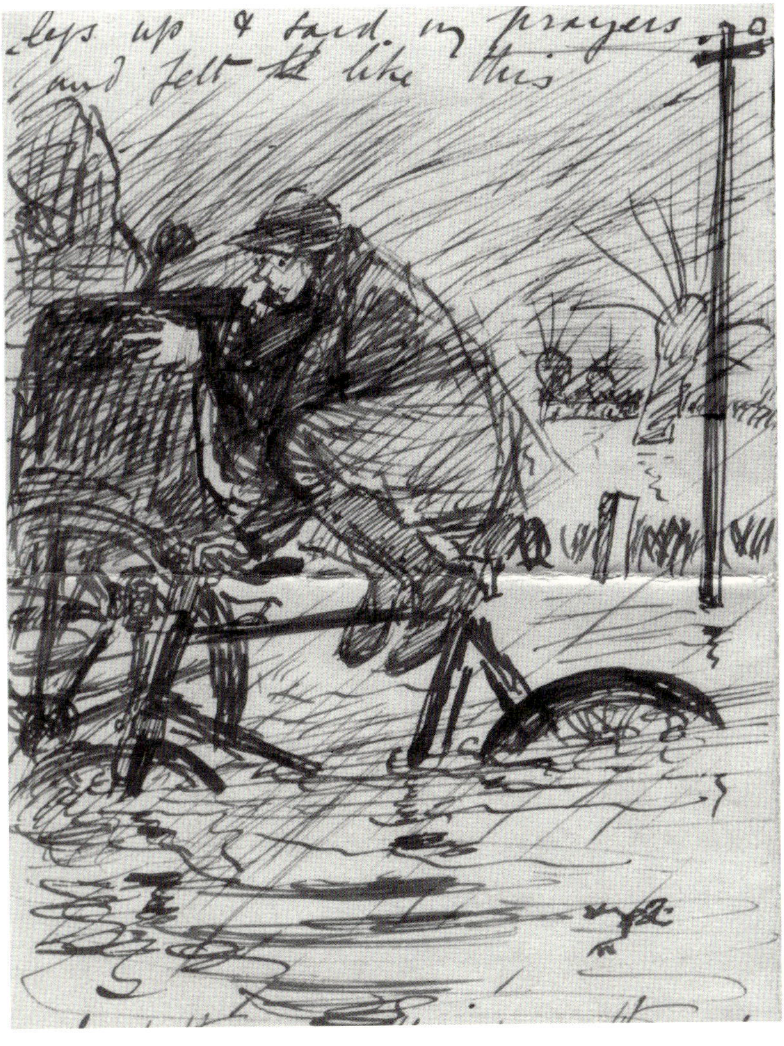

Pencil sketches of a baby (65)
As both children (Graham and Mary) were born at Shamley Green, it can be assumed that these sketches come from the same period. The age of the paper on which they were drawn supports this.

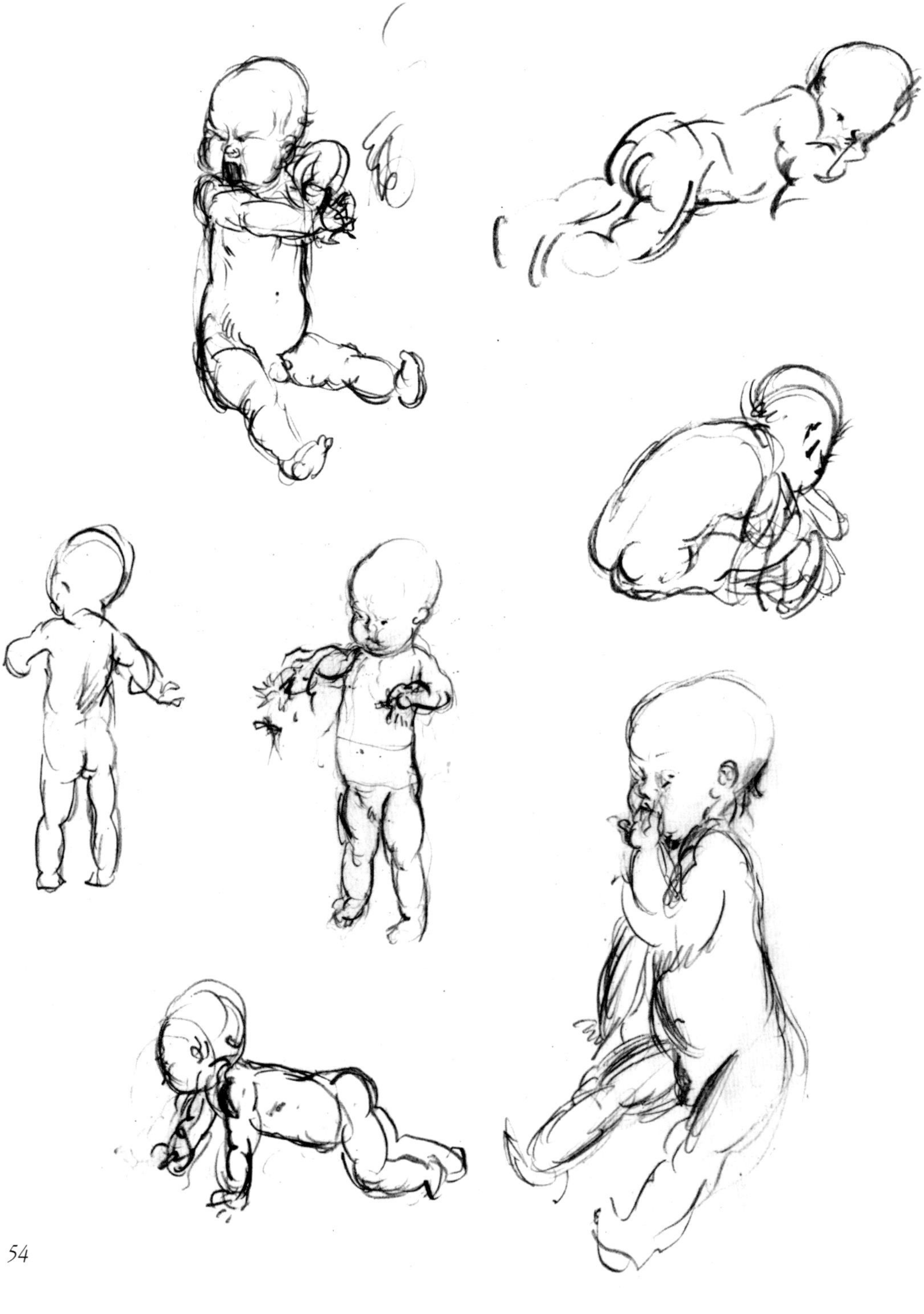

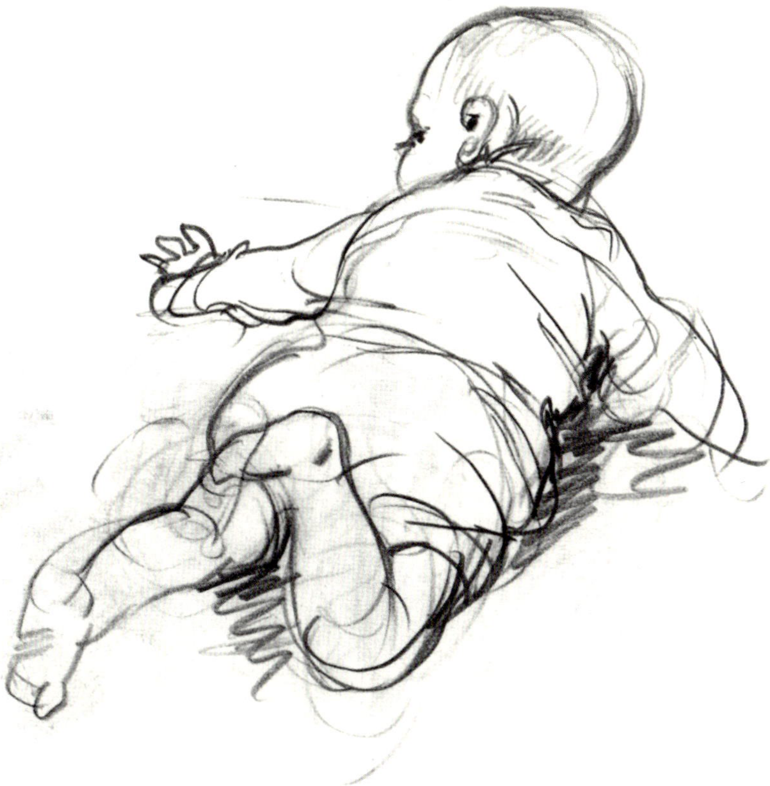

On 7th July 1907 their first child, Graham, was born. The christening took place on 22nd September with a grand tea party to follow. On Christmas Day, two years later, a daughter Mary was born. The two babies inspired a period of child drawings, many of which remain in the Shepard Archive at Surrey University (65).

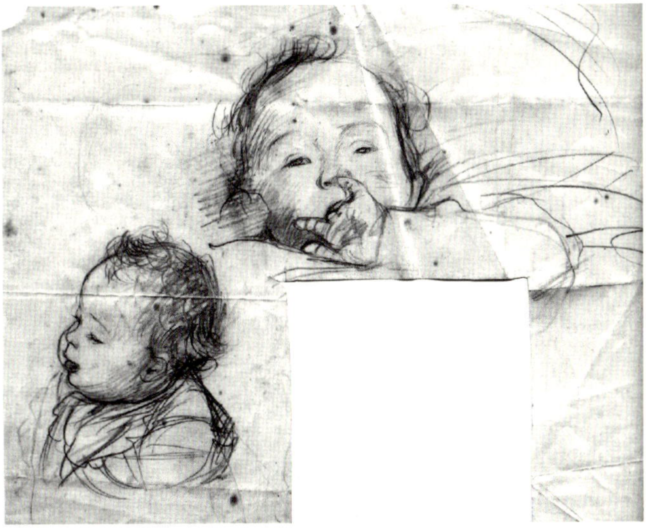

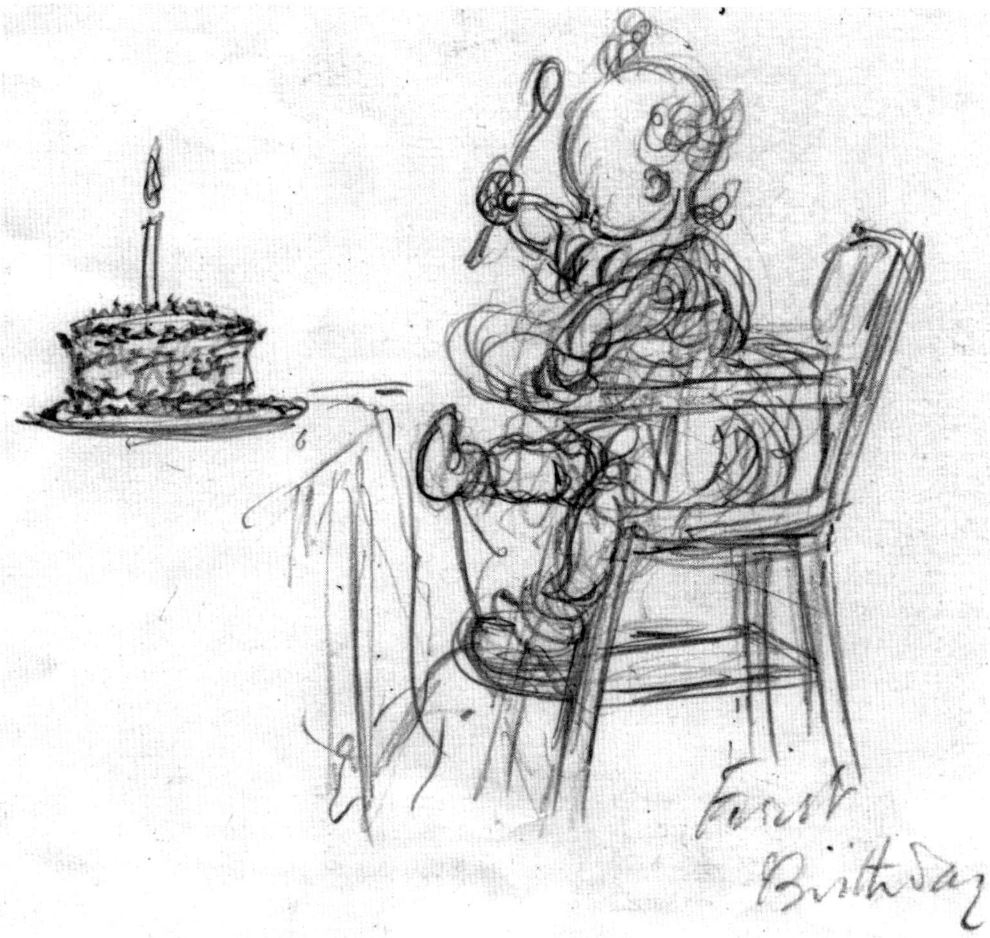

Baby's First Birthday (66)
Although this drawing is used in different forms in later publications, the paper on which it is drawn is that of a notebook used while at 'Red Cottage', Hullbrook Lane.
It can therefore be assumed that this is a drawing of Mary Shepard on her first birthday.

The enlarged family clearly needed more space and they moved to 'Red Cottage' in another part of Shamley Green in the garden of which Shepard had a studio built. It is quite reasonable to imagine Shepard sketching his daughter on her first birthday in 1910. Originally this, like the majority of his sketches, would have been for a personal record but he turned it into an illustration that appeared in various guises from 'First Birthday' to 'What is the matter with Mary Jane?' (66).

For the next five years the parents prospered as the two children grew up in 'Red Cottage', Ernest using his talents as an illustrator enabling them to live a comfortable life in the outskirts of Guildford. Florence (67) continued to use her artistic skills while being a full time mother. The two young children played happily together in the garden while around the corner lurked a very different and horrifying world.

Pie - Photograph and pencil (67)
The head is a photograph but from the neck downwards, the blouse, skirt and the design surrounding the whole area were added in pencil by Shepard

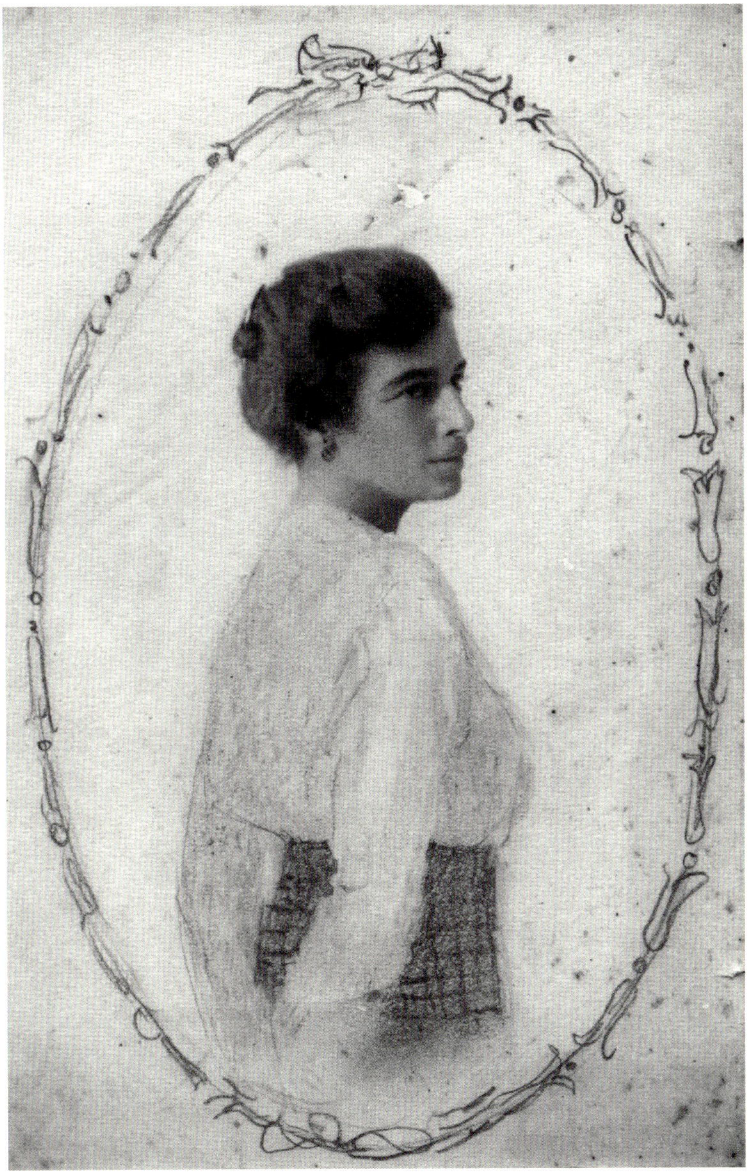

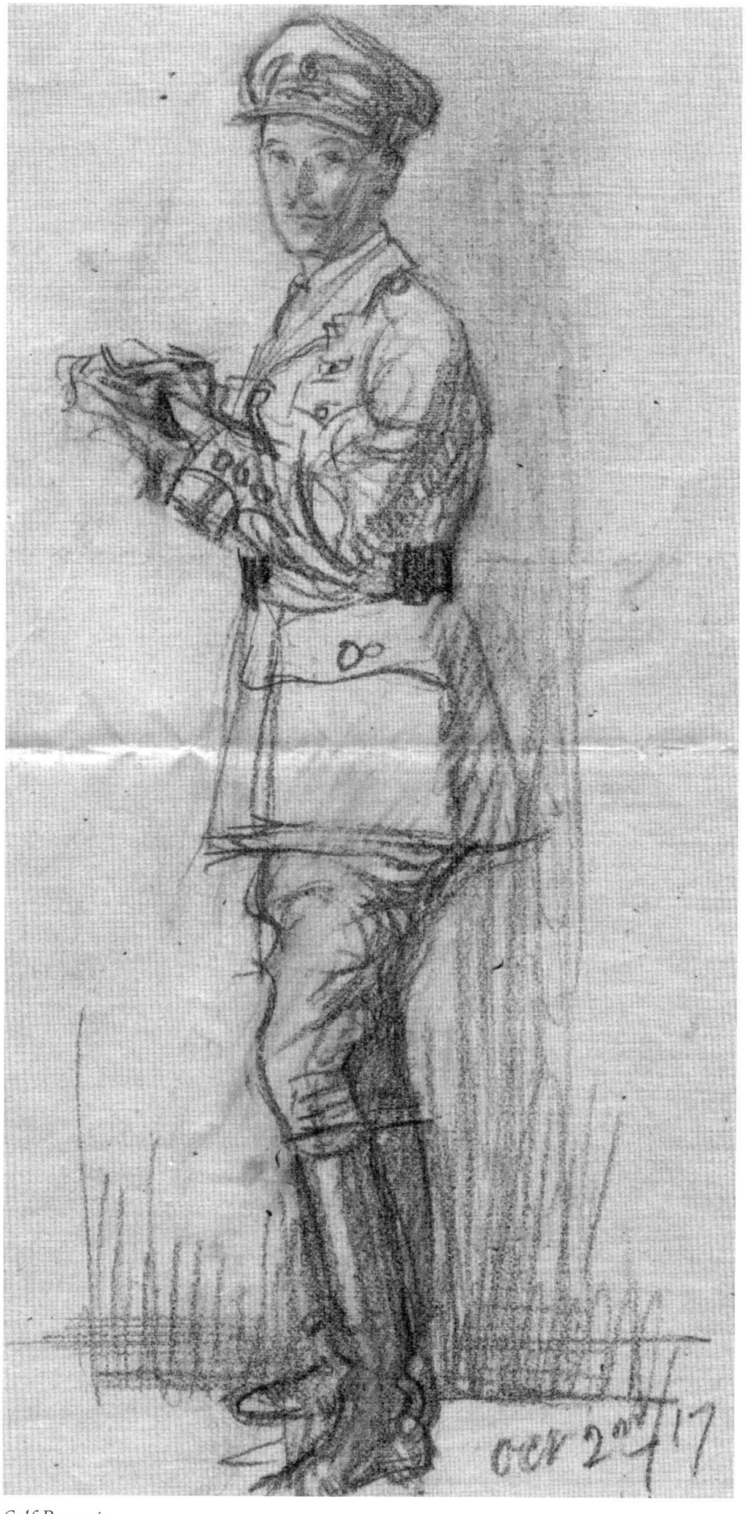

Self Portrait
On 2nd October 1917, Shepard wrote home: "Darling, here's a little wee sketch of your Kits I did most of it before breakfast this morning" (68)

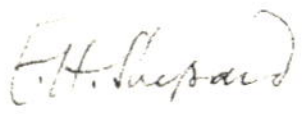

Chapter 6
The Great War 1914 - 1919

As he was a married man Ernest Shepard was not allowed to volunteer for the Forces in 1914. In the following year he applied for a commission in the Royal Artillery. Florence stayed at Shamley Green in 'Red Cottage' with their two children. Ernest was duly commissioned and spent four months training at Weymouth and at Llydd.

In the first half of May 1916, at short notice, his Royal Artillery Battery was ordered to get ready for overseas. He wrote to Pie and arranged for her to come to Llydd the following weekend. They were able to spend two happy days together. She left for home on the Monday and neither of them knew that it would be nine months before they saw each other again.

Two days later on Wednesday 17th May 1916 he tells us through his diary that there was a full moon and although the Regiment was not told he assumed they were going over to France. The journey started from Llydd at 8.15am and they arrived at Southampton at one o'clock. The Regiment boarded a ship at 4.30pm and started to sail across the Channel one and a half hours later. He slept on deck throughout what he described as "a gorgeous night - a very smooth crossing".

At the end of the War Shepard complained that his duties as a gunner had prevented him from making more than half a dozen drawings for *Punch* or for other papers and when peace arrived he found himself out of practice.

Although this was true for his commercial drawings he continued to draw wherever he went with his notebook and pencil always on hand. He regularly sent letters home, often daily. Sometimes he would include drawings of himself, his surroundings or his imaginings (68). Early in July 1917, Pie wrote describing some underwear which she had recently bought. Ernest imagined the effect of it in his sketch included in his letter home later in the month (69).

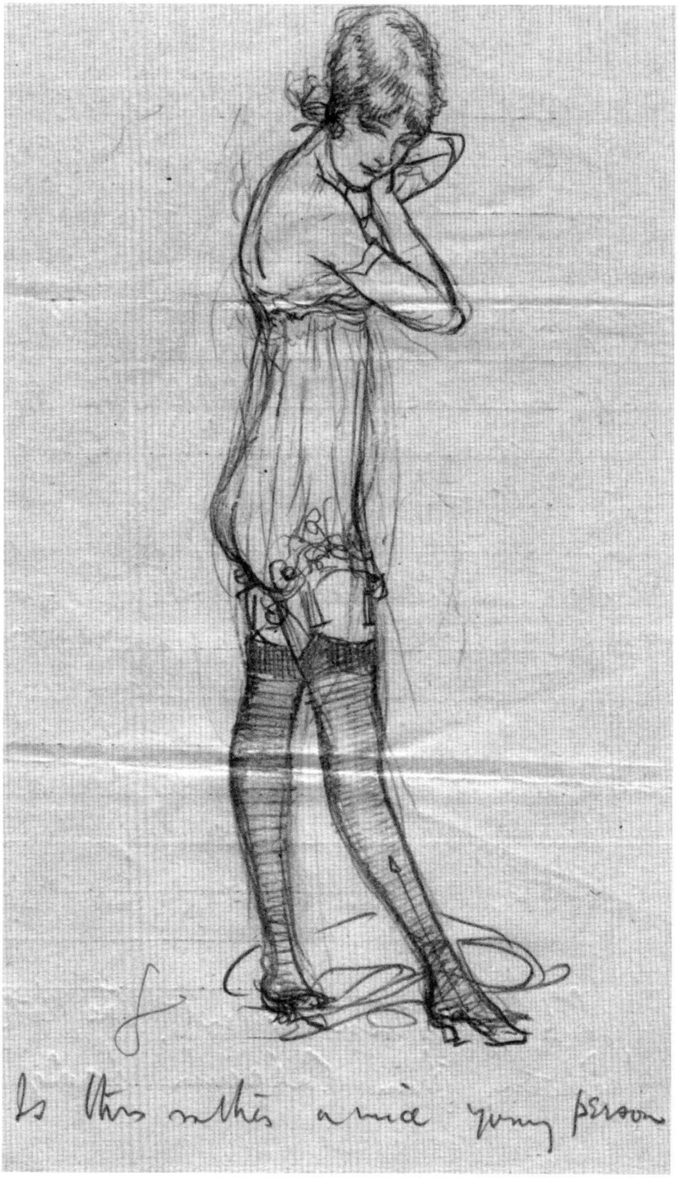

Is this rather a nice young person. Indelible pencil drawing, July 1917 (69)

The Battle of the Somme started in the early hours of the morning of 1st July 1916. The Infantry had gone over the top at 7.30am and Shepard was awake listening to the gunfire that rose to a crescendo at 'zero hour'. He was standing in his Battery controlling the guns when the news came through that the Ninth Devonshire Regiment had captured the enemy trenches. However nearly all their officers were killed or wounded by machine-gun fire. Ernest did not know then that his brother Cyril was among the dead.

When he later had a letter from his sister telling him that Cyril had died, he realised that he was quite near the place where his brother had fallen. He was given permission by his Commanding Officer to seek out Cyril's grave. In Nansell Copse he found the Devonshire Regiment Cemetery that had been made from part of the British Expeditionary Forces front line trench. The area had already been levelled and neatly laid out. Wooden crosses had been erected and the names of the fallen affixed on metal strips. Always having paper and pencil at hand he made two quick sketches of the grave - one for Ethel and one to send to Rosemary, who one assumes was Cyril's girlfriend. In his diary he records "I was grateful to feel so near to Cyril". Unfortunately neither of these sketches can be traced.

Throughout his army service he constantly used his sketchbooks recording the places where he was billeted or fought including a view of St Pierre in October 1917 (4), and Le Rutoire, near Lens (70).

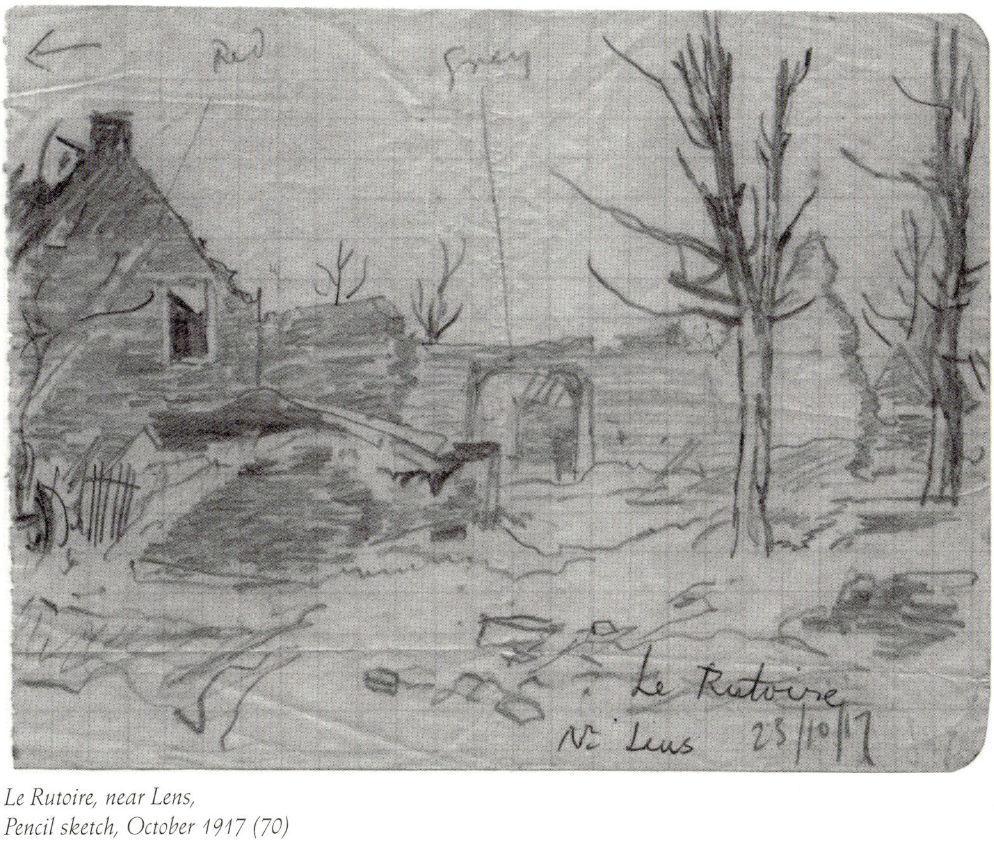

Le Rutoire, near Lens,
Pencil sketch, October 1917 (70)

His cartoonish spirit was kept alive and showed from time to time in his famous drawing of the British Tommy for *Punch* "I ain't but two speeds slow and stop" (71). Not only did he have his sketch book but also his watercolours with him when in France in the summer of 1916 a French biplane officially made 'a bad landing' (pilot wasn't hurt). However, on the back of the painting some years later he wrote, "French plane shot down by our Battery". Today this would be called 'friendly fire' (P2).

In November 1916 he is able to recall the Tea Rooms at Ginchy both by sketch and written word. "The Free Tea Room a bowl of hot tea, some biscuits and a cigarette is given to each man (72). The shed is constructed of stout timber, corrugated iron and sand bagged and has an entrance one end and an exit at the other. It is open day and night and the staff is kept busy practically all the time. The tea is excellent, the place well up to the front so the Infantry can get a hot drink very soon after being relieved from the trenches." Ever being mindful of the use of the back of a drawing, Shepard has sketched, on the back of the Tea Room, a field telephonist and describes the uniform that he wore.

Another drawing for *Punch* that has survived is the sketch that he made of two soldiers in a trench in St Eloi (73). The caption, unfortunately, has been lost. The caption has survived of another rough sketch taken after a village had been captured (74).

He had a strange experience in late October 1916 in the closing stages of the Battle of the Somme. His story of the bob-tailed sheepdog is worth telling here as he recorded it:

THE BOB-TAILED SHEEP DOG

I was standing on the fire-step and leaning my arms on the parapet in an effort to keep my feet from the slushy muck in the bottom of the trench. I was alone but a few yards away some men gathered under a tarpaulin brewing up tea, I could hear the murmur of their voices and the faint roar of a primus stove. No man's land was over two hundred yards wide at this point, so minor noises did not matter. An occasional Verey light went up from the enemy trench opposite and lit up the tangle of wire and the pitted ground in front. It was strangely quiet after the noise and racket of the daytime. Though it was after midnight it was not very dark for there was a half moon behind the clouds and I could just make out the sentry in the bay on my right; he was leaning against the parapet, his rifle with bayonet fixed, beside him.

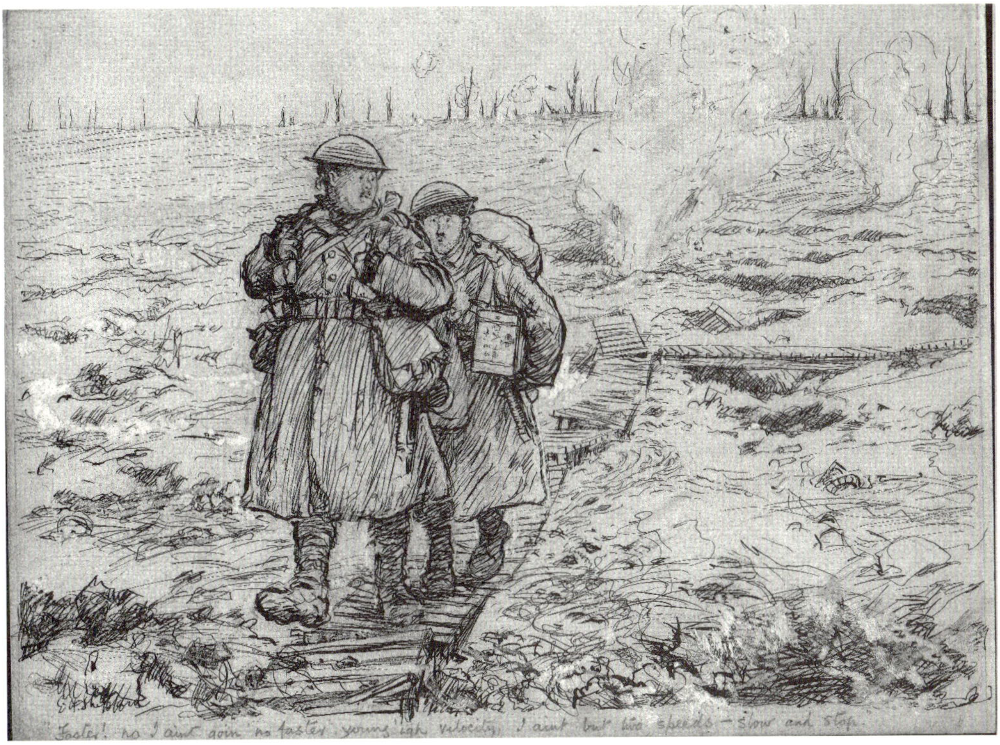

Faster! No, I ain't goin' no faster, young'igh velocity, I ain't but two speeds slow and stop. (71)

I was wearing my British warm and had a woollen scarf around my neck and wished I had put on my Balaclava helmet. I had come on duty at eight o'clock yesterday evening - it was yesterday now - I confirmed this by looking at my wrist-watch.

As a Gunner subaltern my job was to do a twenty-four hour tour of duty in the front trenches and I would be relieved by Oxenham at eight the following evening. My two telephonists, Clarke and Taylor, were tucked away in a cubby-hole scraped in the side of the trench and were probably asleep.

There had been trouble with the telephone line to the battery, in position three miles back, as we came across country, for the Hun had been busy the previous day and the line was cut in many places by shell fire. Taylor and Clarke always came with me and had a habit of sleeping as near me as possible: it was useless to point out to them that one shell might finish us off together if we bunched like that and I had explained this to Taylor, whose only reply was that they felt safer when they were near me.

Our journey on the previous evening had been delayed by having to mend several cuts in the line. As it was dark our only way to check on this was to follow the line, running it through our hands and when we came to a break, stop and join it up. Nearing the front line, the line was divided into two and brought into our trench at different points to give it a better chance of survival.

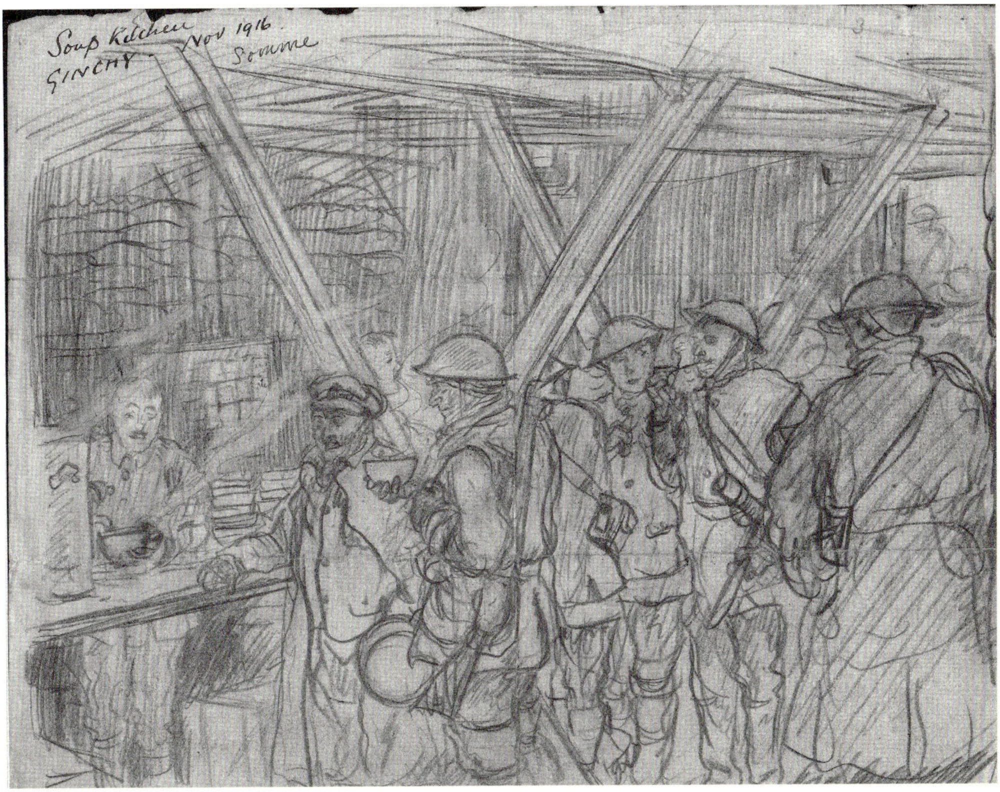

The Free Tea-room, near Ginchy
(sometimes called The Soup Kitchen)
Pencil sketch (72)

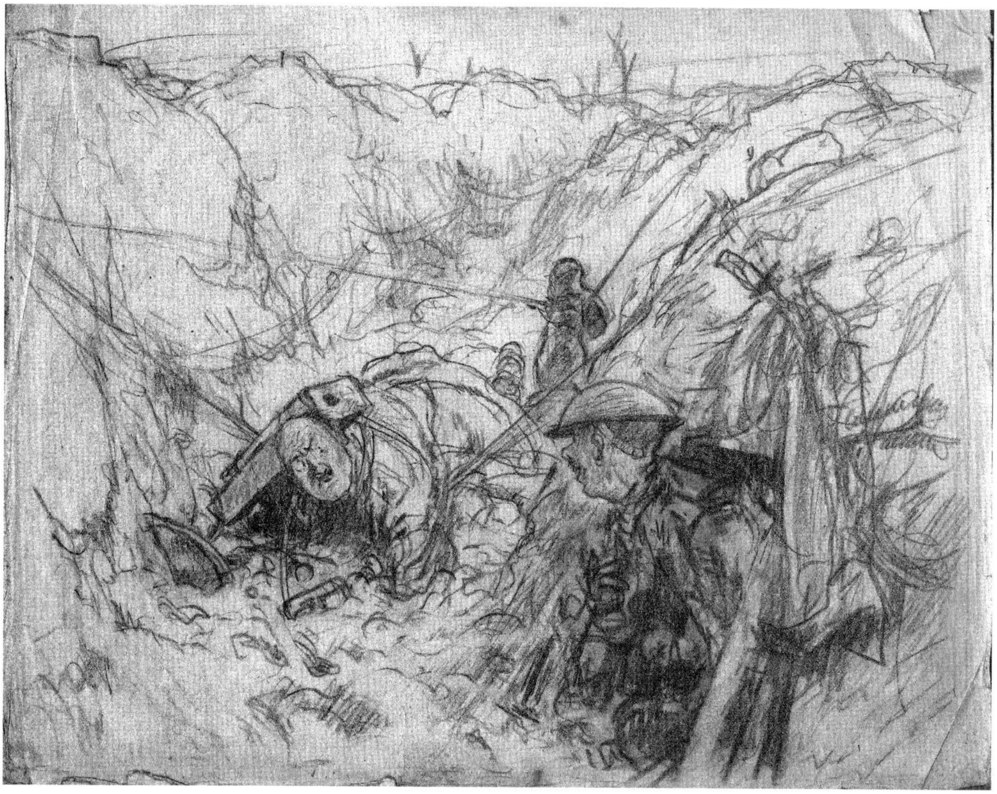

Sketch for Punch drawing made in support trench near St Eloi (73)

I had followed one line and the two men the other; I had mended a break and was moving on when I saw, lying beside a newly made shell hole, a bob-tailed sheep dog. It was lying there quite peacefully as if it were asleep. I stooped down examined it, it was quite cold, as there was no sign of any wound I decided it must have died from shell shock. I had been that same way night after night, but this was the first time I had seen the dog and I wondered how it had got there and to whom it had belonged.

When I joined my men in the trench, I asked them if they had noticed it. No, they had not.

As the night drew on I became more and more sleepy and was dozing when I woke with a start. Away on the right I thought I could see someone moving in no man's land. It was too dark to make anything out but, by the light thrown by a Verey pistol, I saw the figure of a man. He was moving quite slowly towards me. I was wide awake by this time and glanced at the sentry, who appeared to be on the alert but was showing no sign of interest. I was beginning to think that I had imagined things, when the figure appeared quite close to me it was a man dressed in a faded blue jacket and rough grey trousers, he was moving without any sound and was looking from side to side, then he stopped and, speaking in French, said "Have you seen my dog, Fiaton?" I was too startled to answer and the man passed on, shaking his head and saying, "no, no, alas, poor Fiaton". He shuffled on and was soon out of sight. I went over to the sentry "did you see that?" I asked, "what?" answered the man, "that man passing in front?" The sentry looked at me, all he said was "you must have been asleep, cock".

I returned to my post and racked my brains for an explanation. The sentry was right, I must have been asleep, of course it was that dog, I had been dreaming about it.

It was some hours later, I was wide awake now and in the faint light I saw the figure again, it was coming back and it passed in front of me, behind the man trotted the bob-tailed sheep dog. I held my breath, then the man turned and, waving his hand, passed on with his dog.

When I was relieved at eight o'clock, I climbed out of the trench the same way that I had come in, I kept the telephone line in my hand, Taylor and Clarke followed me. "Is this where you saw that dog?" Taylor asked. "Yes", I answered. "Well, he ain't there now!" "No", I said, "I must have dreamt it".

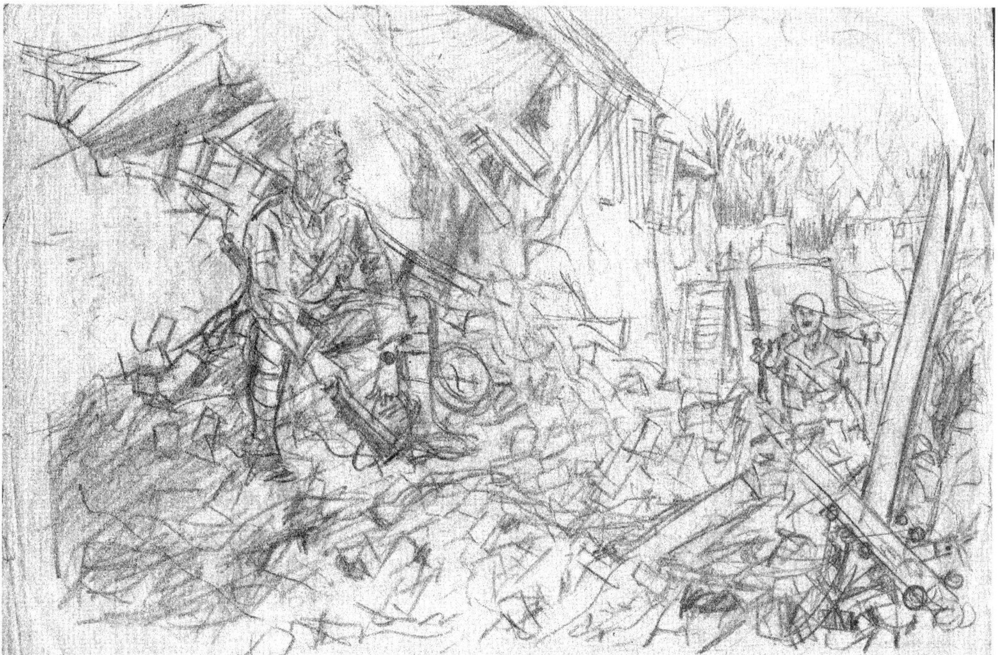

Newcomer: My Village I think!
The One in possession: sorry old sport, I took it half an hour ago
Pencil sketch for Punch *(74)*

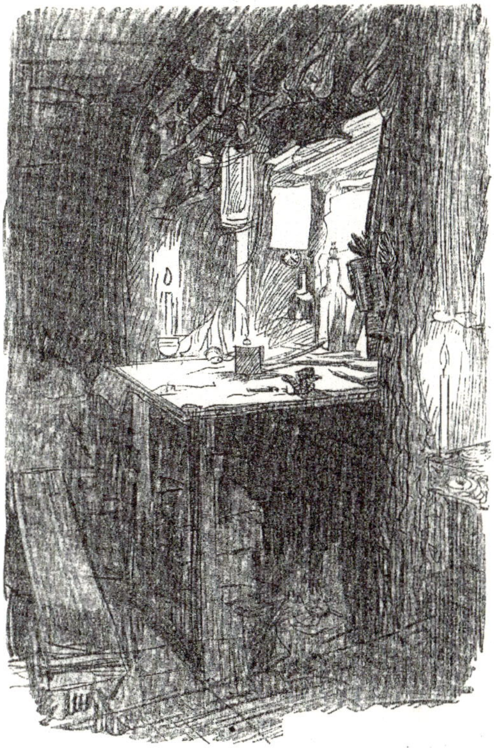

A Battery Dug-out, 1916 (75)

Shepard never lost his ability to draw cartoons. In the midst of the desolation in France he was able to look forward to "Piping times of peace" with a caricature of Captain Herbert, their musical director, when he sketched his fellow officer in a mixture of flamboyant evening dress and war-time steel helmet conducting an orchestra (P4).

Towards the end of 1916 Shepard undertook "a drawing job for the Intelligence Department". This was in fact more the task of an unofficial photographer than that of a war artist. He would sketch everything within view from the dugout used by his battery, which was comparatively civilised (75), to an area after bombardment, which was complete desolation (76). His army notebooks show that throughout 1917 he must have sketched continuously. In March, he sketched the observation station near Rocquigny (77) and in October where he must have been for some time, he sketched the view from his billet in St Pierre (4). A page in his notebook shows Le Rutoire near Lens (70) which he later developed into a full sketch which he notes is the Royal Field Artillery preparing for their position (78).

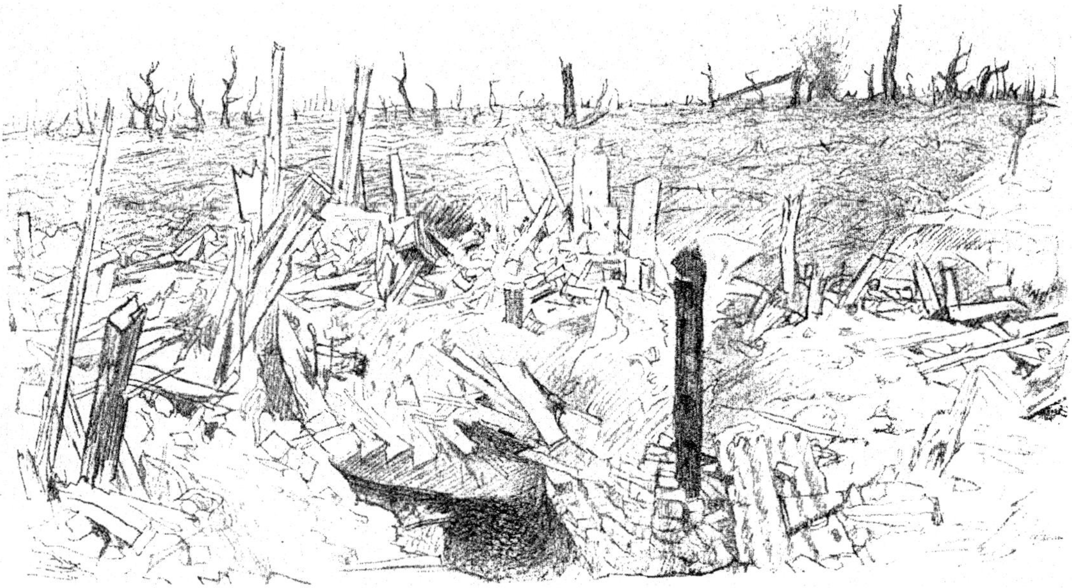

Complete Desolation, 1916 (76)

As we know, Shepard was a prolific letter writer and even under the stress of war he would include drawings, though these seem to be definitive sketches rather than the cartoons which he had included in letters in his younger days. In a letter dated September 1917 he included the drawing of a dress and wrote "I've done you a drawing of a rather nice costume I thought of evolved from one I saw in one of the papers, dark blue linen jumper bodice with blue and white striped skirt, cuffs and collar - nice and simple......... Then I could fancy a big hat am I getting rather dictatorial?" (79).

A month later, in November 1917, his Battery was moved to Italy and he found himself in Verona. Nobody spoke a word of Italian and the Battery had no maps. Shepard had been given the direction to Verona by a local inhabitant soon after they had crossed the border, but they were not certain that they had arrived there until he had passed a statue which he happened to recognise.

Observation Station, 1917 (77)

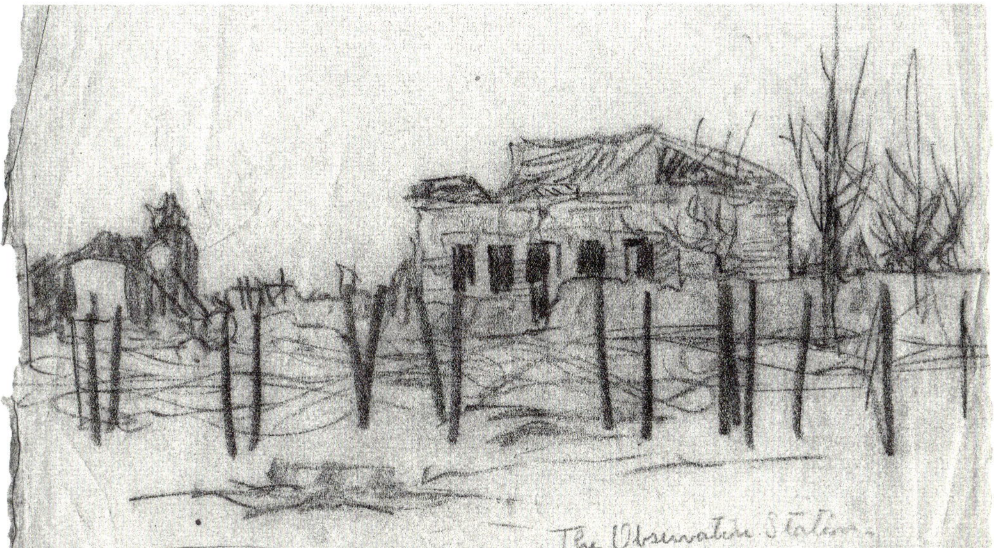

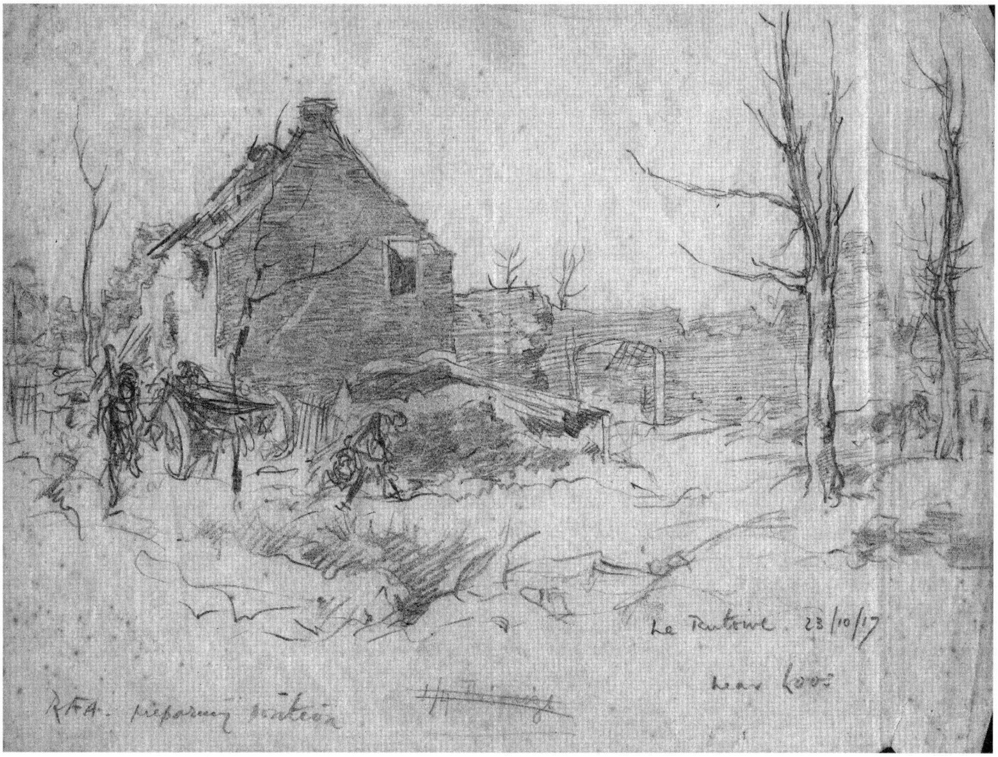

Le Rutoire, near Loos, 1917 (78)

Shepard was soon overcome by a wonderful feeling once he arrived in Italy. He 'felt' for the country of ancient art treasures. Counteracting this feeling of elation he was frustrated in his efforts when trying to negotiate his horse-drawn guns through the many mountainous roads of Italy (80). The terrain made it difficult to move as the local people evacuating from the areas of battle were tired, hungry and rather naturally uncooperative.

At Christmas time 1917 Shepard found himself in a farmhouse kitchen. He was helping to prepare the turkey when he saw some red tabbed staff officers arriving. Hastily dusting himself down, he went to the door to find that General Gaythorne-Hardy, the Corps Commander and the Prince of Wales were standing there. Shepard apologised for his unmilitary appearance that evoked a broad grin on the Prince's face. The new year was celebrated with a very successful concert party that had been instigated by Shepard. He also painted all the scenery.

With winter gone, the Asiago plateau had become a place of prime importance to the allied troops and Shepard's battery prepared to move up there. The mountains on the Italian side were about one thousand five hundred metres high. Those on the Austrian side were considerably higher. The plateau was four and a half kilometres across and eleven kilometres wide as the Battery viewed it. They found that only by climbing a tree could they get a really good view of the plateau

Design for a dress
Sent by Shepard to his wife,
September 1917 (79)

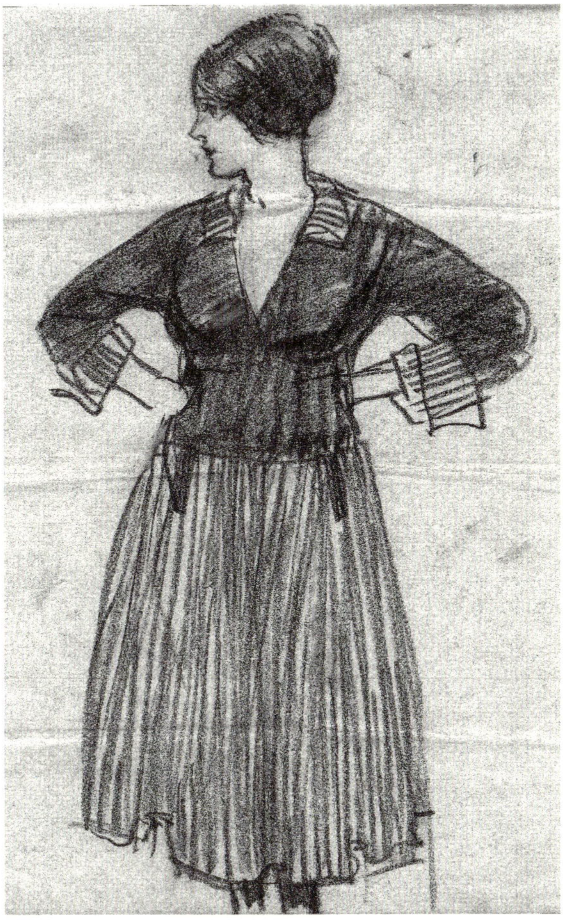

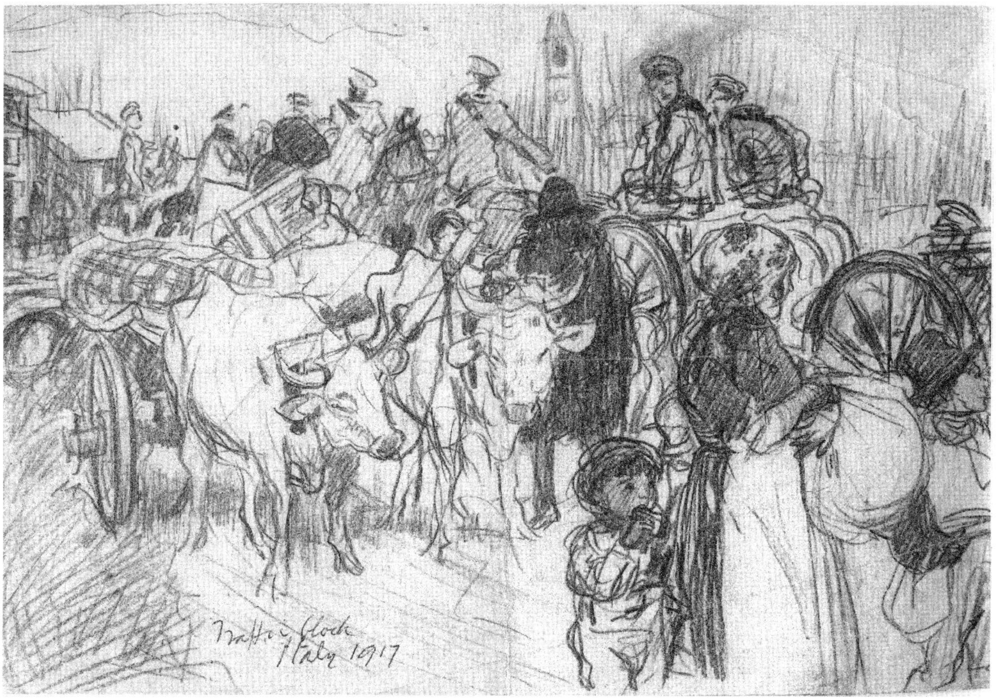

Traffic Block, Italy 1917 (80)

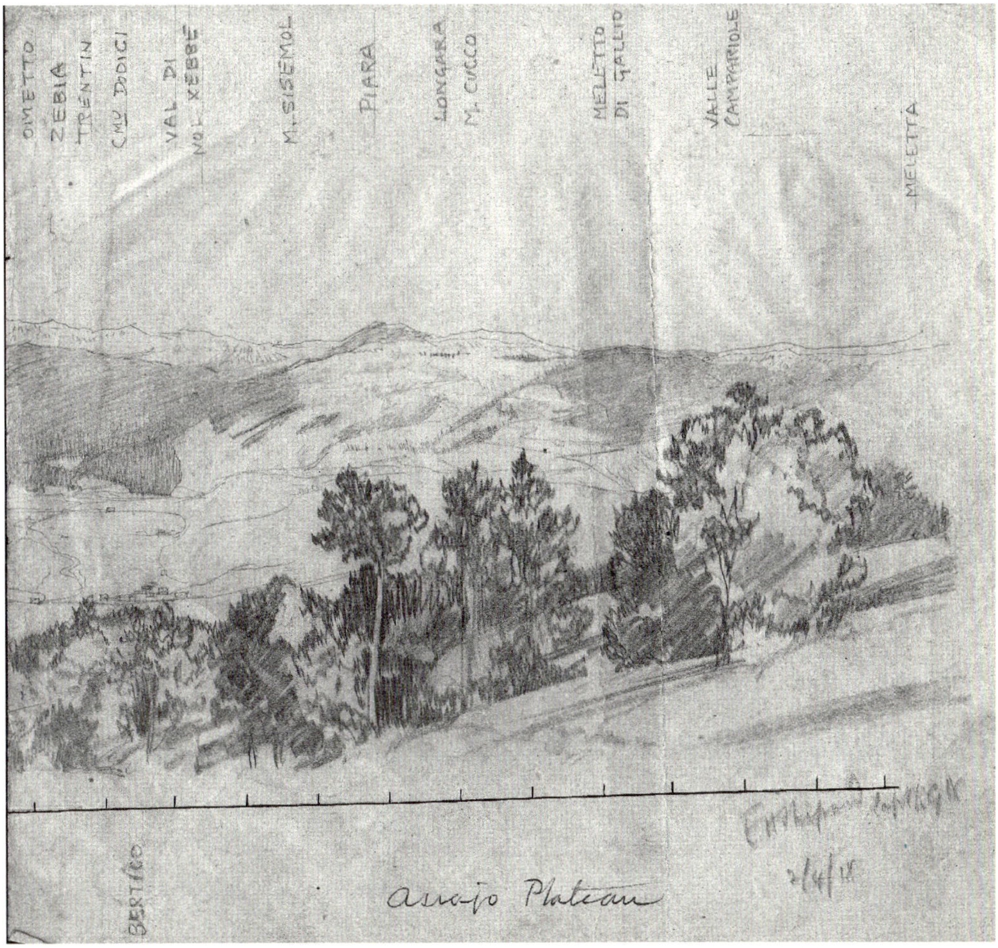

Asiago Plateau, April 1918 (81)

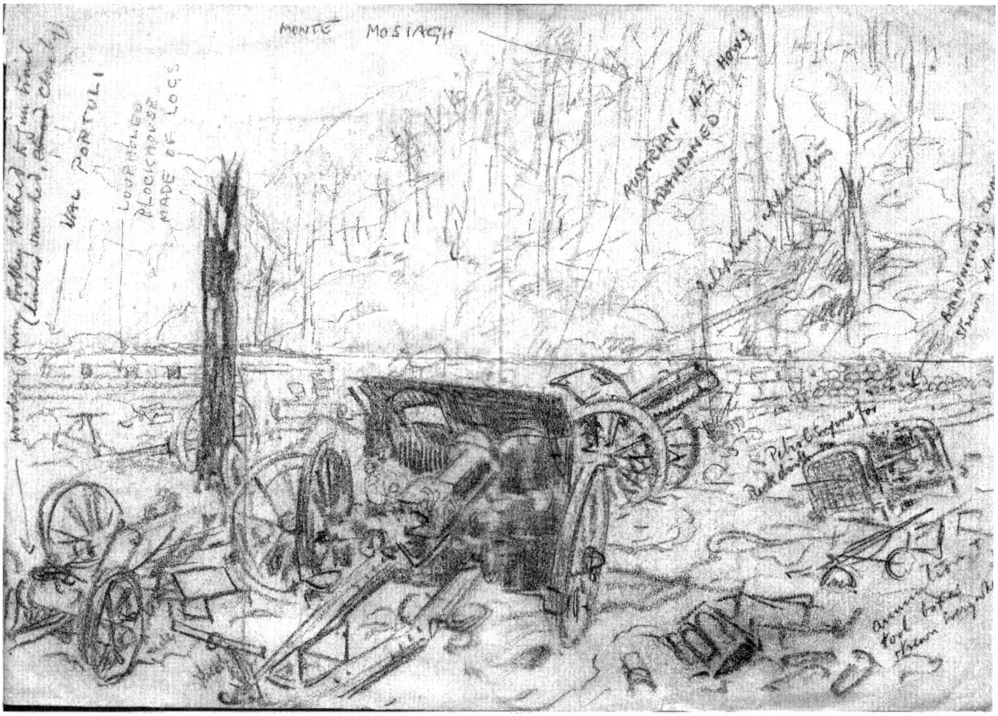

Monte Mosiagh (82)
Pencil
An abandoned Austrian position showing detail of equipment left behind.
Note explanation of items to be shown on completed picture.

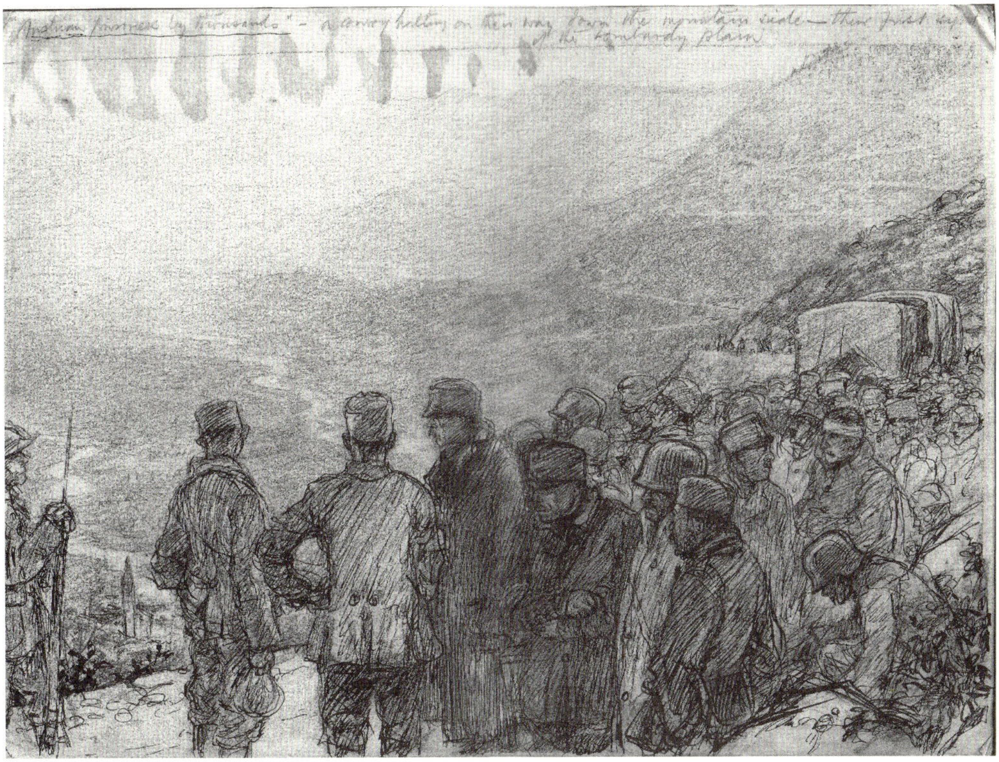

Austrian Prisoners by Thousands
Pencil
A convoy halting on their way down the mountain side their first sight of the Lombardy Plain (83)

The Battery was ordered to register certain points of the plateau and Shepard was detailed to do this. The original drawings of the plateau are still in existence (81). Also preserved in the archives is a panorama of the area that could be viewed by Shepard's Battery together with the appropriate gun readings. This document is about thirty centimetres in height and is two metres in width. Having seen the Battery safely established on the plateau Shepard went on leave. On 19th January 1918 he woke up at Southampton, quickly caught a train and reached London by noon. He then travelled to Guildford where Pie met him and they were both home by 6.30pm. A week later he was in London discussing possible sketches and visiting the *Punch* office. His leave ended on 2nd February when he returned to Europe. Later in the summer, Shepard was ordered to attend an advanced gunnery course back home.

Another period of leave commenced on 4th May when he returned home to find that Graham had mumps. He then attended gunnery lectures and military examinations but managed to find time to go to the Royal Academy and to visit Salisbury although that was part of the course. In mid June he went to the War Office in order to get a week's extension of his leave although the Austrian offensive started at the same time. During this period he was given some days leave when Pie accompanied him to Buckingham Palace to receive the Military Cross from King George V. Within a few days of this Investiture, he had finished and sent off a series of cartoons and illustrations to *Punch* before his leave ended on 24th June.

He returned to Italy for the final stages of the War. His diary mixes business with pleasure. He was now able to send cartoons to *Punch* as well as undertaking official sketches as part of his military duties. On 4th and 5th July he records "*Punches*". August 13th he records "On duty - painted". On the following day he wrote "painted - no shooting". On October 6th the enemy asked for an armistice and it seems that for the rest of the month his interests were more in designing scenery and taking rehearsals than in worrying himself with what, in his area, was quickly becoming a 'peacetime army'. On 3rd November Austria surrendered. The pace of his military activities slowed down and his sketching interests moved to record abandoned military sites (82) and the gatherings of thousands of enemy Prisoners of War (83).

In November his cartoons showed his realisation of peace and the return of normality (85). He suddenly was able to stage a regimental review that he had been preparing in his mind for some weeks. Imagination produced 'Grand Peace Ballet' for the close of the Italian season where his immediate group of officers was shown as ballet dancers in the regimental magazine *Venti Quatro* which he produced in January 1919 (86). The other ranks were not spared Shepard's pen when he drew a cartoon of the referee, Gunner Jackson, at a regimental football match, the title of which was *The Accusing Finger* (P5).

Sketch for a self-portrait just before he left Italy (84)

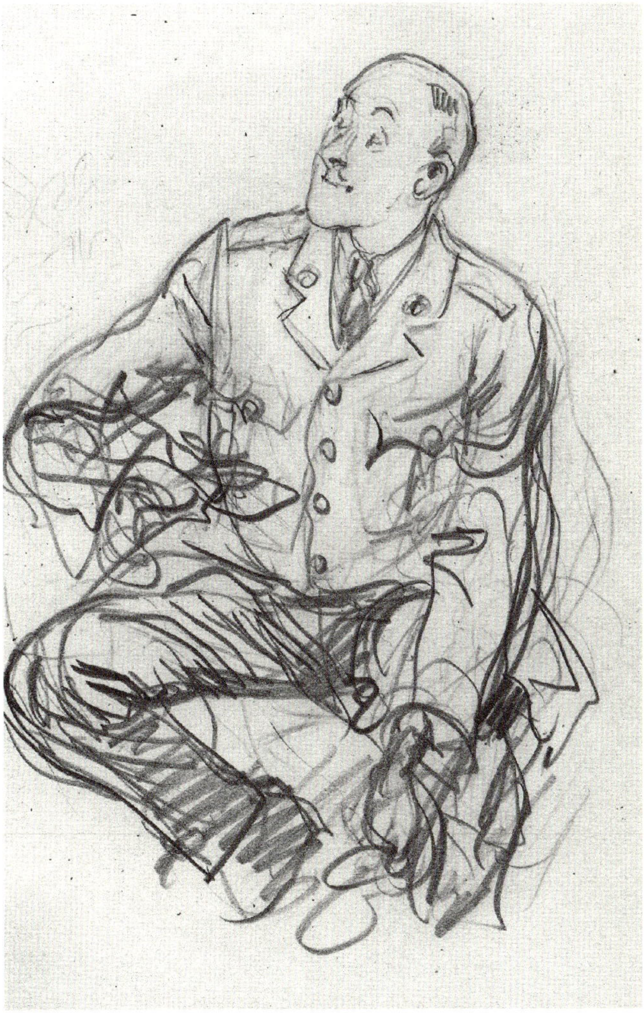

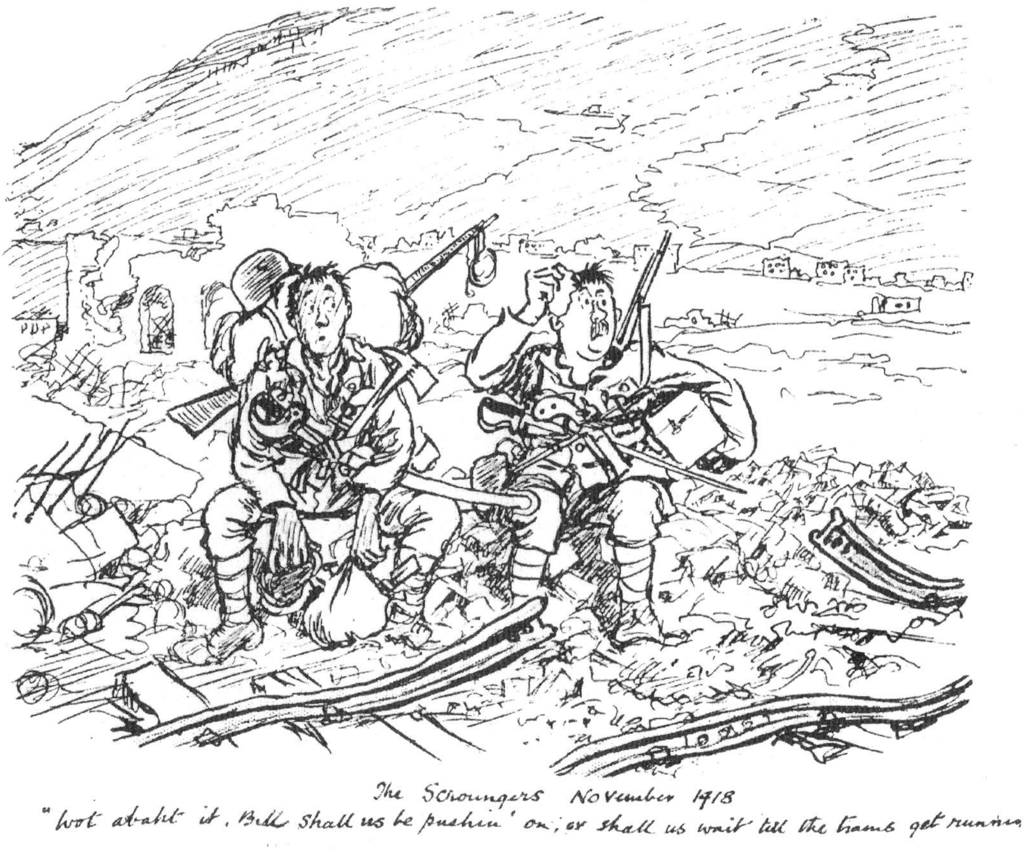

The Scroungers, November 1918
Wot abaht it, Bill, shall us be pushin' on, or
Shall us wait till the trams get runnin (85)

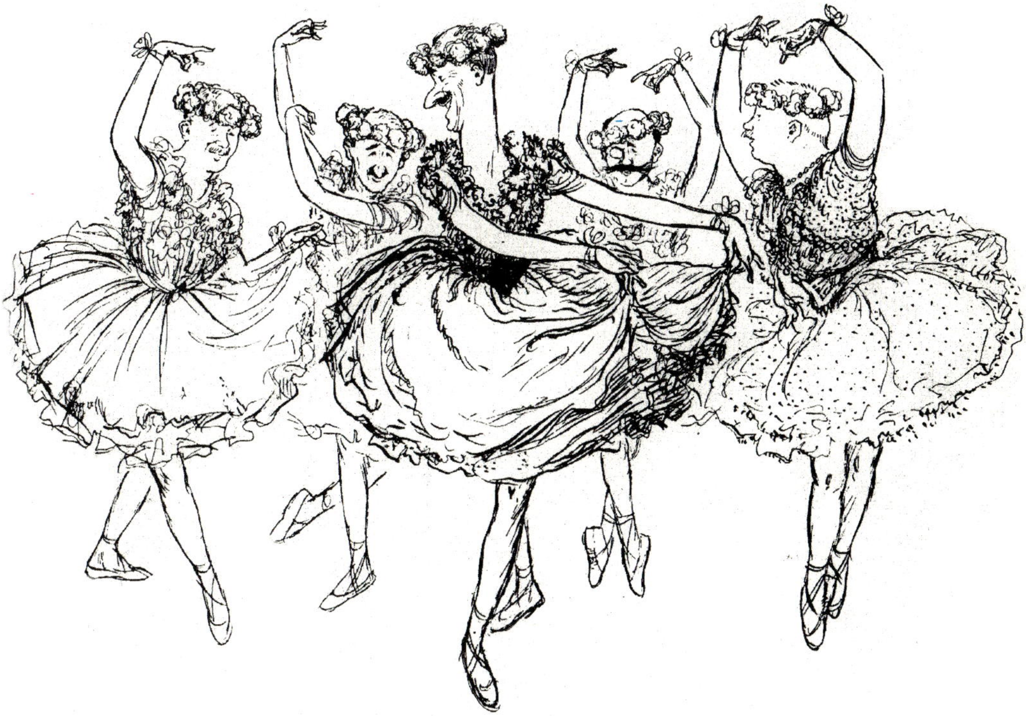

Close of the Italian Season
'Grand Peace Ballet' Finale (86)

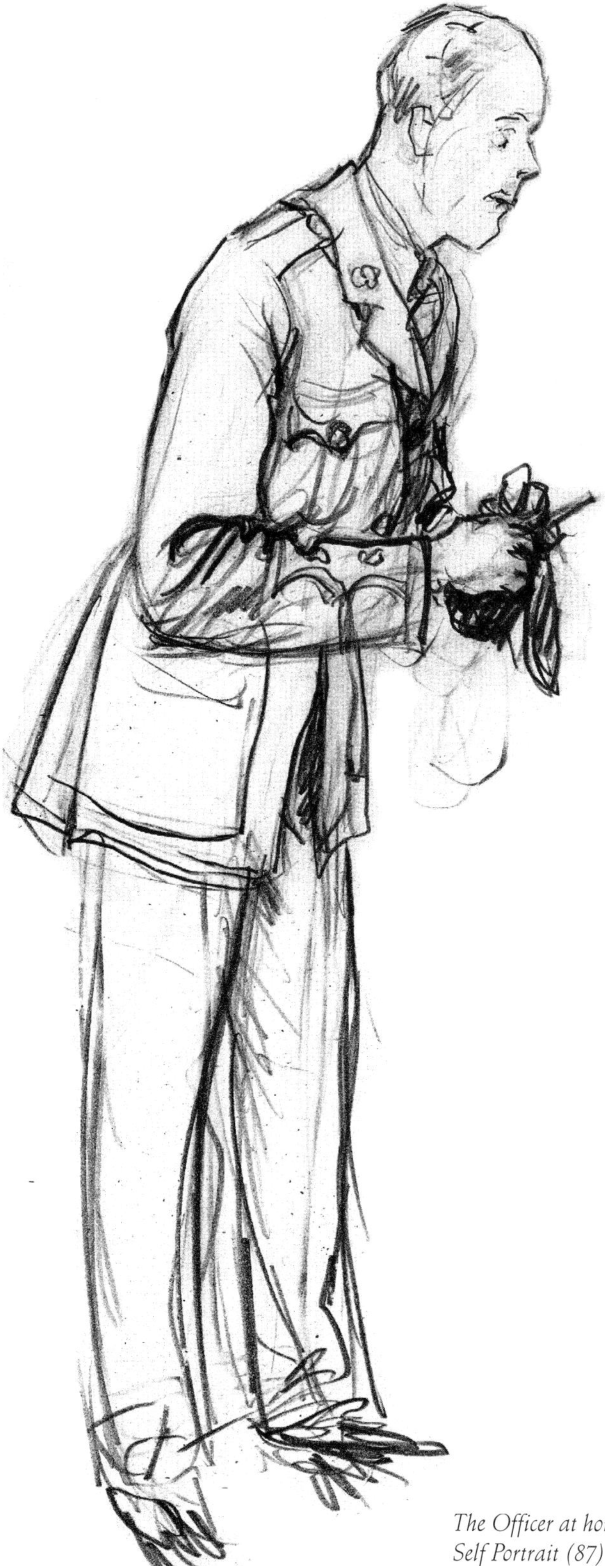

The Officer at home
Self Portrait (87)

E.H. Shepard

Chapter 7
RETURN TO FAMILY LIFE 1919 - 1928

The War was over. Major Shepard's army life was nearing its end. He managed to snatch forty-eight hours' leave in Venice before his Regiment returned across the Channel and made its way to Crystal Palace in South London where one by one the men were given a fortnight's leave with pay and demobbed from His Majesty's service. He records that he found it a very queer feeling standing on the platform at Crystal Palace waiting for a train to Clapham Junction whence he would take another train to Guildford.

It was hard for him to realise that he was no longer a soldier. He had brought with him from Italy and France photographs, maps and field glasses that he had used throughout the War. Like all old soldiers, he brought back his 'war souvenirs' a revolver, two brass shell cases and an Austrian carbine all packed in a wooden case marked 'ammunition, for the use of'. The most precious items were his army notebooks (87) and his sketchbooks (88), which he was to refer to many times in future years. The sketchbooks contained pictures of places and events of the War. In the latter part of the conflict he had started to draw civilians and children and this eased his way into the years of peace.

Upon his arrival at 'Red Cottage' in Shamley Green the children, Graham and Mary, became very excited on seeing him. They couldn't restrain themselves because 'daddy' was home. The first thing that he wanted to do was to have a hot bath.

His personal present for Pie was Venetian lace, which he had purchased on his return journey through Italy. Pie had saved sixty pounds from her army pay allowance and Ernest had twenty-five pounds in his pocket, being a major's salary for his two weeks leave. They therefore had a reasonable amount of money, for those days, on which to resume their married life.

In May the couple decided to take a holiday having accepted an invitation to join Pie's cousins for two weeks at Chideock in Dorset. They travelled by motorbike and sidecar for the one hundred mile journey. As it was term time they left the two children in the charge of a friend. At that time Mary was at Tormead School and Graham at Ferndene Preparatory School.

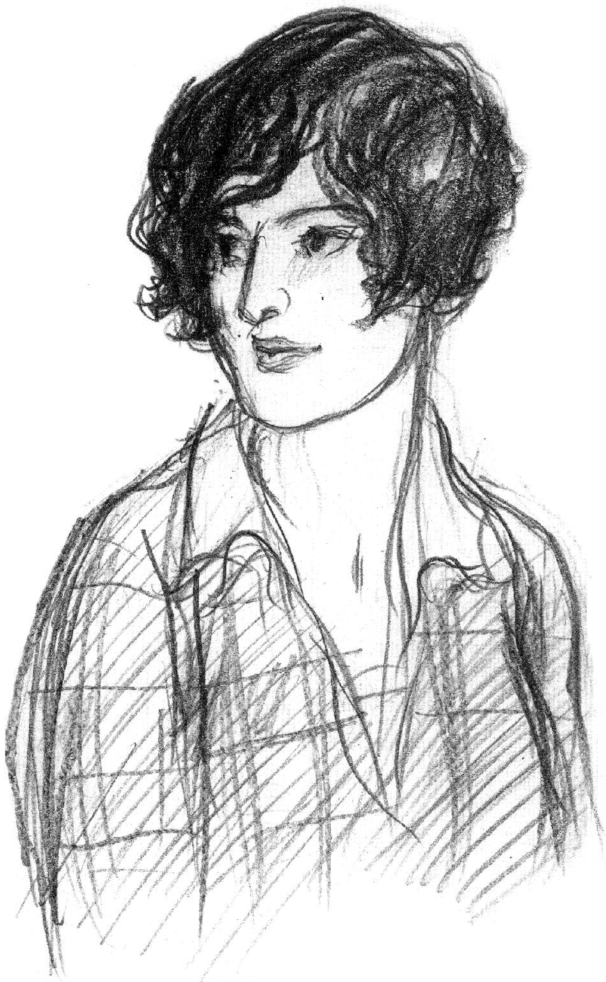

Pie
Pencil sketch by Ernest (88)

Before he went on this holiday Shepard had been considerably worried lest he was not able to paint again for the commercial world. Pie had been painting throughout hostilities and had submitted a watercolour for the Royal Academy Exhibition in March 1919. Shepard felt that he would have difficulty in taking an interest in anything that did not have a military theme. In a letter to his wife he said he felt that he had "a lot of leeway to make up, I've got to relearn so much how to think about painting, probably when I get home with the smell of the food and the old studio things will improve". He should not have worried as he had drawn constantly throughout the War mainly through 'military experience'. In actual fact this turned out to be another 'life experience' in the same way as his childhood for him had been.

He now put his military life behind him and concentrated on re-establishing himself as an illustrator and cartoonist. He was able to send a few drawings to *Punch* during the War and began sending them ideas, some of which were accepted. The managing director of G Bell and Sons wrote to Shepard inviting him to illustrate an abridged edition of *Pepys' Diary*. Shepard considered that this would be a full year's work and asked six hundred pounds. The publisher said that they could not pay such a sum on a book with a doubtful saleable value and suggested an advance payment of £150 plus a royalty of ten per cent on sales. Shepard reluctantly agreed to this but it proved a worthwhile risk as he continued to receive royalties from the book some fifty years later! The chairman of G Bell was called Bickers. He had also served as a gunner and it was his firm that was to produce the *Royal Artillery War Commemoration Book* for which Shepard was asked to submit detailed sketches of observations (see 75 & 76, Chapter 6).

In pursuit of accuracy for his Pepys illustrations he used to hire the appropriate costumes and wigs, sometimes using models to wear them. One of his models was Lettice Spence of whom he said "She was such a lovely sight. A pure white skin and a figure like a Greek goddess. I had seen many models but never anything like her". All his professional work was carried out in his studio (89) in the grounds of 'Red Cottage'. He never ceased to draw his wife whenever he could.

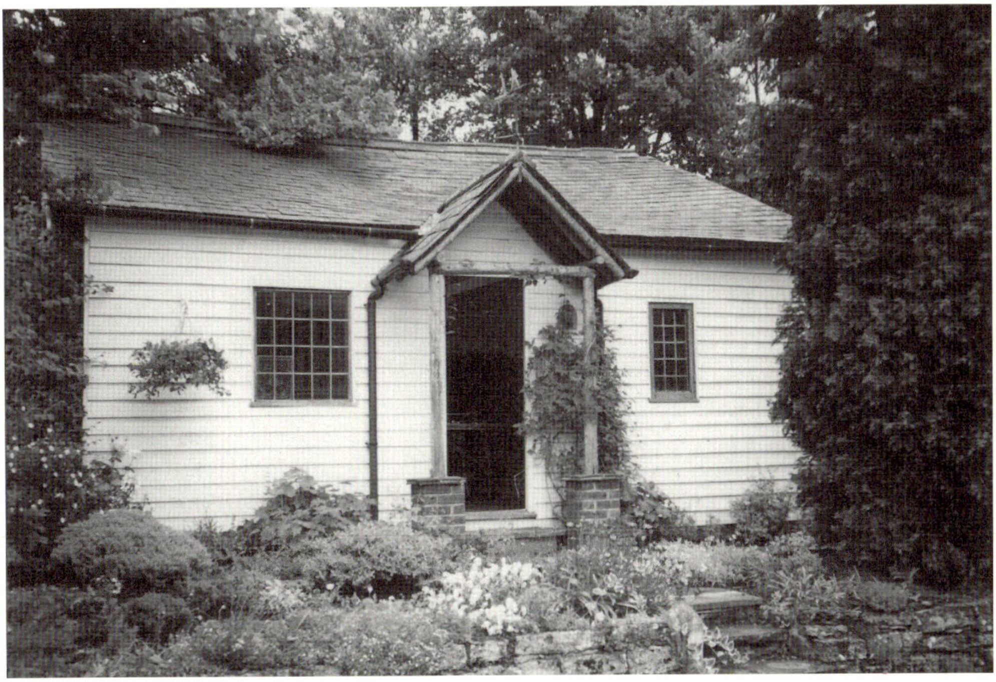

The Studio at 'Red Cottage'
where all the Milne illustrations were drawn (89)

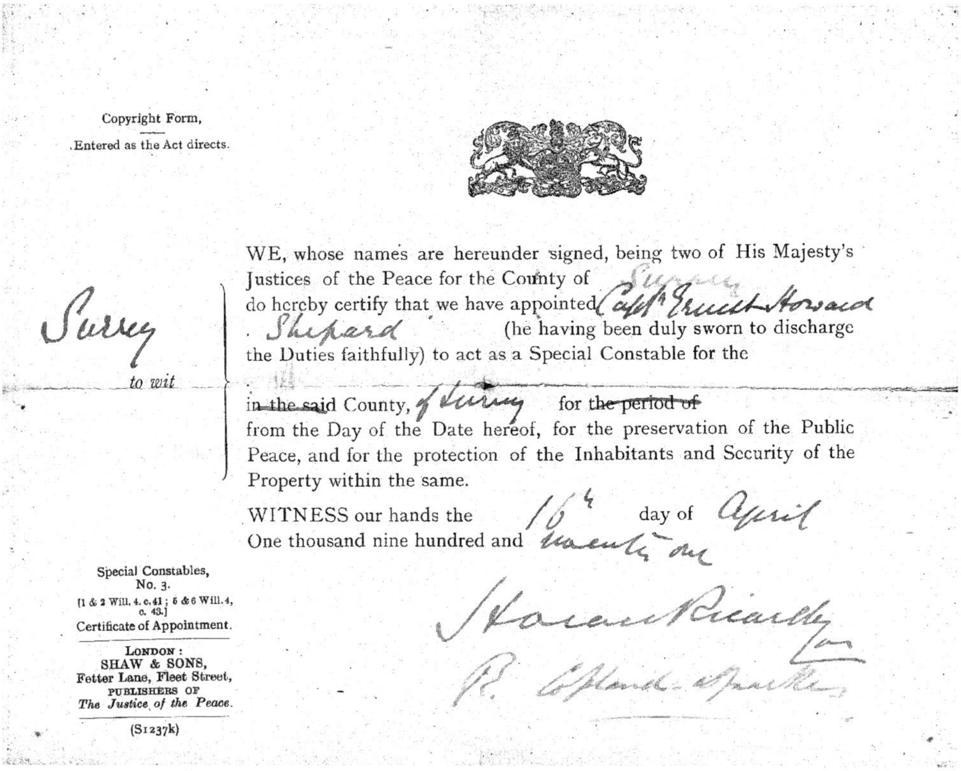

Copyright Form,

Entered as the Act directs.

Surrey to wit

WE, whose names are hereunder signed, being two of His Majesty's Justices of the Peace for the County of Surrey do hereby certify that we have appointed Capt Ernest Howard Shepard (he having been duly sworn to discharge the Duties faithfully) to act as a Special Constable for the

in the said County, of Surrey for the period of from the Day of the Date hereof, for the preservation of the Public Peace, and for the protection of the Inhabitants and Security of the Property within the same.

WITNESS our hands the 16th day of April One thousand nine hundred and twenty one

J Horace Ricardo

R. Copland-Sparkes

Special Constables, No. 3. [1 & 2 Will. 4. c. 41; 5 & 6 Will. 4, c. 43.] Certificate of Appointment.

LONDON: SHAW & SONS, Fetter Lane, Fleet Street, PUBLISHERS OF *The Justice of the Peace*.

(S1237k)

Certificate of Appointment as Special Constable (90)

On 16th April 1921 Captain Ernest Howard Shepard was sworn in as a special constable for the County of Surrey. His truncheon now resides in the Shepard Archive. His idea of service to the community comes out in many of his activities both for church and state (90).

In the summer of 1921 he was invited to join the *Punch* Table. This was a great honour for him. The table had been founded soon after the paper was born in 1842, to be a gathering of the original founders with one to be chosen as editor. It had to meet every week, dine, and make plans for the policy of the paper. The members were both writers and artists. The word 'table' meant the administrative staff and once elected you were a life member even if you ceased to contribute to *Punch*. Shepard's original place at the table was next to Bernard Partridge who was then the chief cartoonist. Very unusual for that time, members of the Table called each other by their Christian names (91).

Ernest thoroughly enjoyed his Wednesdays at *Punch*. His one problem was the need to catch his last train back to Guildford. Eventually he found a studio in Holland Park Road where he could stay overnight and finish his cartoon the following day and he would take it straight to the printers in Mount Royal on the Friday.

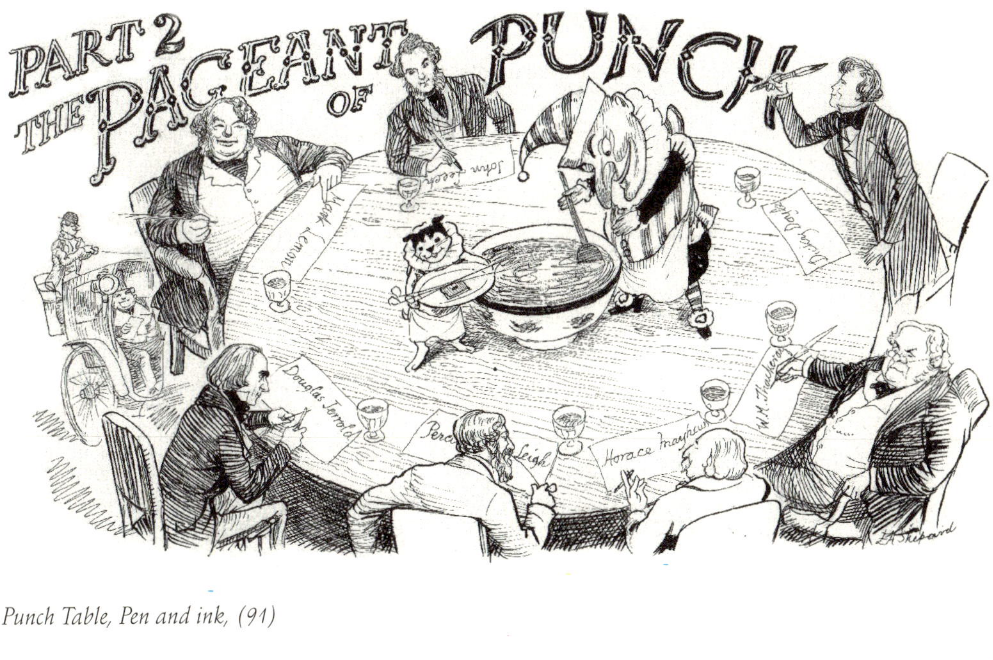

Punch Table, Pen and ink, (91)

In 1922 he consolidated his work as an illustrator, family holidays were taken, but his sketchbooks were always to the fore (92) (94). In November he attended the Third Annual Dinner of the 24th Brigade for which he had drawn the cover of the menu (93).

One evening at the *Punch* Table Shepard was sitting next to E V Lucas who was then chairman of Methuen's, the publishers. They had been offered some verses for children by A A Milne and wanted an artist to illustrate them. Shepard jumped at the opportunity. Author and illustrator met and it at once became obvious that they would be able to work happily together. Shepard expected to do about fifty drawings on this project and he looked around, as was his custom, to find actual models for his drawings. When writing his notes on this he said "My son, Graham, had a teddy to which he had been deeply attached as a child and I used this bear as my model. I also had a number of drawings I had made of Graham as a boy of six and these were very useful when, later on, I came to draw Christopher Robin".

1923 was probably the most important year of his career because his meeting with Milne and Milne's acceptance of him as a brilliant illustrator led to a second book of poems and the two books of Pooh.

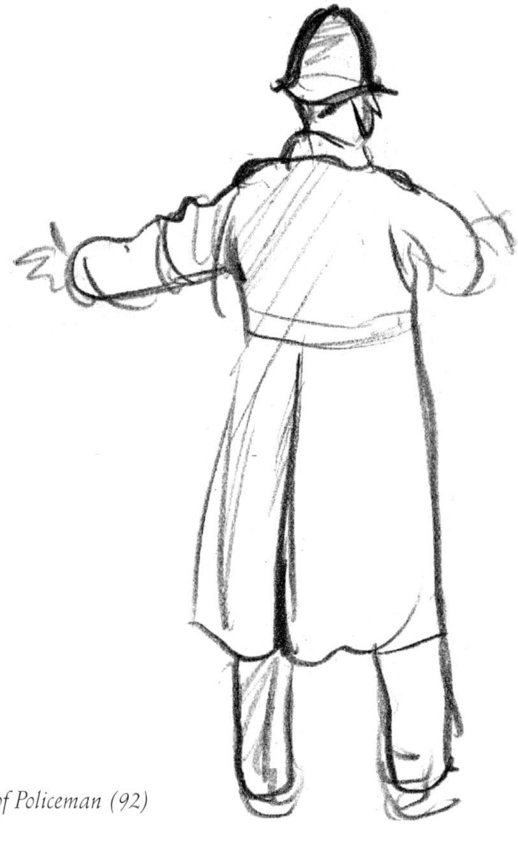

Pencil sketch of Policeman (92)

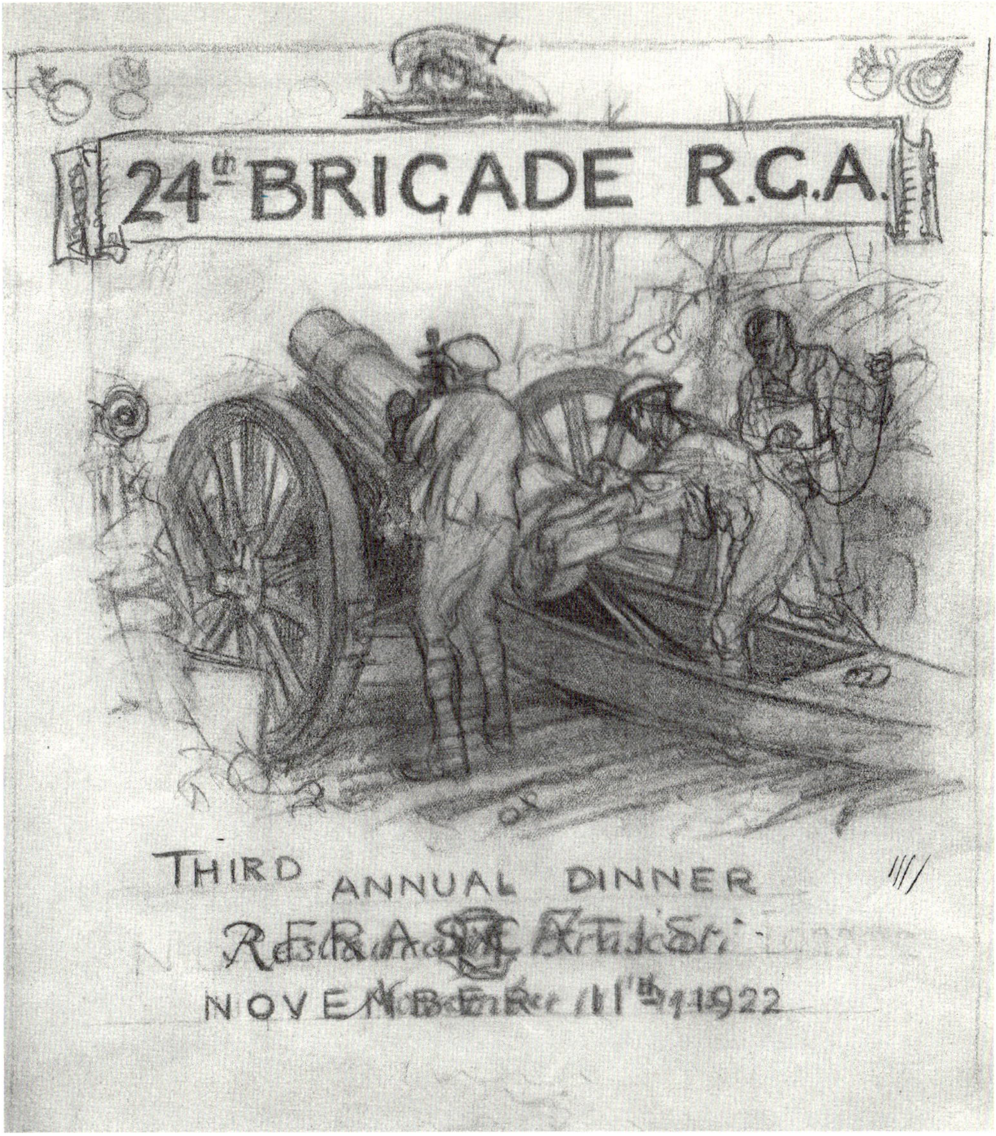

Pencil sketch for 3rd Annual Dinner 24th Brigade R.G.A.
Drawn September 1922 (93)

Because of his commitment to the *Punch* Table and the need to keep to other publication deadlines, Ernest could not take the long holidays that he had in previous years. In March 1923 he and Pie went off to Rapallo in Italy for a month's holiday but after a few days he had to return to London because of publication commitments. He did manage to go back to Italy for the final week but while Pie was on her own he wrote to her daily as he had done when they were separated in earlier years. One of these letters, in which he expresses both his joys and sorrows of working for *Punch*, he wrote while on the train in which he spent a fair amount of time between Guildford and London. Sometimes his travel between home and office and return would take up to four and a half hours a day. In June of the same year his notebook contains, amongst many other drawings, two sketches of a lady in a train (95) (96). His notebooks never failed to capture an interesting moment in the same way that a press photographer today might capture a special moment or a memorable scene.

Methuen had invited Milne to produce another book for children but the author was not to be hurried. He told Shepard that he would do so in due course and then added "In any case I shall want you to illustrate it".

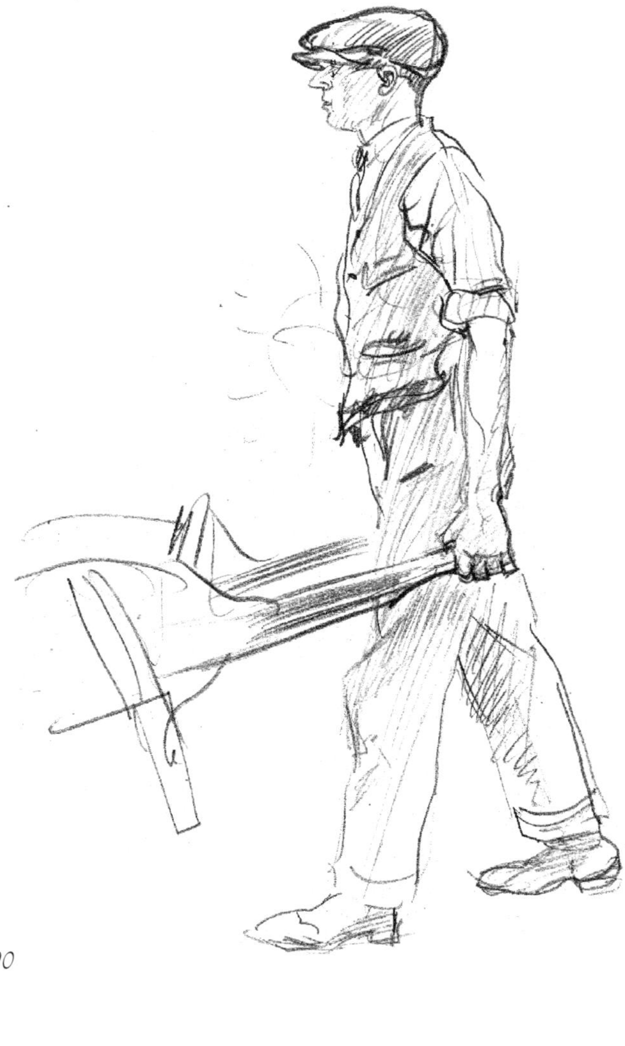

Pencil sketch, 1924:
Man with wheelbarrow (94)

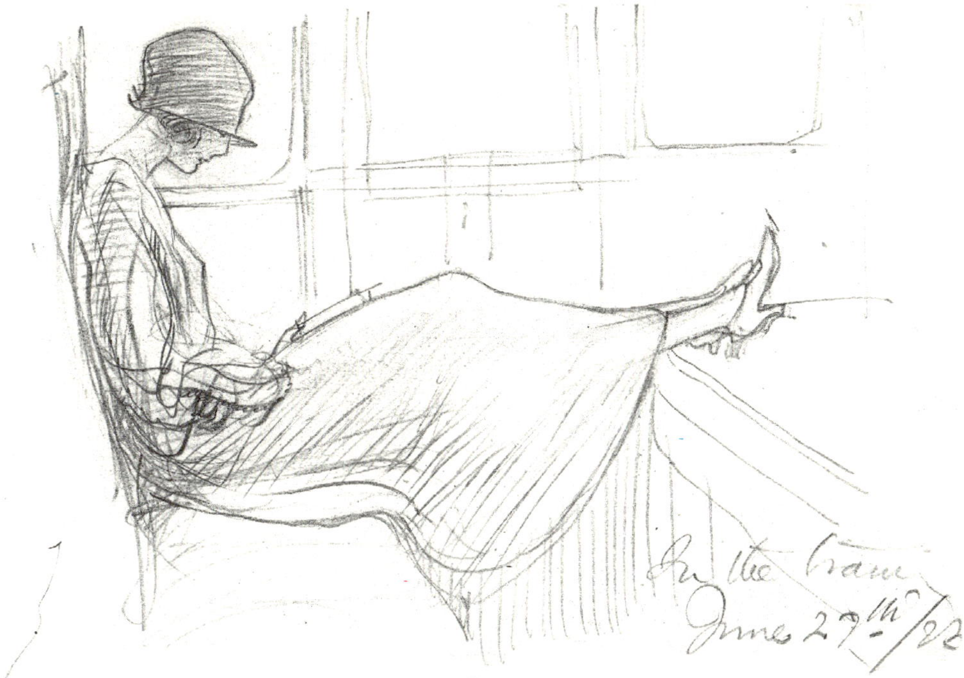

Pencil sketch (95)

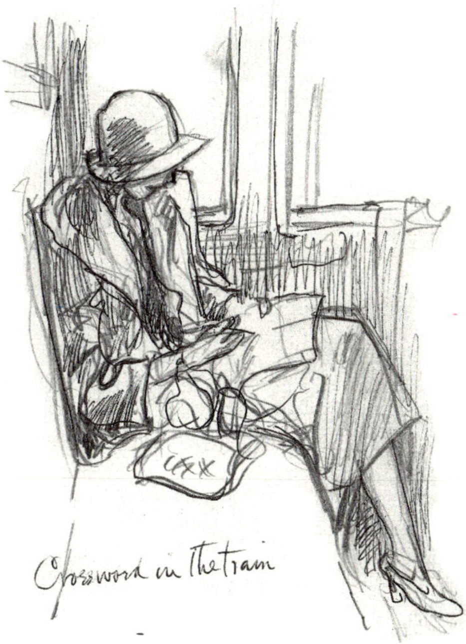

By the spring of 1924 the illustrations for the poems were ready and these were published in the November as *When We Were Very Young* (99). He had now been commissioned to undertake illustrations for *Winnie-the-Pooh* and *Now We Are Six* (101) (102). Throughout 1924 he spent hours with A A Milne in Ashdown Forest going over the ground that was to be the scene of the adventures with Pooh, Piglet, Kanga, Roo, Eeyore and Tigger.

He drew the pine trees, the house where Wol lived and Piglet's home and watched A A Milne's son, Christopher Robin (97) making mud pies with his own son, Graham, in Milne's garden Hartfield, East Sussex.

Pencil sketch drawn between Guildford and London, June 1923 (96)

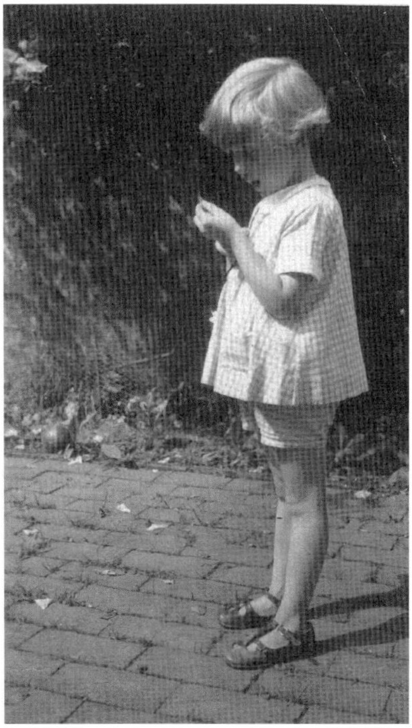

Photograph of
Christopher Robin Milne (97)

There are many stories told of the origins of Pooh, but in his notes, written in later years, Shepard states "The bear that I used as a model belonged to my son Graham (98). He was a wonderful bear, quite the best I have seen, and seemed to have a character all of his own. He had a chequered career but lived long enough for my son to hand him on to his own child, my granddaughter (Minette) who, when war broke out in 1939, was taken to Canada by her mother to grandparents there. Pooh went too, only to die at the hands, or teeth, of a neighbour's dog. Piglet, I fear, met the same fate in this country, so Milne told me".

Christmas 1924 saw the Shepard family and some of their friends giving a performance of A A Milne's play *Once Upon A Time*. It was chosen partly to please Milne but a powerful consideration was that it had two parts for children exactly suited to Graham and Mary.

Playtime and Company, published in 1925, was written by E V Lucas, described as 'a great man of letters'. He was a member of the *Punch* Table and a director of Methuen. This delightful anthology of verse was illustrated by Shepard and well received by the public.

Pie suffered from asthma and spent an Easter holiday in the South of France where Edith Rupell, a friend from Shalford, accompanied her. At the beginning of the school holidays Ernest and the children joined them. He and Pie painted most of the time. In the summer the family went to the Quantocks in Somerset.

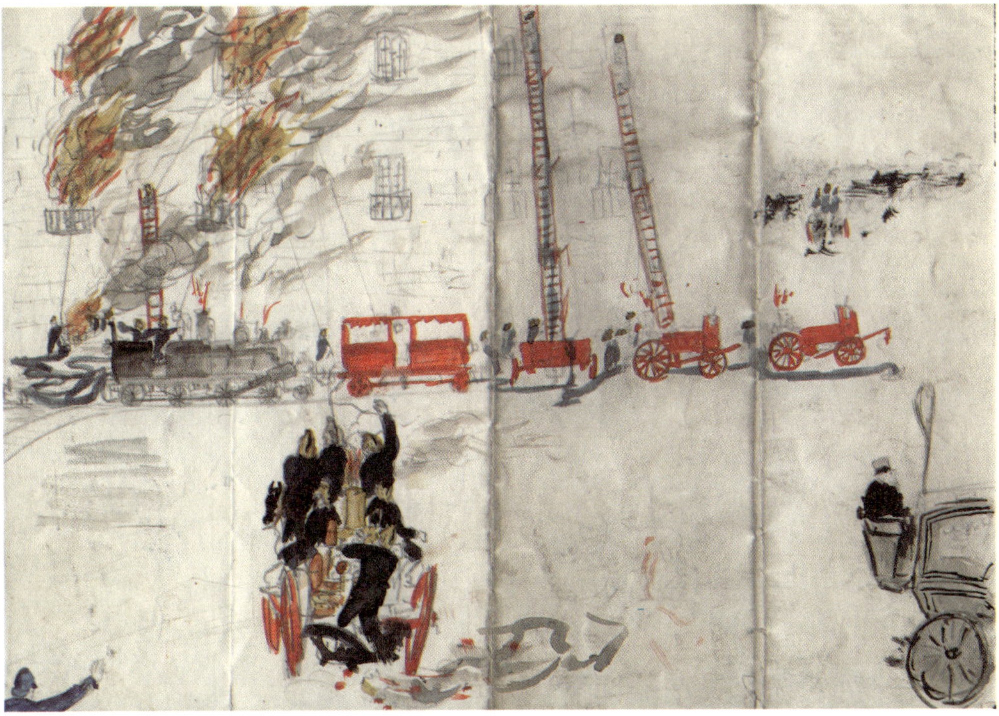

Plate 1a Whiteley's Fire

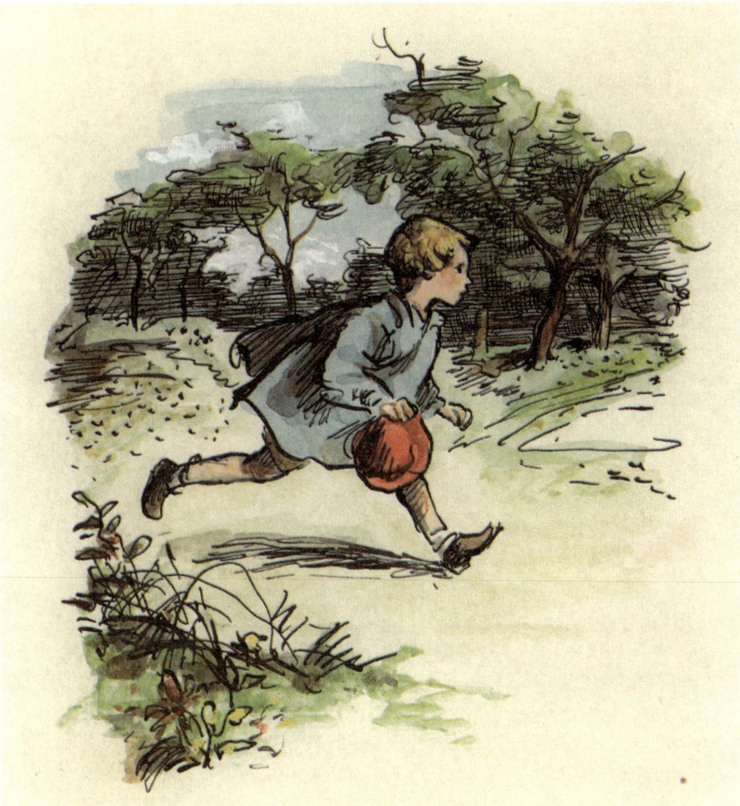

Plate 1b Roman Road
It is believed that this illustration was never used fot the story
Roman Road

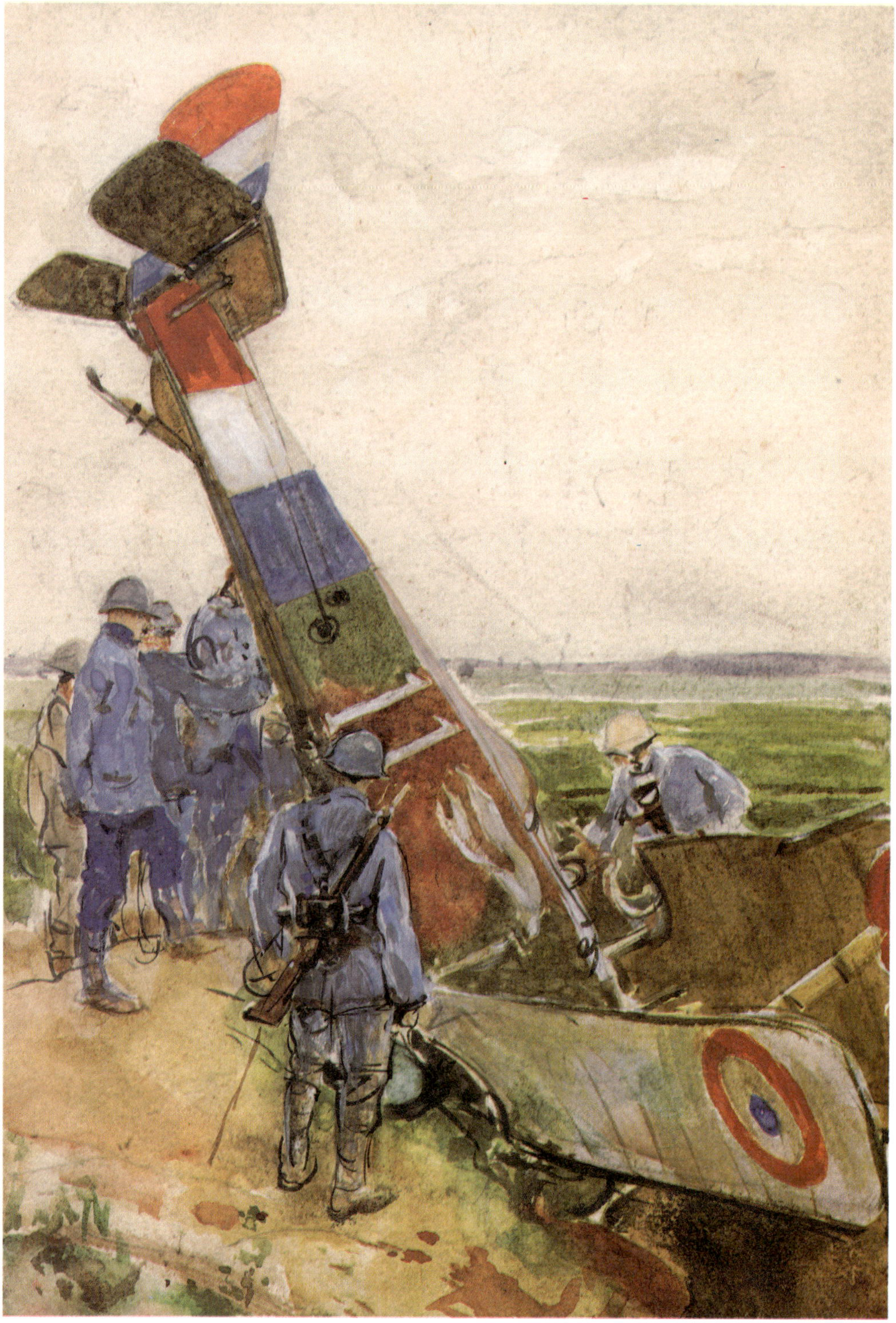

Plate 2 French Plane after crash

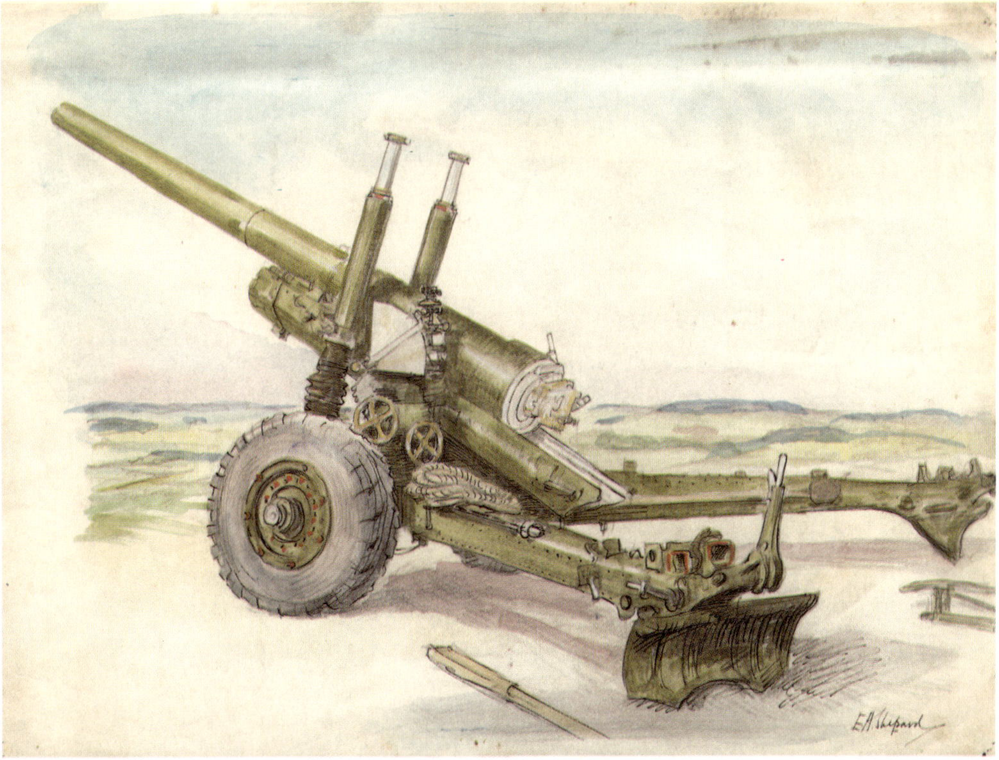

Plate 3a American Machine Gun

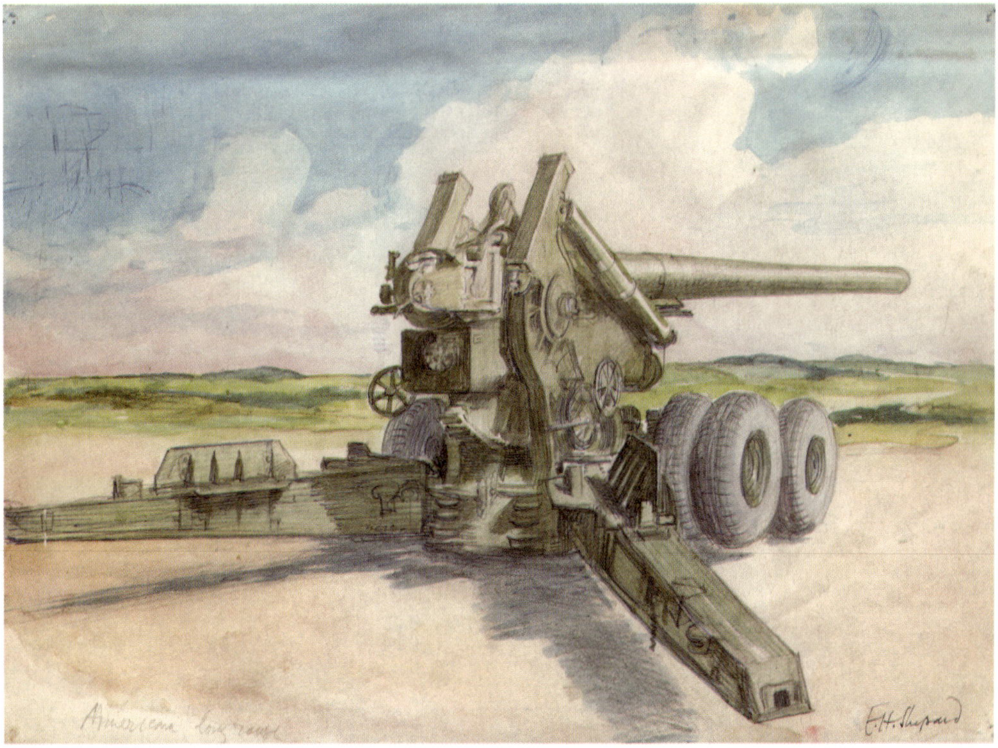

Plate 3b American Long Gun - both drawn by Shepard in France while waiting to go to Italy

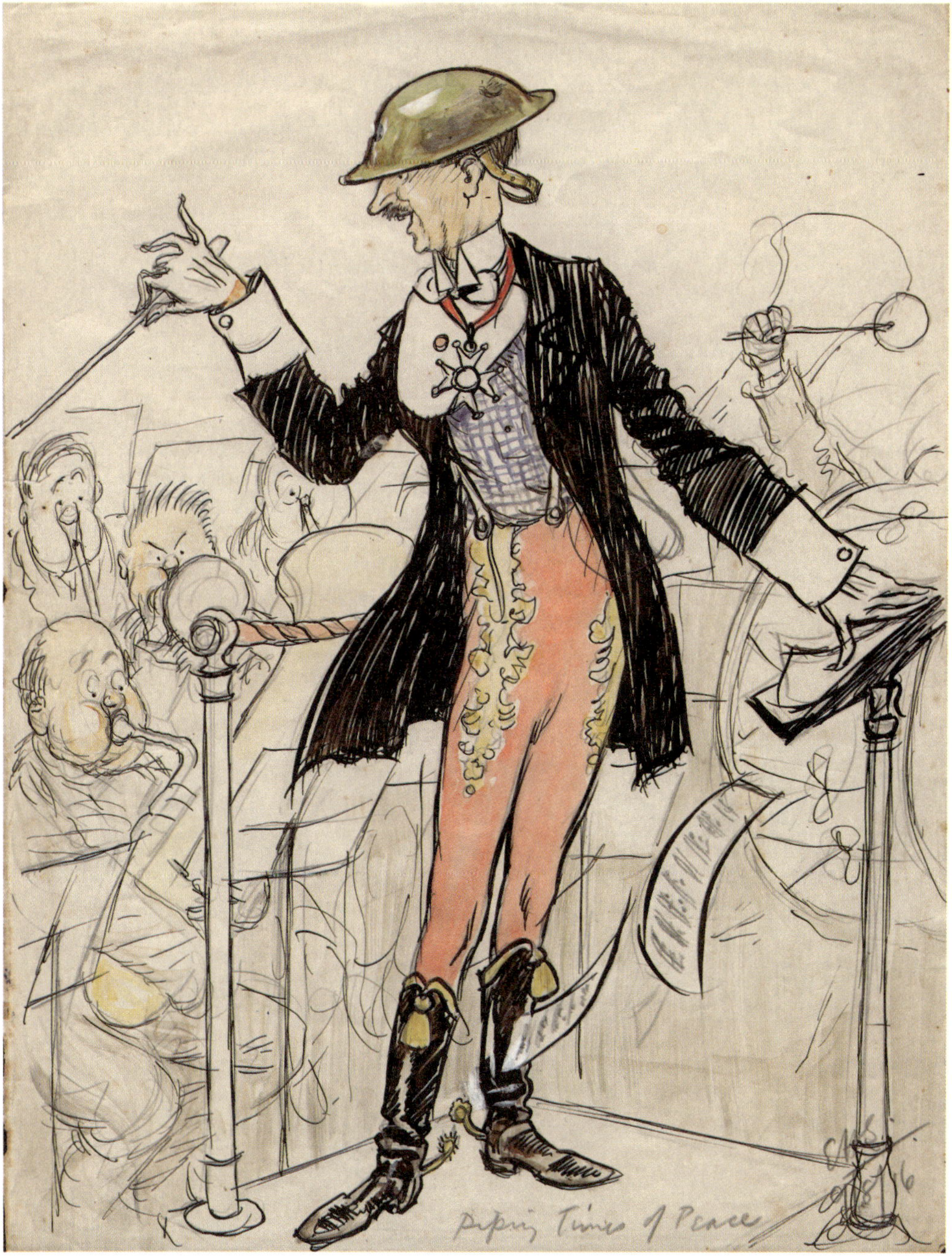

Plate 4 The Piping Times of Peace

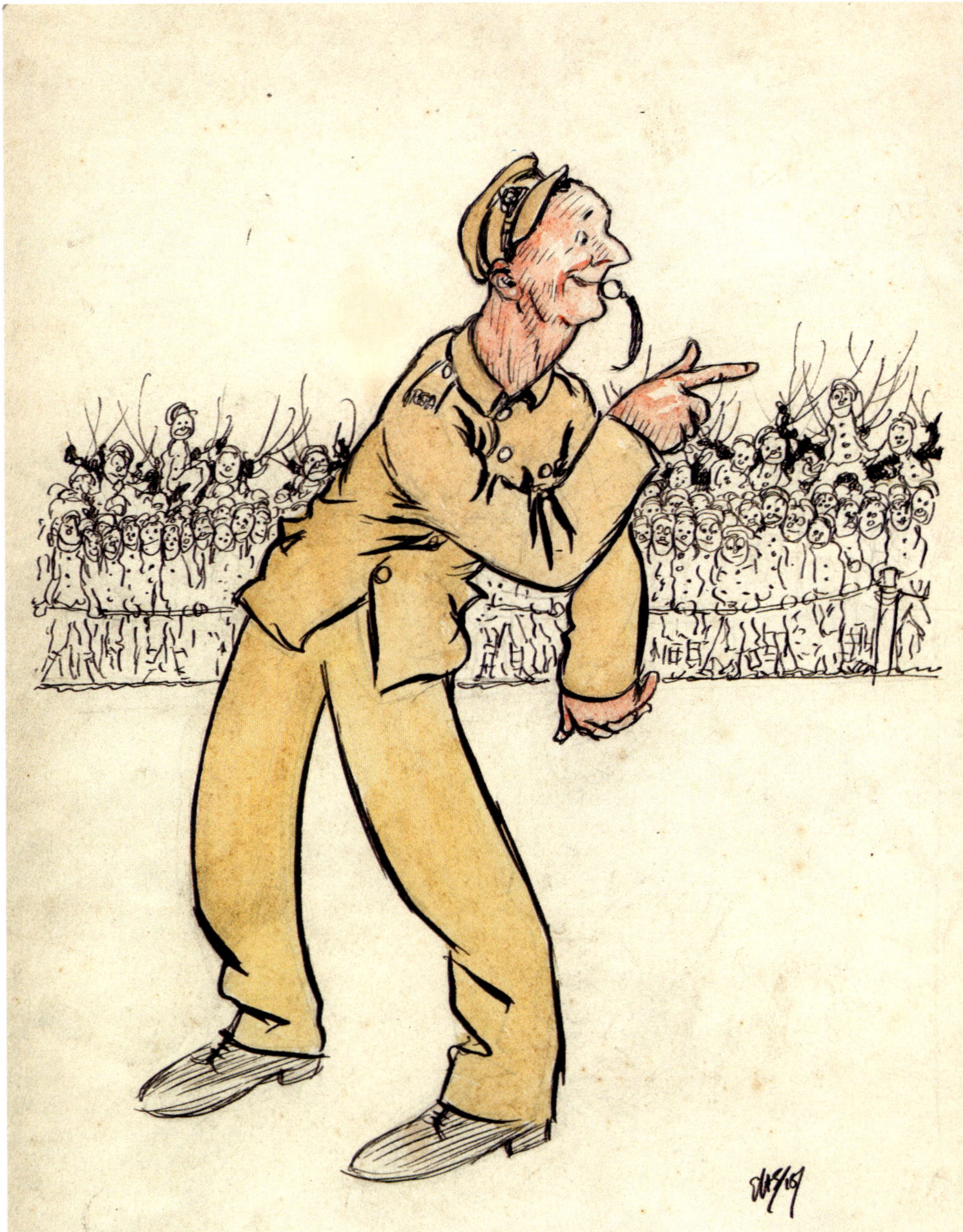

Plate 5 The Accusing Finger

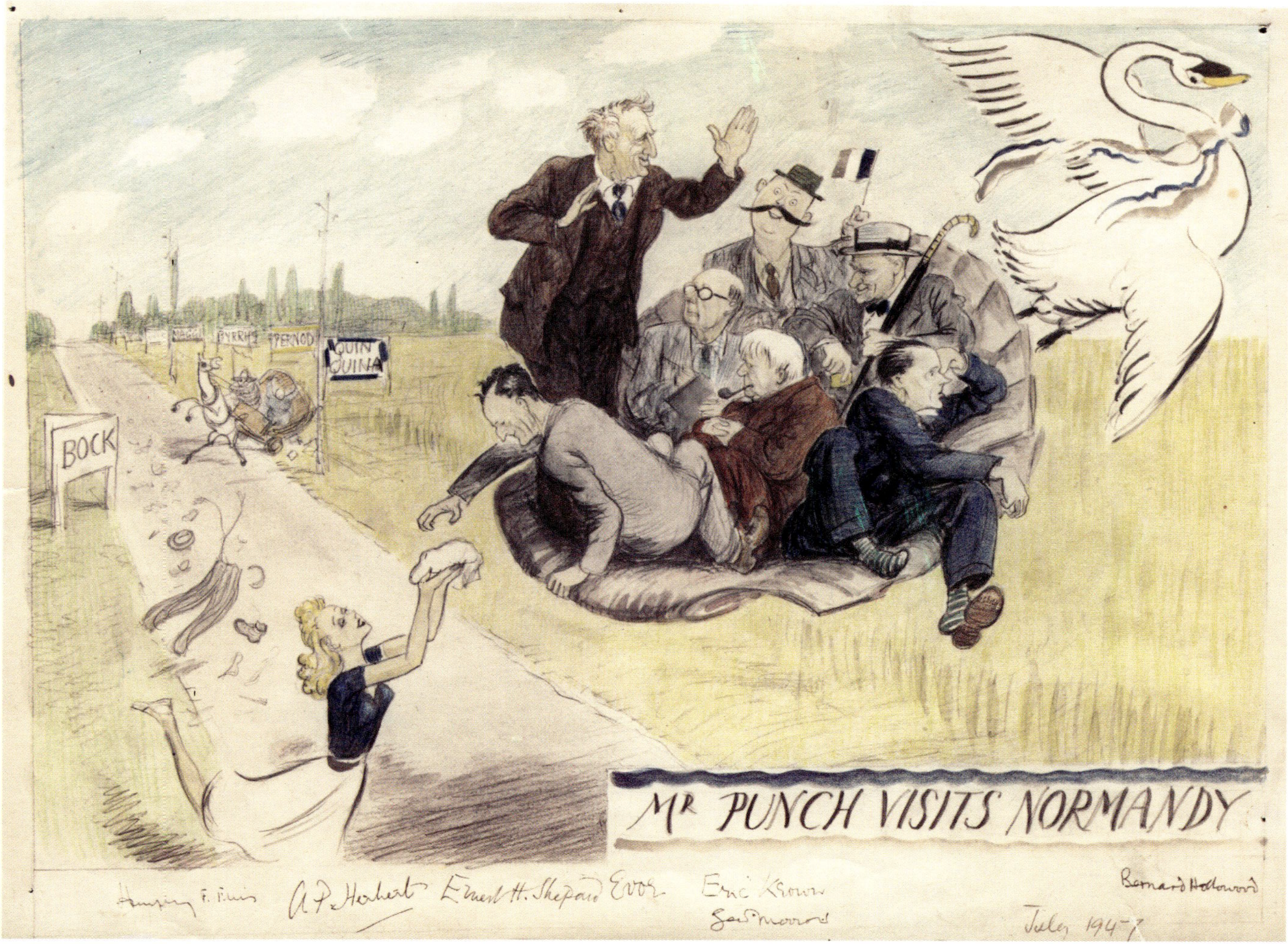

Plate 6 Mr Punch Visits Normandy

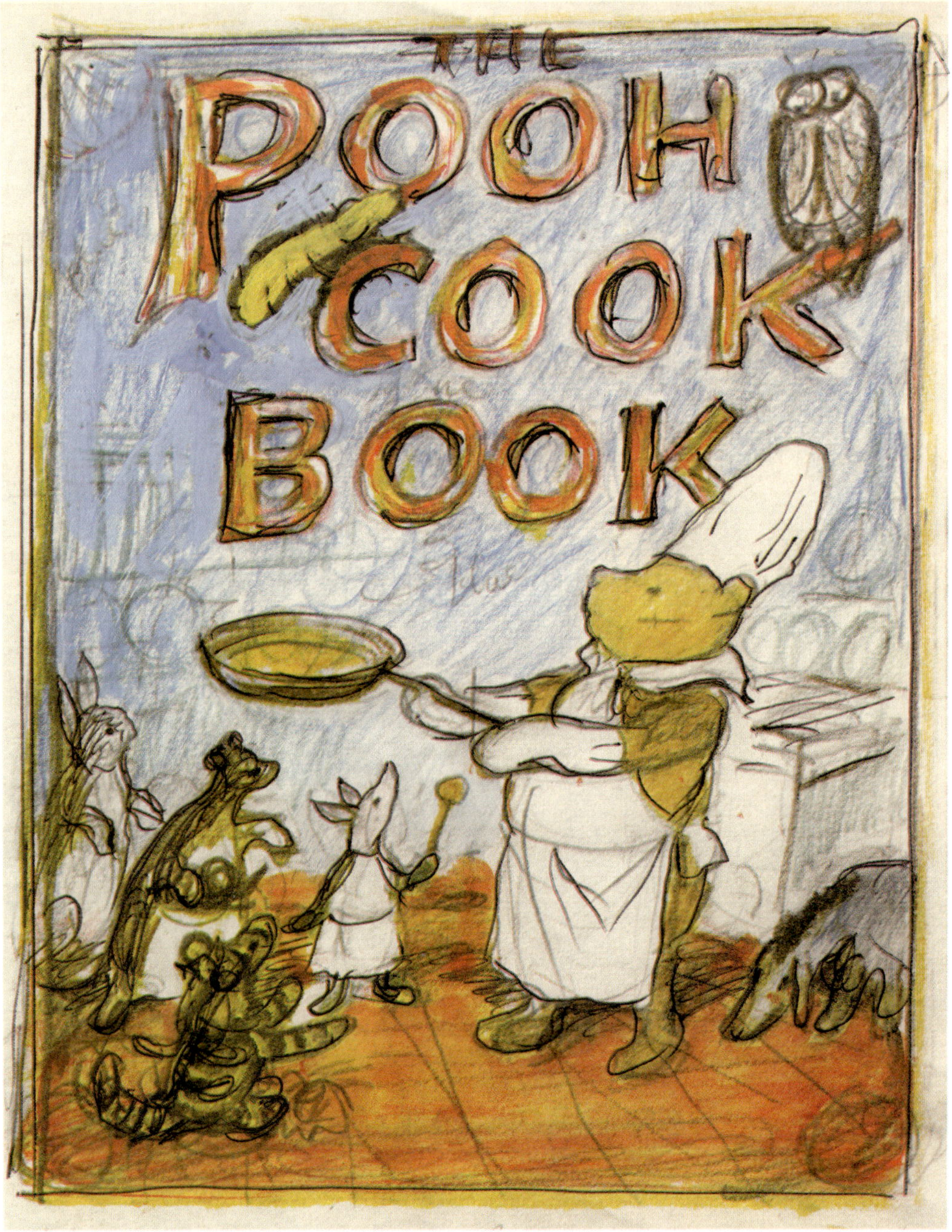

Plate 7 The Pooh Cook Book

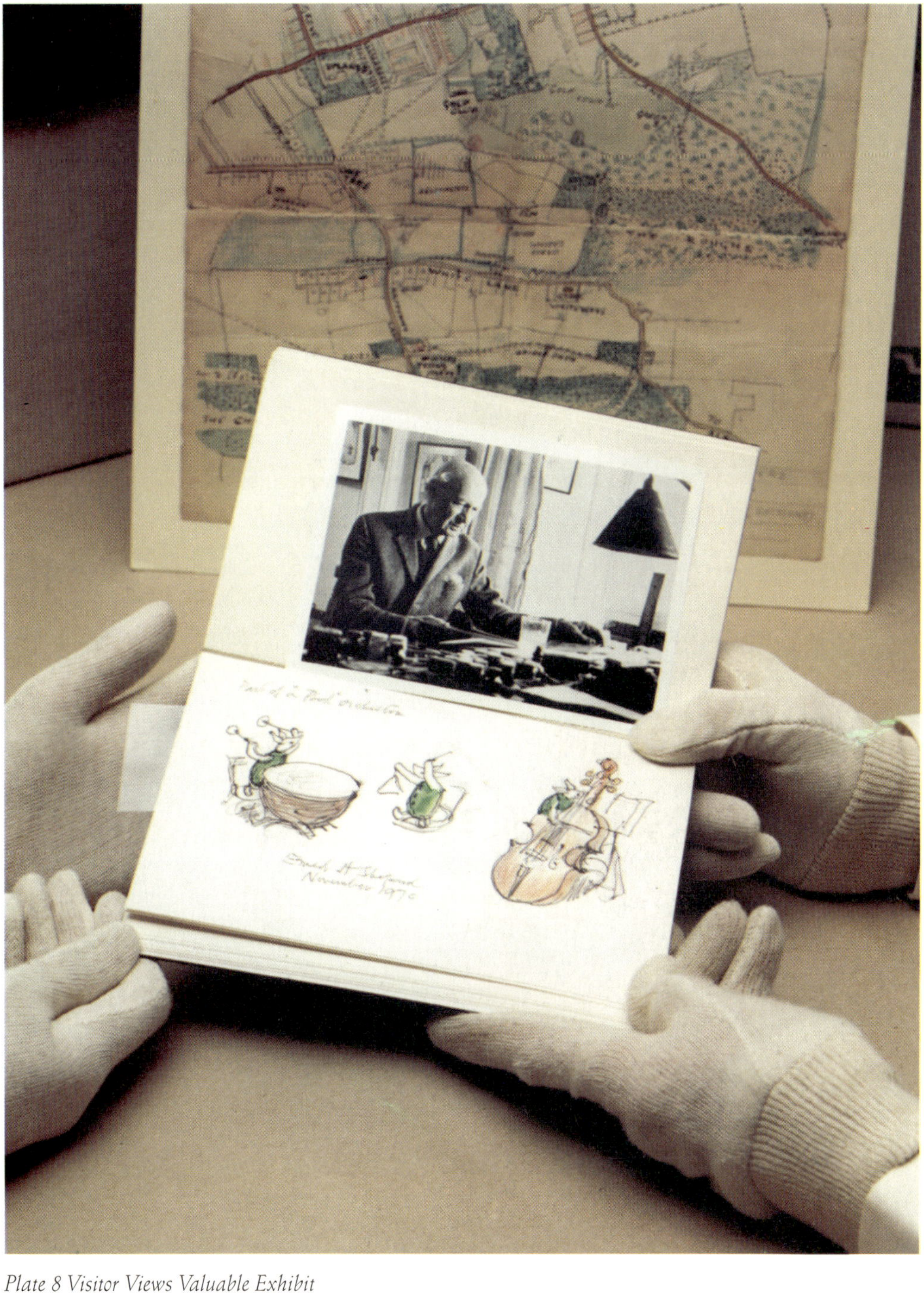

Plate 8 Visitor Views Valuable Exhibit

Commission requests were constantly arriving and there was no need to worry about income. In fact the workload put him under great strain. He even worked on a revision of his *Pepys'* drawings on Boxing Day. Pressure was building up on Ernest's time. The Pooh books were well on their way, he had begun work on *Now We Are Six* and had finished the illustrations for *The Holly Tree* by Charles Dickens.

Although Pie had as many holidays as possible away from the pressures and always enjoyed her visits abroad, her asthma never improved while she was at Shamley Green. Dr Eric Sheaf, a family friend, suggested that Pie, because of her asthma, should live on higher ground. It was decided, therefore, that such a move must happen. They looked at Pewley Down and decided they would build a new house there.

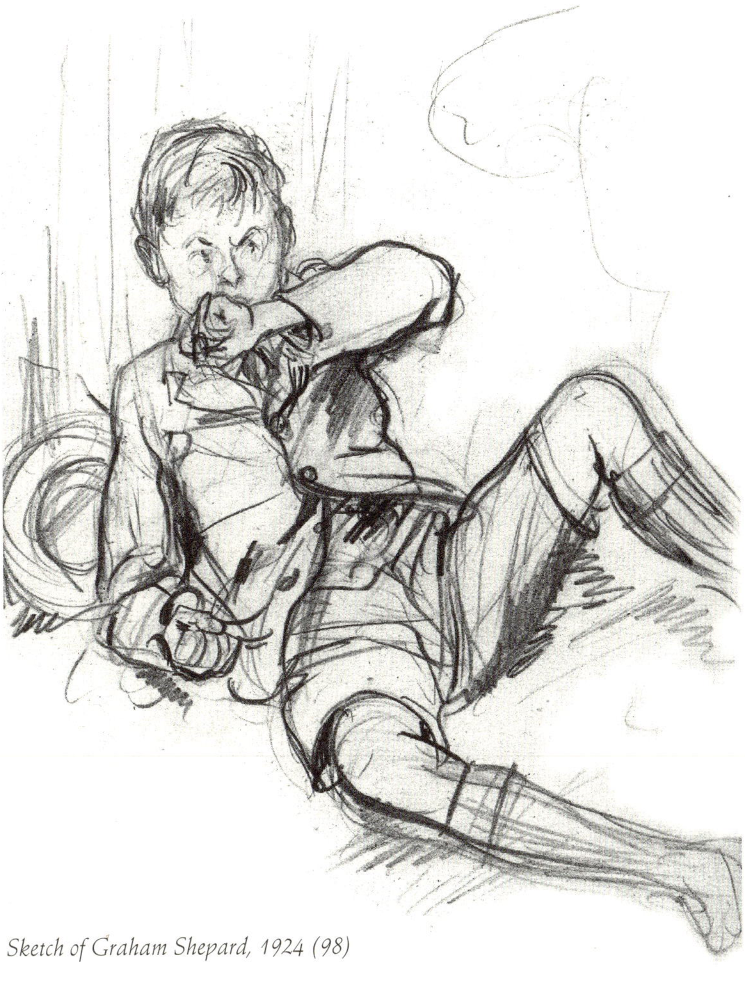

Sketch of Graham Shepard, 1924 (98)

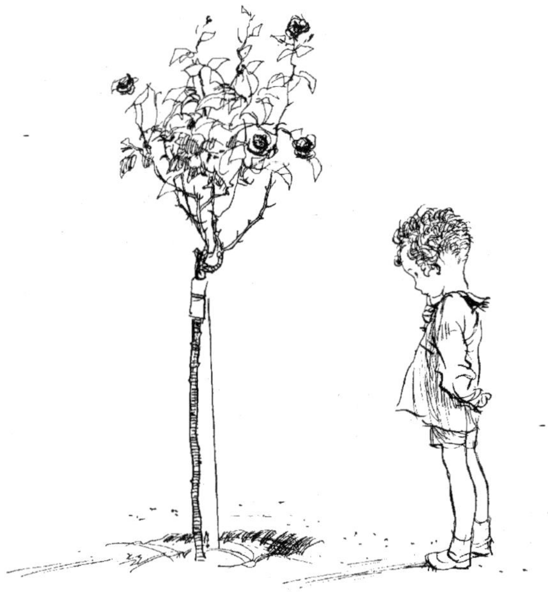

'An early version of the christening in When We Were Very Young' *(99)*

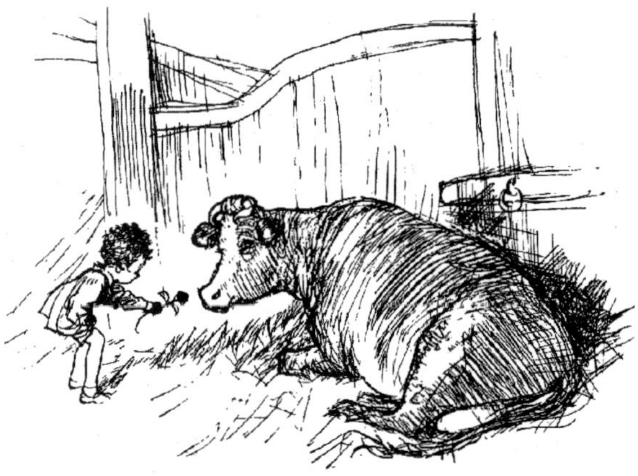

Everybody's Pepys (100), was published in the autumn of 1926 and was immediately a great success. Following this Bells the publisher considered an abridged edition of Boswell's *Life of Johnson.* This was to be in the same form as *Pepys.* In order to produce authentic drawings Shepard was to spend considerable time in the print room of the British Museum studying engravings of old London. He hired period clothes and had two special wigs made at Nathan's.

As soon as the launch of *Pepys* was completed, Ernest began a set of drawings for *Little One's Log.* Then, with Pie and Graham, he went on holiday to Paris, and from there they visited Cyril's grave on the Somme.

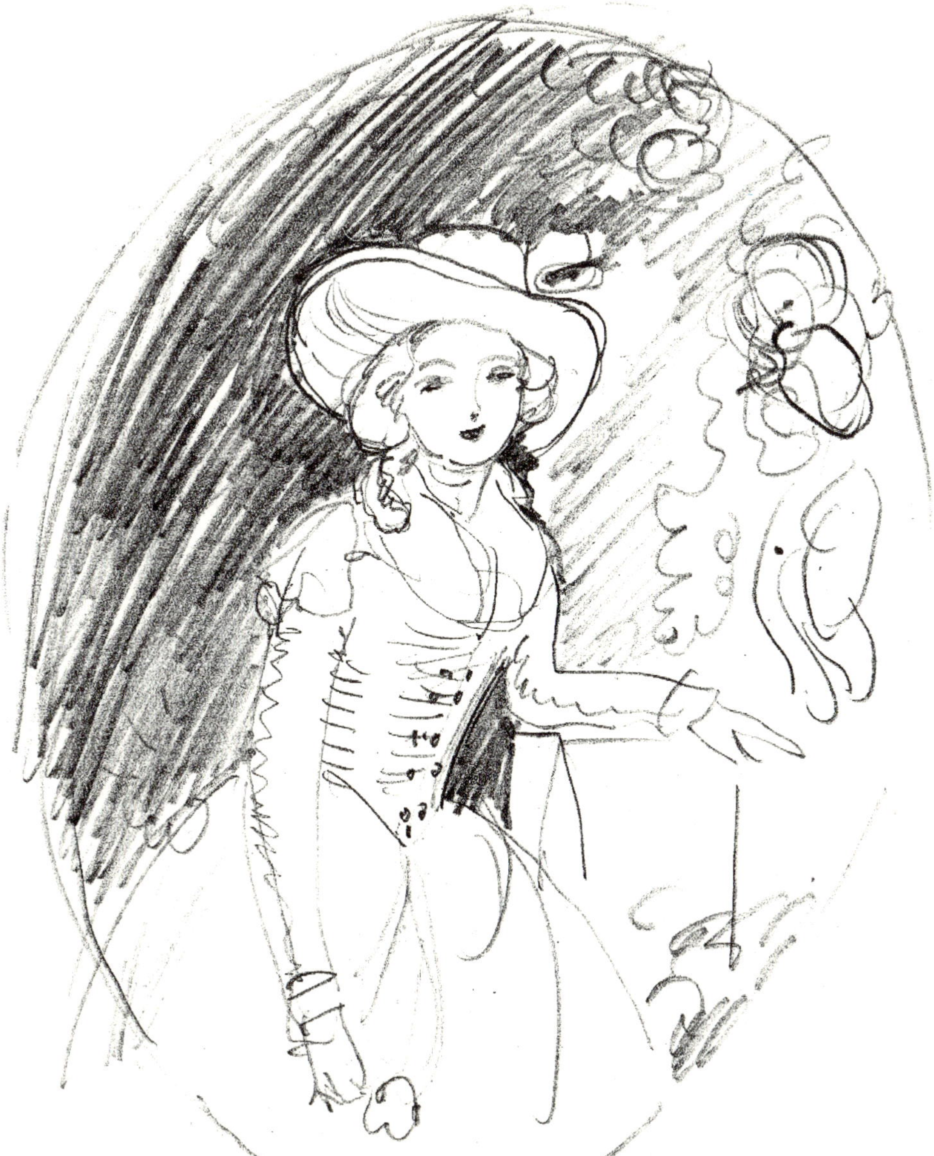

Experimental sketch for Everybody's Pepys (100)

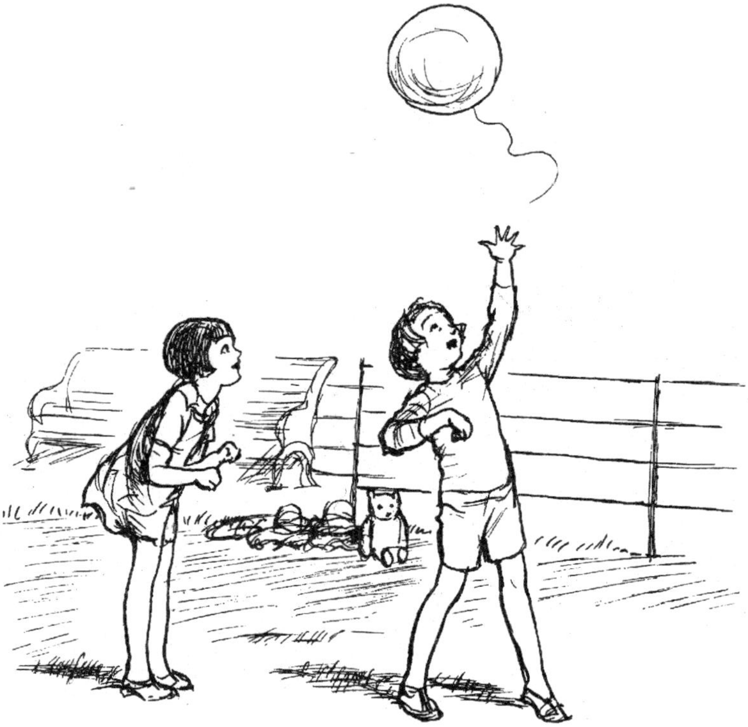

Sketches from the morning walk from Now We Are Six *(101)*

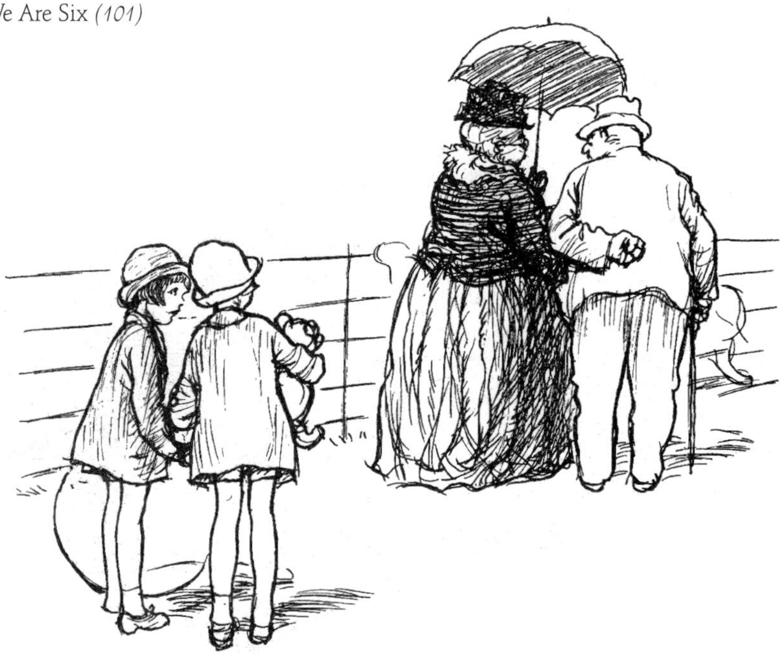

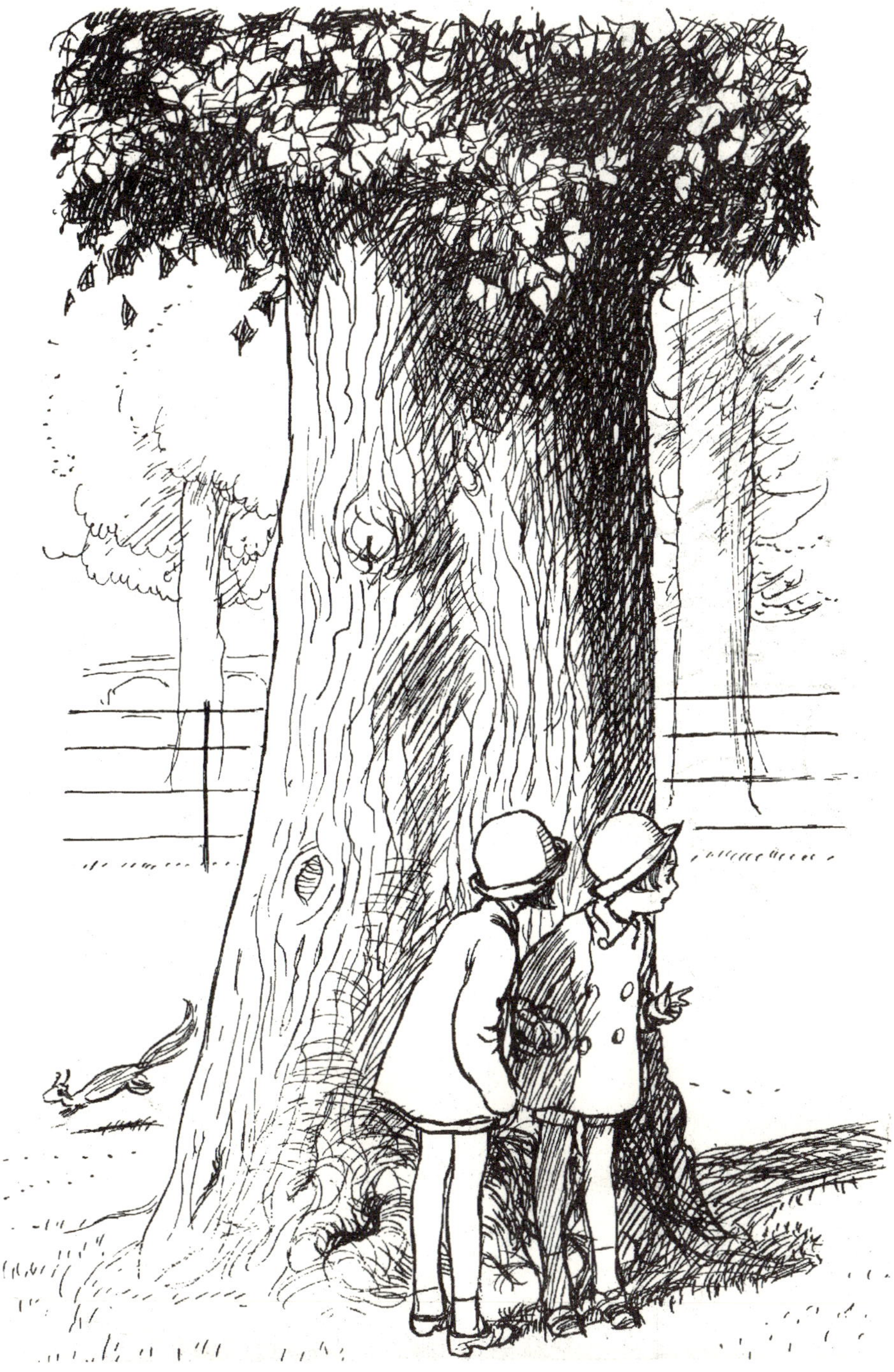

Sketches from the morning walk
from Now We Are Six *(102)*

The year 1926 saw the fruition of the co-operation of Shepard and Milne with the publication of *Winnie the Pooh.* Pooh and his chums were to establish themselves as some of the leading characters in the forefront of children's books from that time on. The few original sketches held in the Surrey Archive are of great interest to all visitors (103) (104) (105) (106).

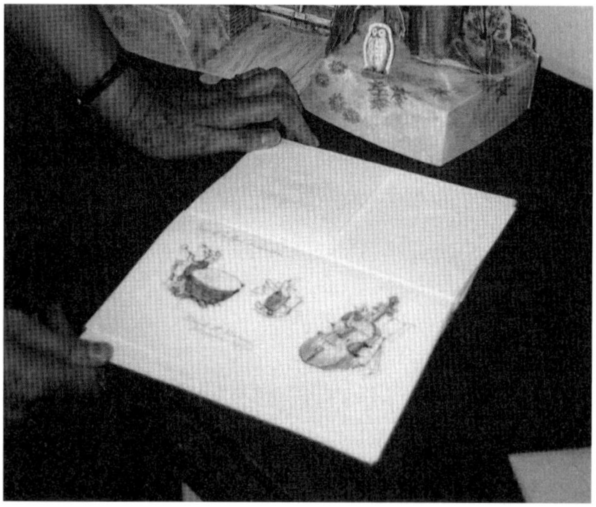

Photograph: Visitor Viewing the Shepard Archive (103)

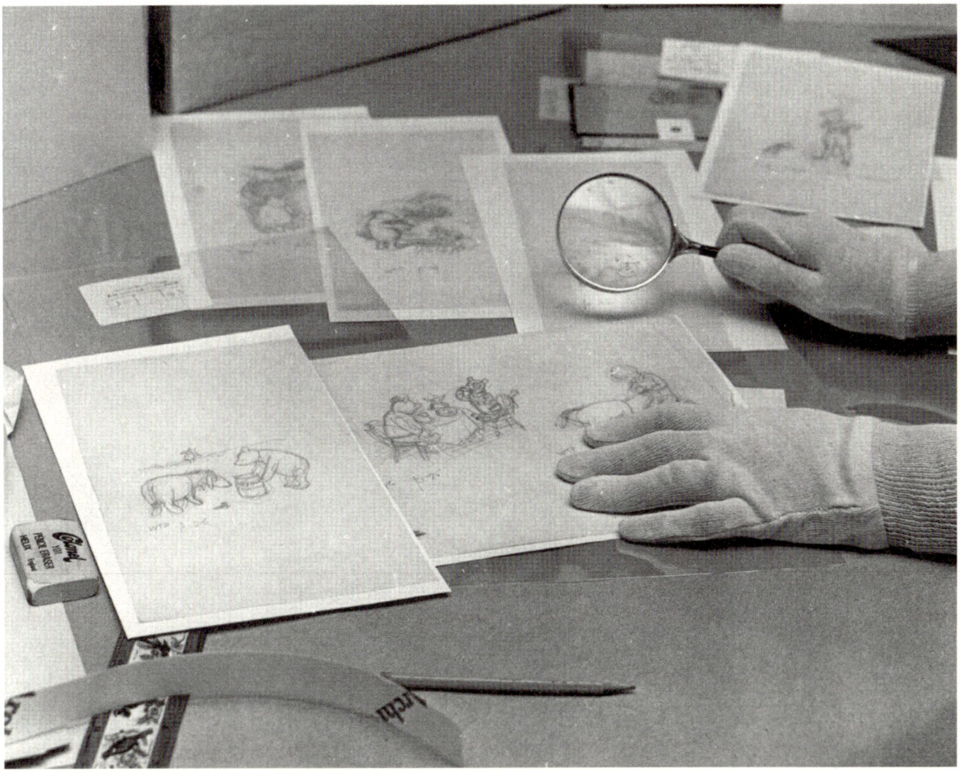

Photograph: Conservation Work within the Archive - 1 (104)

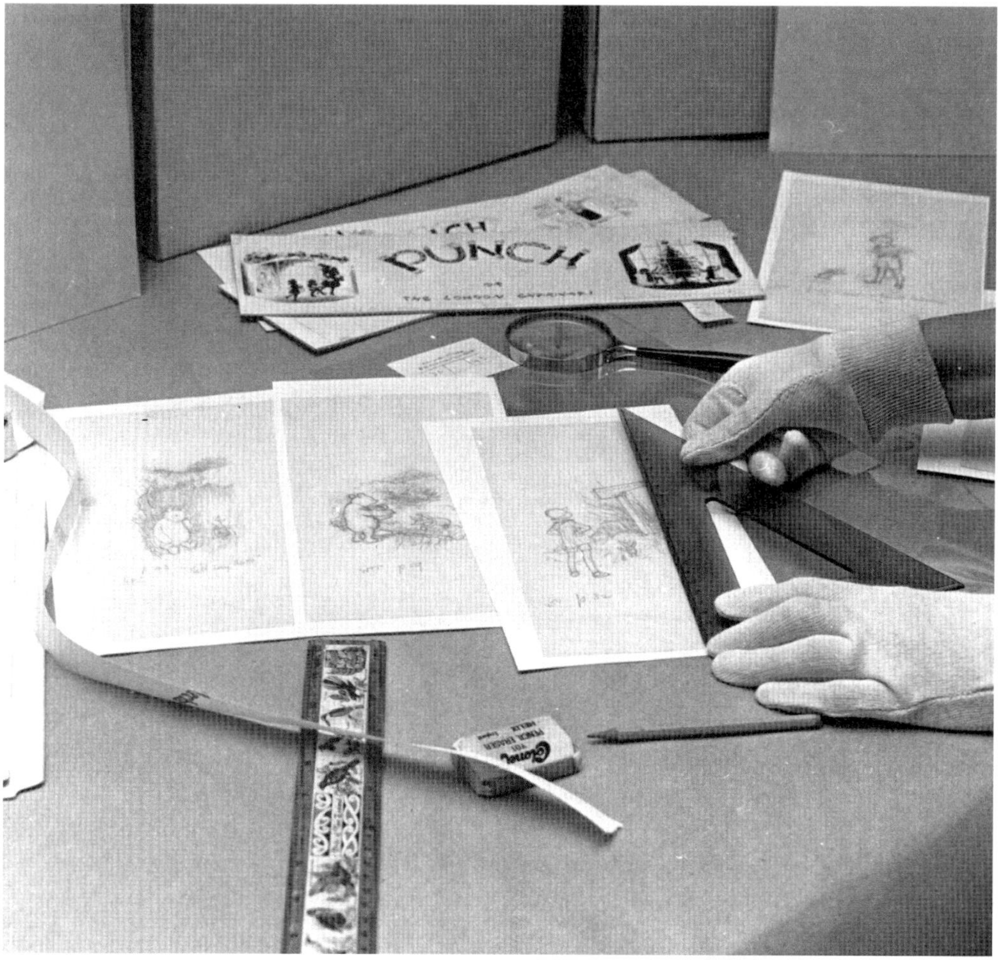

Photograph: Conservation Work within the Archive - 2 (105)

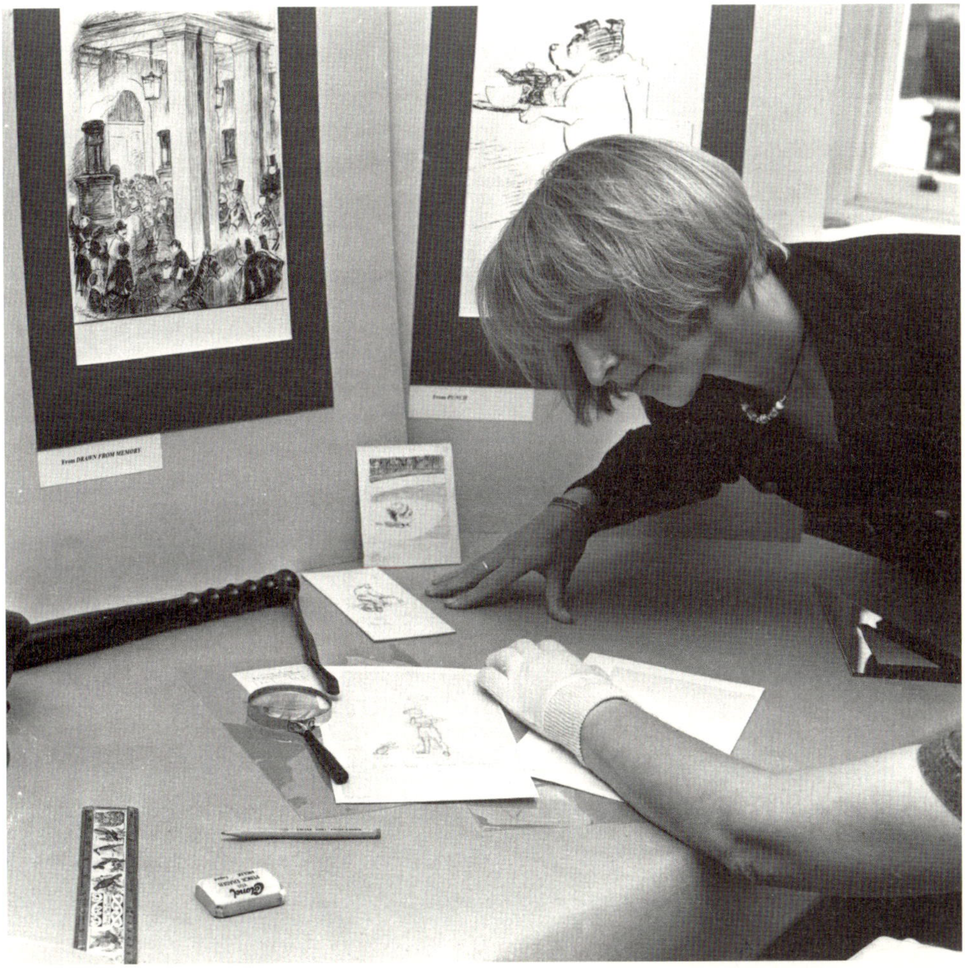

Photograph: Conservation Work within the Archive 3 (106)

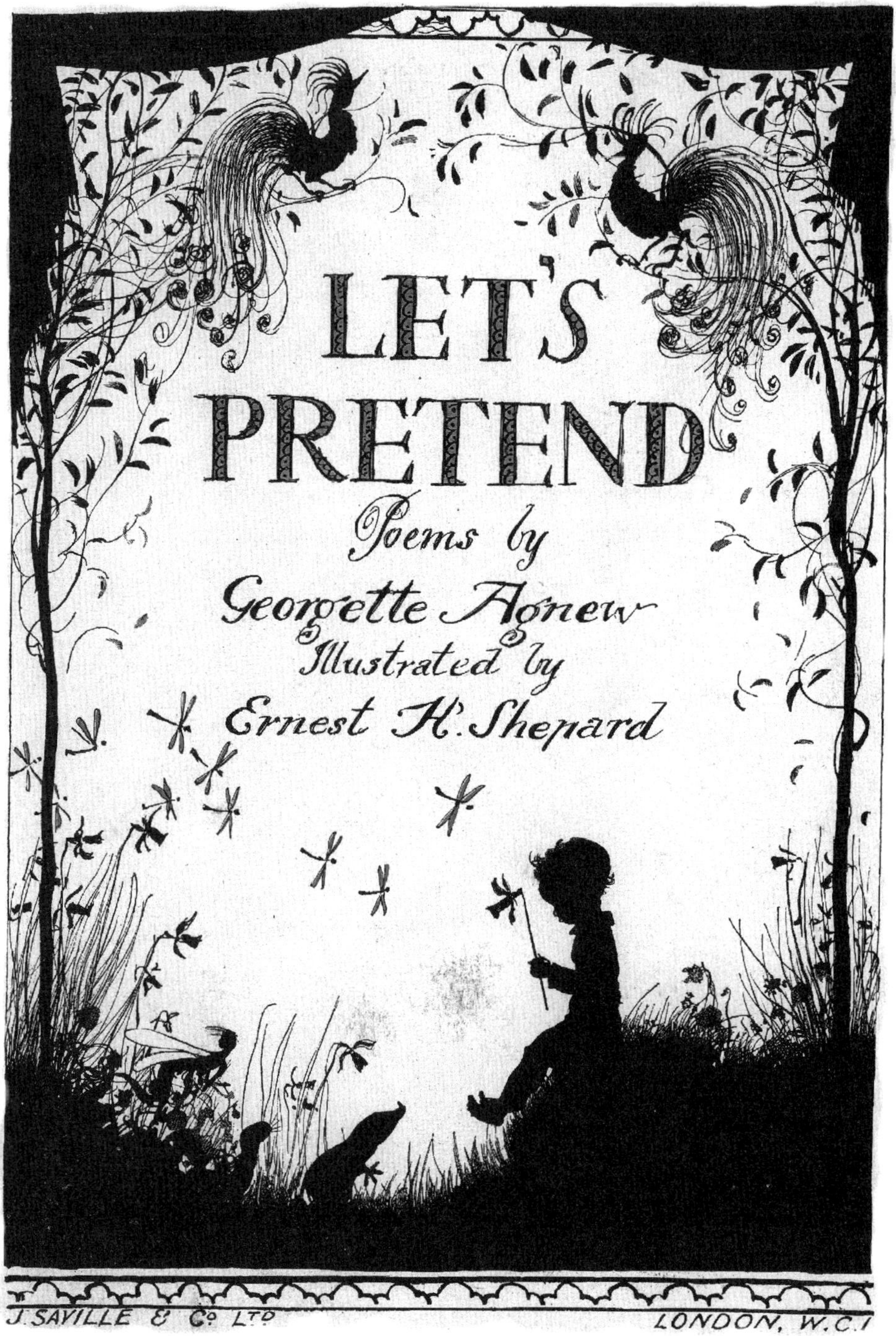

Cover for Let's Pretend *(107)*

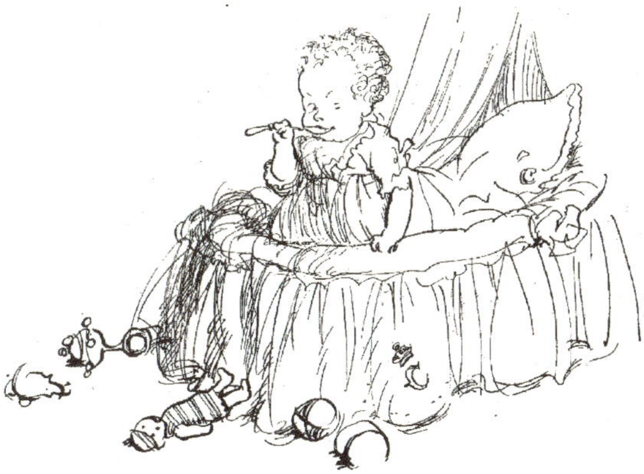

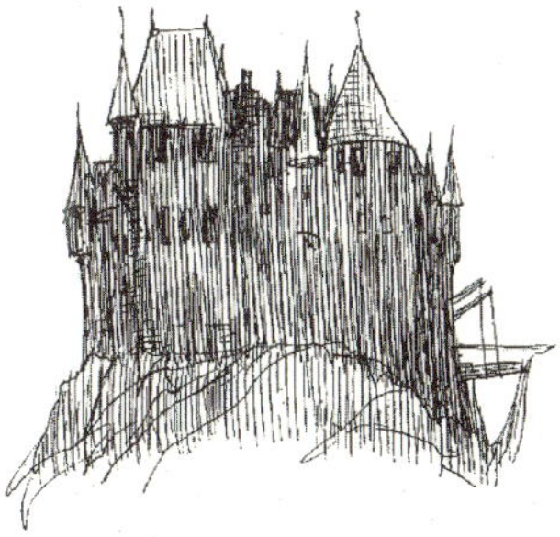

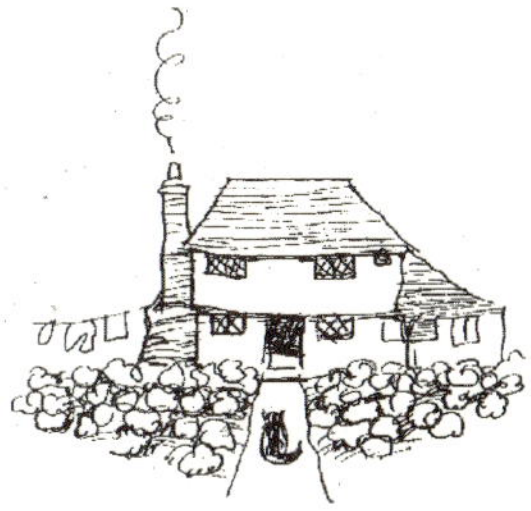

Sketches from Let's Pretend *(108)*

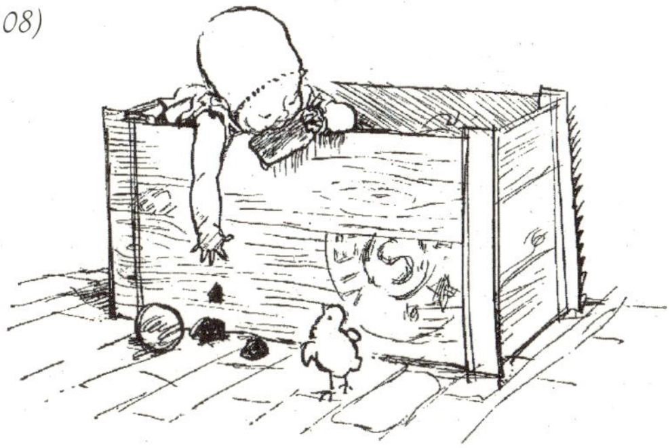

Life prospered and travel for the Shepard family was to progress in December from a motorbike and sidecar to an Austin Ten.

1927 saw the blossoming of the published works that he had illustrated. *Little One's Log* by Eva Erleigh, Marchioness of Reading, was a book recording an individual child's progress. *Let's Pretend,* a book of poems by Georgette Agnew (107) (108) (110), *Now We Are Six,* and *Fun and Fantasy* (109) a book of drawings by Shepard with verses by E V (Evoe) Knox, later to be Shepard's son-in-law.

Ernest was receiving regular royalties from *Winnie the Pooh, When We Were Very Young, Playtime and Company, Holly Tree* and *Everybody's Pepys*, which, in addition to his work for *Punch*, provided a considerable income. This enabled them to proceed with their plan for the new house at Pewley Down. The house was to be built of red brick with a tiled roof and include a large studio with a floor suitable for dancing for Mary and Graham to enjoy with their friends. There was to be central heating, electric light and a large loft for storage and, probably the most important of all, there was to be a veranda with a door to Pie's bedroom where she could sit out in the sunshine and cure her asthma (the real reason for the proposed move).

Graham, now aged twenty, was at Oxford. Mary, aged eighteen, was in her last year at school looking forward to studying at the Slade and any financial worries of previous years had disappeared. Graham and Mary had planted a conker from a chestnut tree at 'Red Cottage' with the idea of re-planting it in the grounds of the new house and all were looking forward to this exciting move and a bright future when tragedy was to strike hard.

In order to alleviate her asthma, arrangements had been made for Pie to have a straightforward nasal operation at a nursing home in London. On the afternoon of 26th September 1927 Ernest drove her and Mary to the nursing home and, with one of Pie's friends, they had a tea party after which Ernest and Mary drove back to Shamley Green.

At eleven o'clock the following morning Ernest answered the telephone to be told the news that his wife "had died under the anaesthetic". His love of over a quarter of a century had gone - there was a complete void in his life. He sent a telegram to Graham and then with Mary immediately drove to London. They were taken to Pie's room where "she was lying on her back, beautiful and serene". Graham soon arrived from Oxford. They then went out and bought "a tiny bunch of violets" which were placed under Pie's crossed hands.

Ethel, Shepard's sister, was on leave in London from her sisterhood in Lahore. She was a great comfort to the family and an immense help with the funeral arrangements. Two days later Ernest returned to the undertakers in London, watched while the coffin was closed and then followed the hearse to Shamley Green where the coffin remained overnight until the funeral on 1st October. The church was full with family, friends, locals and staff from *Punch*. For the first time in his life he did not use his sketchbook. On 27th September his diary records "Pie died", on 1st October he wrote "Funeral Shamley Green" - there were no further diary entries that year.

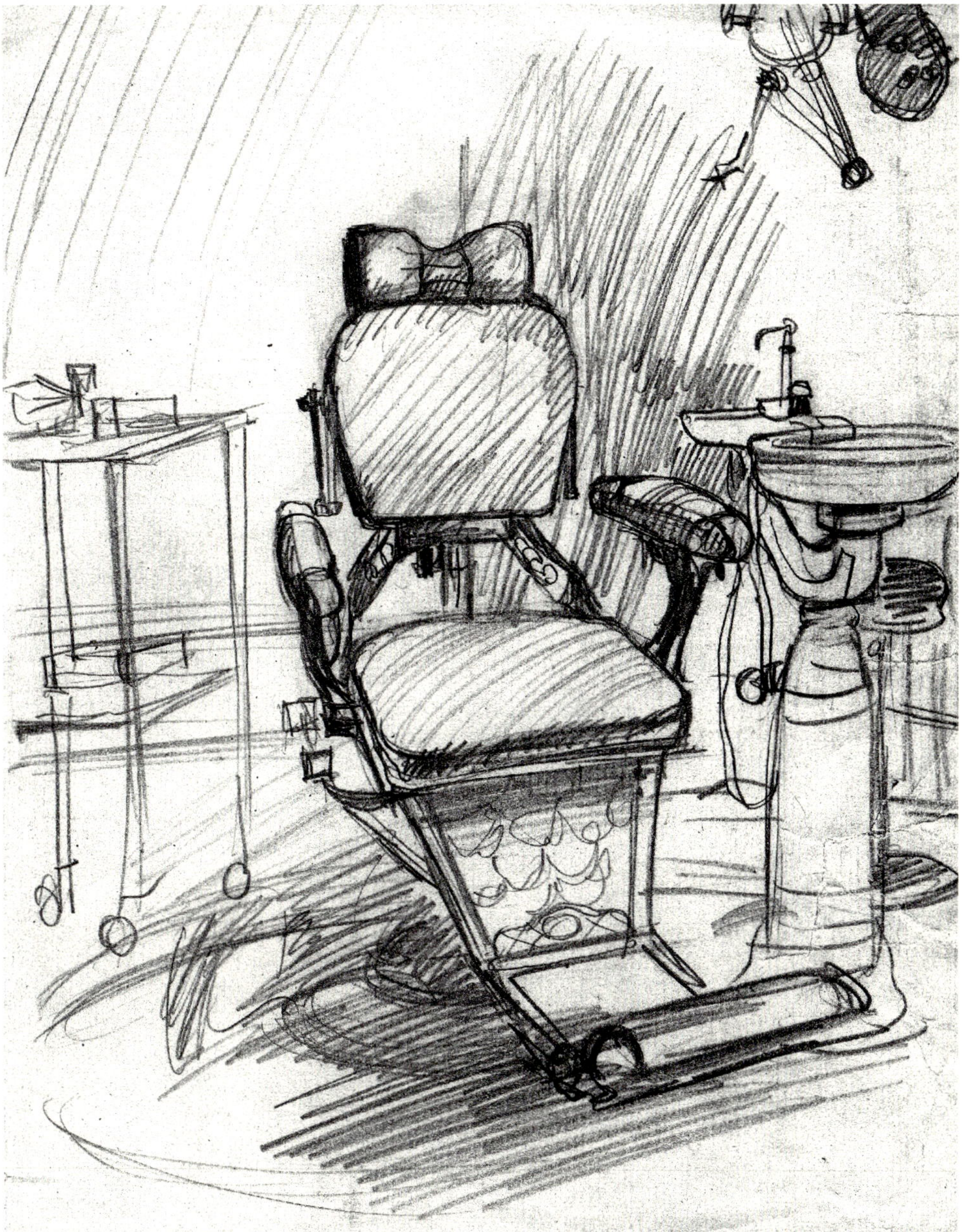

The Dentist's Chair
published in Punch, *February 1925*
and in Fun and Fantasy, *1927 (109)*

In his sorrow he immediately turned to the drawings for *The House at Pooh Corner* which he had only just started. This work kept him busy through the autumn, over Christmas and well into the New Year.

He had to steel himself to visit the building site at Pewley Down. During the Christmas holidays Mary helped him choose curtains and carpets and Sarah, their housekeeper, made visits to see her kitchen and to check where the furniture was to go. On 28th May 1928 all was ready and the move took place. A contractor was then called in to lay paths, create a tennis court, and to plant beech and yew trees. The chestnut planted at 'Red Cottage' was now a very small tree. It was dug up with great care by Graham and Mary and planted with due ceremony at the new house which was to be called 'Long Meadow' as part of the land had been called the Long Meadow in times gone by. It was now possible to look forward to a new life.

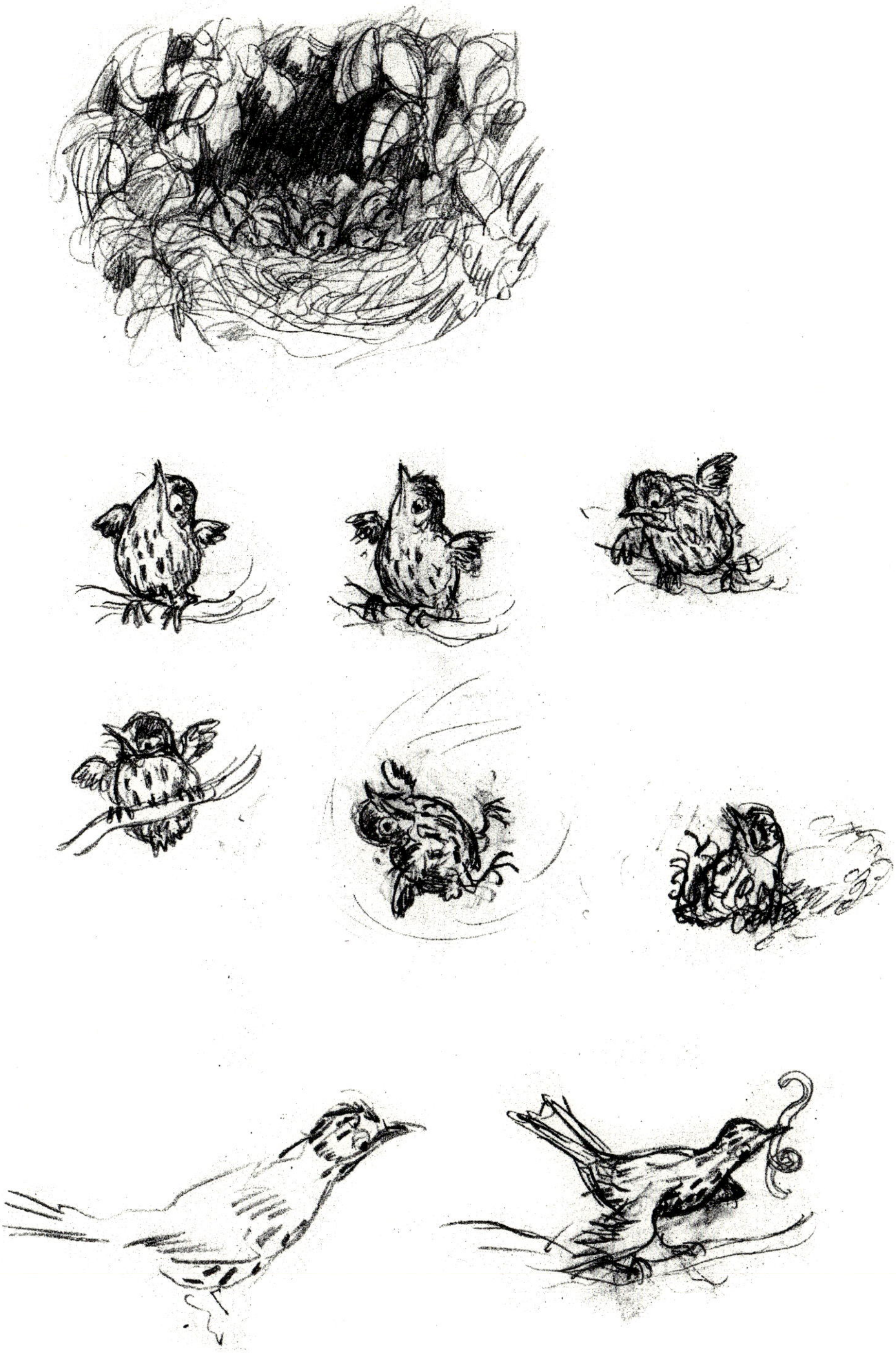

Sketches of young birds for use in Let's Pretend *(110)*

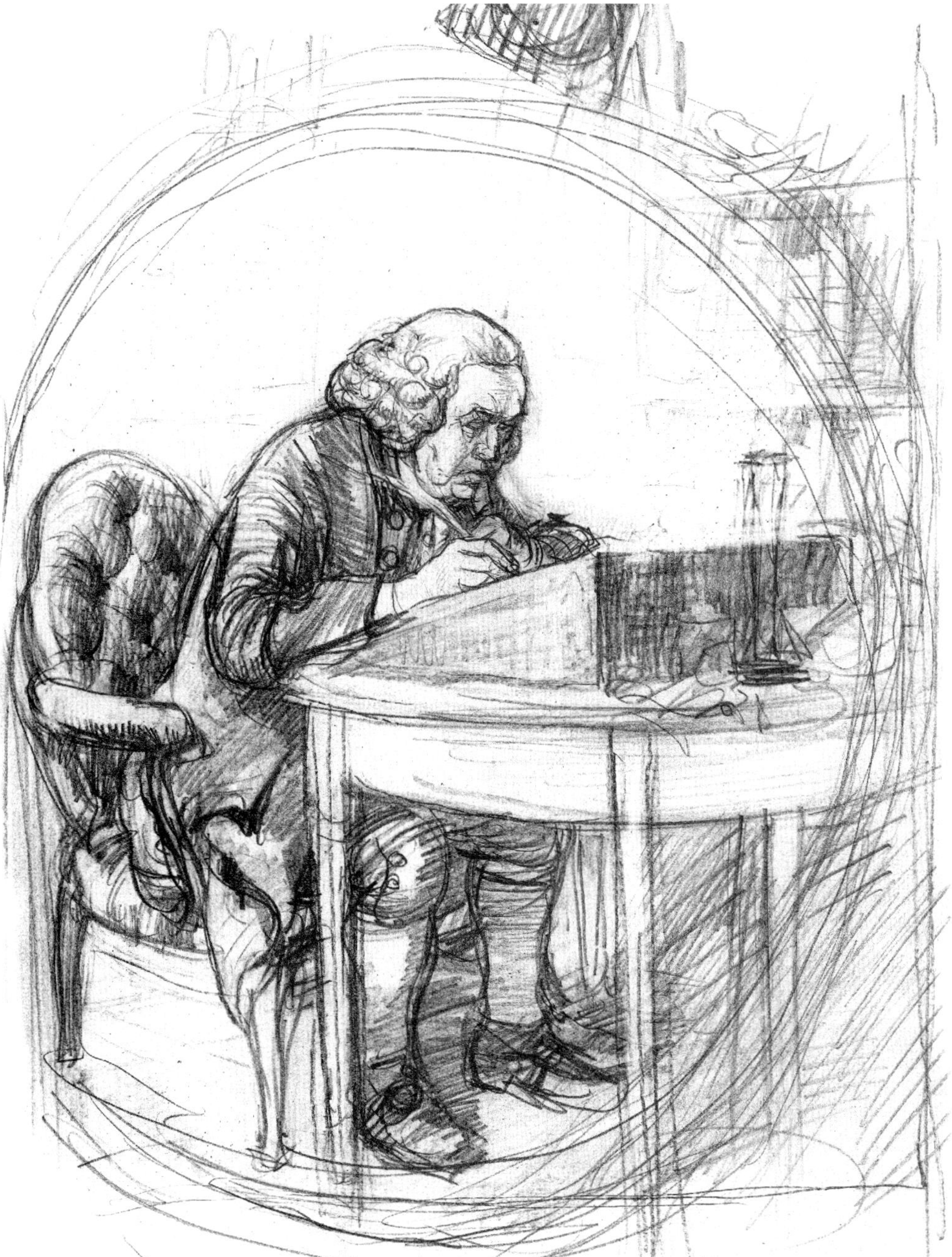

Dr Johnson at his desk
Pencil drawing by Shepard
Based on the picture in the National Gallery, 1930 (111)

E.H. Shepard

Chapter 8
Long Meadow 1928 - 1939

For the first few days in 'Long Meadow' Shepard seemed to have difficulty with his drawings. One day in his diary he admitted he had tried to do a sketch for *Punch* but had failed. However, he bounced back and on the 7th June was attending a rehearsal of the Aldershot Tattoo. He produced a drawing of it for *Punch* some five days later. By the 14th June he was happily drawing Pooh.

The first big event at the new house was his son's 21st birthday dance held early in July. Graham had just started working at *The Illustrated London News* for Bruce Ingram and Mary had settled in happily at the Slade. The dance took place in the studio. There was a four-piece band from London and a bar outside in a marquee. Graham's friends came from Oxford and Marlborough. Mary's friends also attended. Osbert Lancaster, another great cartoonist, was among the many guests. It was a real house warming.

Ernest travelled to Oxford frequently and became very involved in Mary's life especially because of her chosen profession. He was her chauffeur and companion, they shopped together, went to the theatre and cinemas and often ate out. At the same time, however, he developed an inner circle of friends of his own.

He worked incredibly hard throughout the whole year even on his sailing holiday. Work for *Punch* was not just bread and butter but included the jam while other illustrations provided the cream. Since arriving at 'Long Meadow', alongside his other work he had been drawing illustrations for *Golden Age* by Kenneth Grahame. This book and *Dream Days* which was to follow two years later are really stories of Kenneth Grahame's boyhood with his sister and brother and their constant warfare with the grown-ups. The stories were full of charm and humour. The clothes that the children were pictured in were those of Shepard's own childhood, pinafore dresses and black stockings for the girls and ankle-boots for the boys. He enjoyed these illustrations very much for he felt he was delving back into his own past.

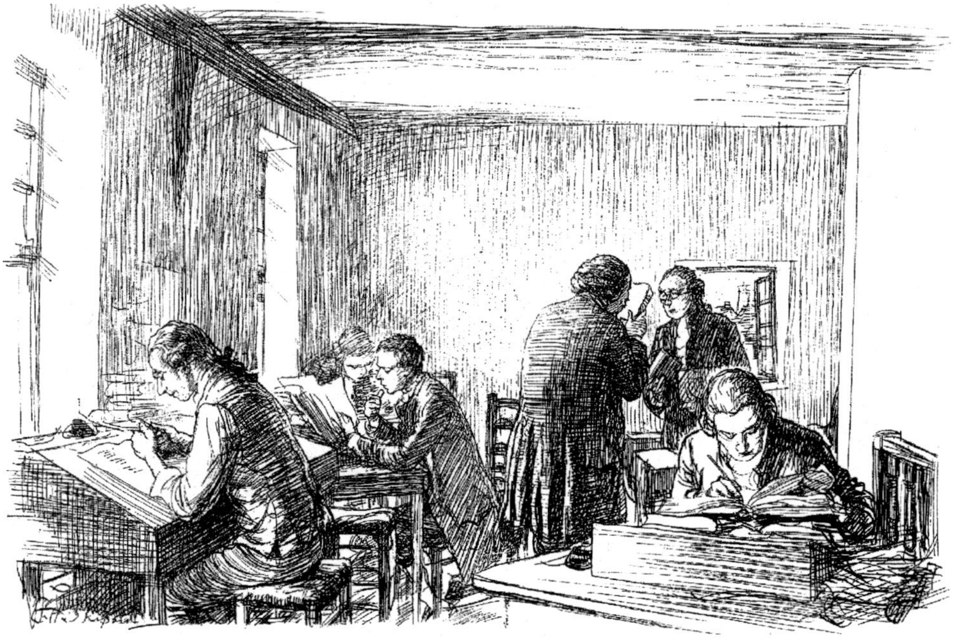

The Garrett at Gough's Square
Pen and ink drawing of the room in which Johnson created his English dictionary (112)

On 11th October, *The House at Pooh Corner* was published and was another immediate success. Throughout 1929 his special efforts were concentrated on *Everybody's Boswell* originally called *Boswell's Johnson (111) (112).* This was the life of Dr Johnson and enabled Shepard to hire more costumes for authenticity and to visit such places as Gough Square where Johnson had created the first English dictionary. As a counteraction to these serious literary illustrations he was producing *Dream Days,* the companion volume to *The Golden Age* published in the previous year.

He loved sailing and was given the opportunity to own a boat when visiting Cowes off the Isle of Wight. He saw 'White Owl', a ketch of ten tons with an auxiliary engine. She was about fifteen years old and painted white and had been dismantled and stored in a shed for some time when Shepard decided to buy her. She was then owned by a retired colonel who was a member of the Royal Yacht Squadron. The boat had been used very little, in fact possibly only in Cowes Week each year.

There was a paid 'hand' called Ireland who was happy to stay in his post and Shepard had the boat moved from Cowes to the River Humble where moorings were less expensive. Ireland was paid five pounds during the season and one pound a week as a retainer during the winter. His home was at Brixham in Devon and once the boat had been restored Ernest, Mary and Graham sailed the boat there to make a base. They sailed around local waters reaching Dartmouth and the jetty at Kingswear bringing back memories of his student holidays there.

His work on the illustrations for *Everybody's Boswell* continued for three-quarters of the year and his notes show that it was finally completed on 24th September. He had also spent some time drawing statues and the city churches and had taken a holiday in Scotland, possibly with Boswell and Johnson in mind. In addition he had been on various boating trips. Obviously he had a very full life, he spent time with friends, swam, rode, played squash and danced but always he was drawing, drawing, drawing people, views, various commissions. On Christmas Day 1930 with Mary abroad and Graham in Birmingham he accepted four different invitations to meals, beginning with breakfast! Three months before he had shared the cost of renting a house in Cleveland Square with Michael Solomon, a family friend. Neither of Shepard's children was living at home and he really needed a semi-permanent place in London where he could sleep and paint. He rented a first floor room that served as a bed-sitter cum studio. The rest of the house was shared by the Solomons, their children and their friends. He was comparatively rich with his fees from *Punch* and the royalties from the books he had illustrated so could well afford to have his London 'pad'.

In 1930 he was invited to illustrate *The Wind in the Willows*. In his hand-written notes he reflected:

"*When I was commissioned to illustrate The Wind in the Willows in 1930, I hesitated, as I considered it so perfect a work of art in itself that no pictures could do justice to it, but I learnt that it had been illustrated already by various artists, none of whom, to my mind, had made a success of it. I suppose I felt that I could do better than this, anyway, I could try.*

I was lucky to have an introduction to Kenneth Grahame given me by a friend and armed with this I went over to his house at Pangbourne on the Thames, he was very kind but I think he rather feared another illustrator! He told me of the spots on the river where his little animals lived and where to find them all, where was Toad hall, where Rat kept his little boat. He said he himself would take me to these places but he was too infirm.

Armed with his instructions & my sketch book I set out. It was very peaceful in the meadows by the river and I kept as quiet as possible as I moved along the bank - some movement in the grass might perhaps mean that mole was about or the line of bubbles on the water told me that rat was not far away. I looked for the tiny boat among the rushes and peered into the dark hole in the bank, fancying that I could see a pair of tiny eyes watching me. I stayed and sketched till the light failed, then I picked my way carefully across the fields, back to reality.

I was to see Kenneth Grahame once again. When I had made some drawings for the book I took them to Pangbourne. He was critical but I think he was pleased with my efforts and when he handed the drawings back to me he said "I'm glad you've made them real". I always regret that he did not live long enough to see the new edition completed."

On 23rd November a diary entry reads "Ruth's birthday". Is this Ruth Draper the actress for whom he drew a special birthday card with his favourite characters. (113)

Once he had accepted the task of illustrating *The Wind in the Willows* the first half of the year 1931 was mostly devoted to these drawings but at the same time he was producing illustrations for *Christmas Poems* by John Drinkwater to be published in December that year (114).

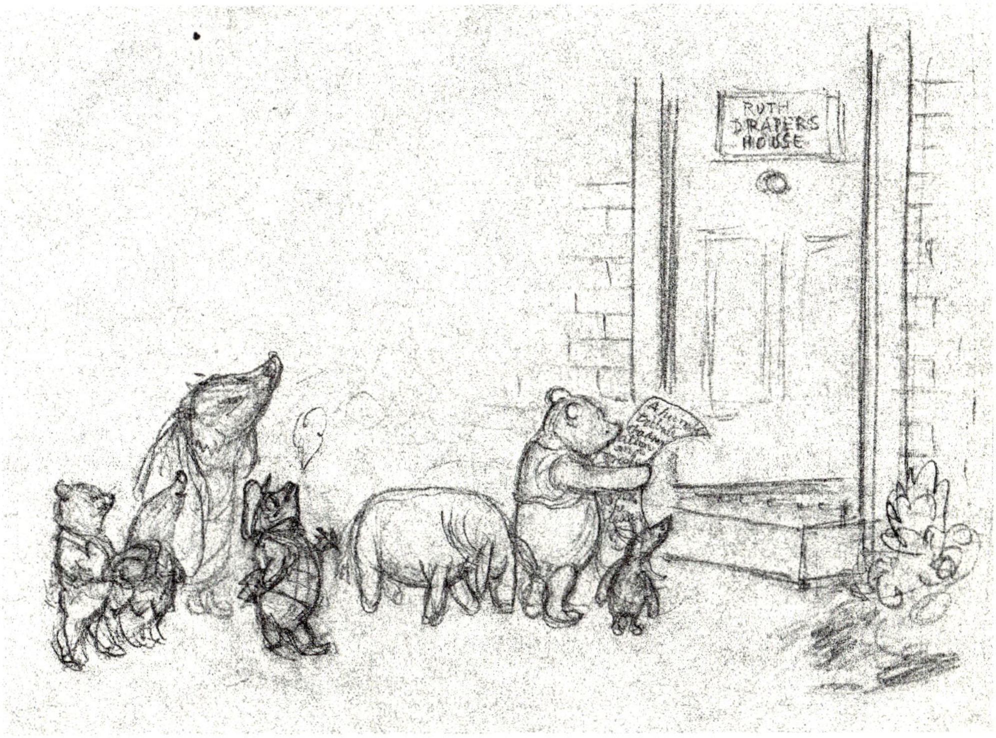

Ruth's birthday card
Pencil sketch, 1930 (113)

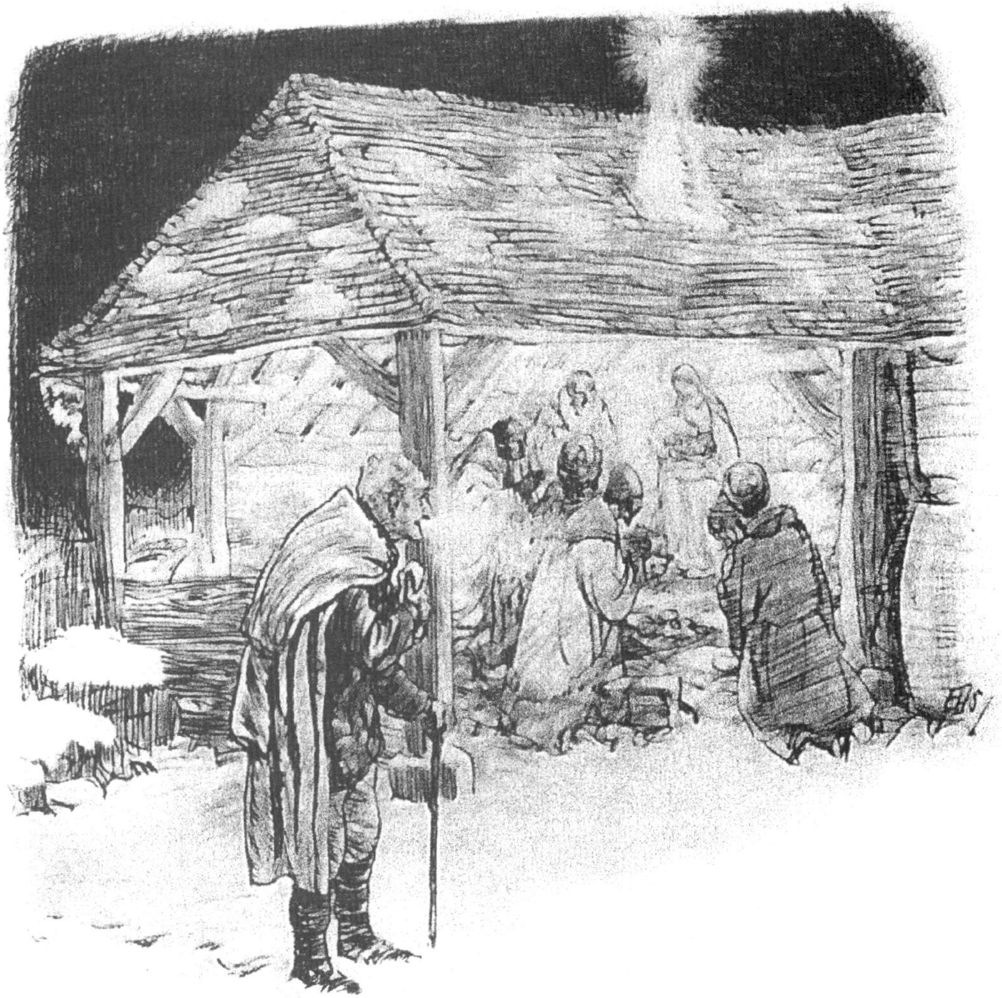

Dick Mapletoft's Christmas
One of a series of pen and ink drawings
to illustrate Christmas poems *by John Drinkwater (114)*

On 14th September the name of Ann Gibbon, from Montreal, appears in Shepard's diary for the first time. In October his son Graham and Ann, who had met each other the previous summer, became engaged and were married at Holy Trinity Church, Guildford, in the same month. After their honeymoon they joined Ernest, Mary and Osbert Lancaster on the 'White Owl' at Salcombe but work called Ernest as usual and he left them all on board and drove home.

G Bell and Sons came up with a third book in their literary series. Charles Lamb was to be the subject for this new volume. As a boy he had been at Christ's Hospital, which gave Ernest an excuse to visit the school and draw the pupils. *Everybody's Lamb*, which was a collection of his writings and edited by A C Ward, inspired the same enthusiasm and meticulous detail from Shepard that he had put into the two companion books (115) (116).

1932 saw the publication of four 'minor' books that Shepard had illustrated. *The Kenneth Grahame Book, The Christopher Robin Verses* by A A Milne for which twelve colour plates had been produced, and *Bevis: The Story of a Boy* by Richard Jefferies. Shepard 'loved it' and, following his custom, visited the Swindon area in order to get a sense of the place. The fourth book was *Sycamore Square* by Jan Struther.

In the following year *Everybody's Lamb* and *The Cricket in the Cage* by Patrick R Chambers reached the bookshops.

On 1st January 1934 Ernest bought a five year lease on an old house in Melina Place off St John's Wood Road. It had a small garden but its main attraction was a large studio that had once been owned by Phil May, a lesser known artist of the period. Gas and electricity were installed and Graham and Ann moved their furniture there from Cleveland Square in March. A small bedroom was fitted into the second floor so that Mary could have a London base. Ernest used an ante-room attached to the studio as his bedroom and a wash room next to the garage for his ablutions. When the three parts of the family were safely installed in their London quarters at Melina Place, he gave up the tenancy on their rooms in Cleveland Square.

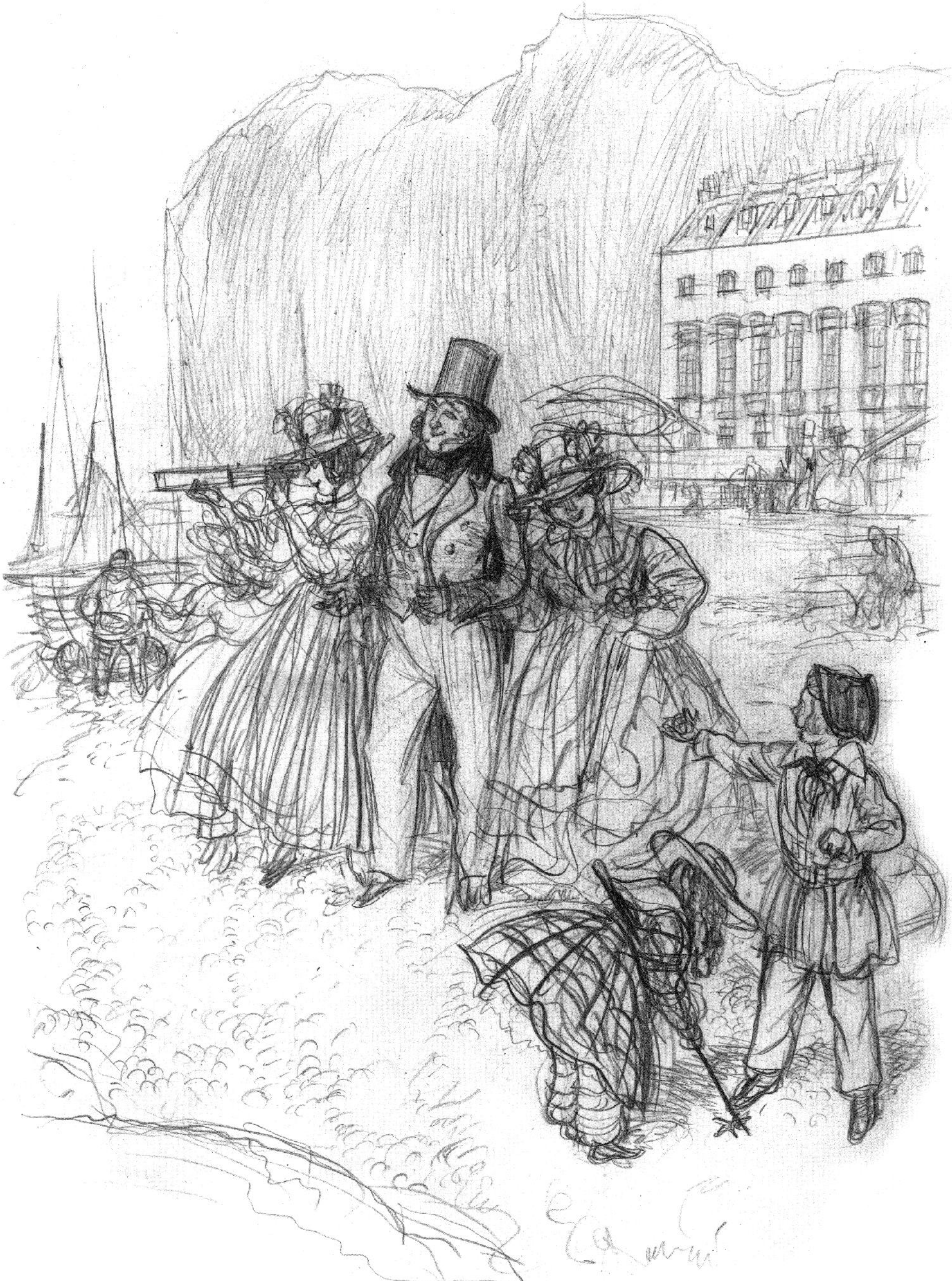

A seaside scene
Pencil sketch drawn from
Everybody's Lamb*, circa 1931 (115)*

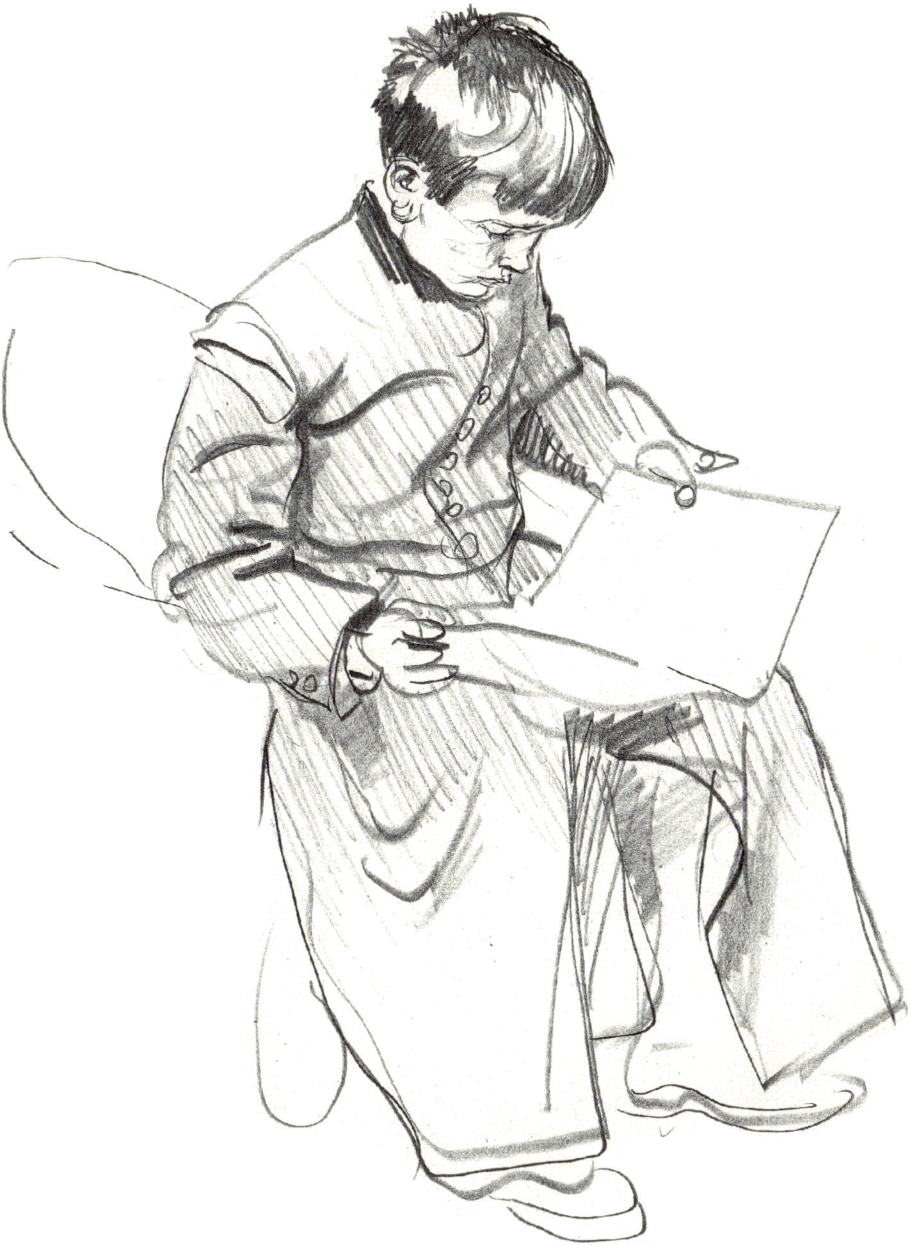

Pencil sketch of a Christ's Hospital boy
Charles Lamb was a pupil at Christ's Hospital (116)

Later in the year he travelled to Street in Somerset in order to discuss with Laurence Housman his 'Palace Plays'. The first of these was *Victoria Regina.* A great deal of of research was called for including visits to Windsor Castle and Osborne House on the Isle of Wight where Queen Victoria died. The two other books to follow were *Golden Sovereign* and *Gracious Majesty* although the latter was not published until 1941.

He was now Deputy Art Editor of *Punch,* which took much more time than his routine cartoons yet he seemed to have more time available for travel including visits to France, although some were connected with his illustrations to *Perfume From Provence* by Winifred Fortescue. Lady Fortescue (known as Peggy although she used 'Winifred' as an authoress) was the perfect hostess for Ernest and Mary at her villa near Cannes where she was pleased to show Ernest her late husband's library. He showed a great interest in the places and some of the people who figured in these books.

Perfume from Provence was published in 1935 with *The Modern Struwelpeter* the following year. While the country was concerned with the Silver Jubilee of George V, then his death, the abdication crisis and the accession of George VI, the flow of new books illustrated by Shepard slowed down considerably.

Golden Sovereign, already mentioned, was published in 1937 as was *As the Bee Sucks*, with words by E V Lucas, and *Cheddar Gorge* a book about cheese edited by Sir John Squire. Although these new books appeared there is a feeling that life was a little artificial, there was a lot more travel, a lot more play and a lot less hard work.

Shepard's first grandchild was born to Ann, wife of Graham, on 22nd April 1937. Named Harriet on her birth certificate, presumably after her paternal grandmother, she was known as Minette throughout her life. She was christened at St Martha's-on-the-Hill on Saturday 26th June 1937.

At the same church Mary Shepard and Evoe Knox, a widower and the editor of *Punch*, were married on 2nd October 1937. The guests were brought back to 'Long Meadow' for 'a very good lunch', provided by Guildford Caterers, in the studio. Ethel, Ernest's sister, came home for her annual leave too late for the wedding but stayed a fortnight before returning to Lahore. By then she was the head deaconess and also played the organ in the cathedral, not so surprising considering her ability to accompany on the piano at a very early age.

While travelling around England enjoying himself in 1938, Shepard wrote "We all knew we were living on a volcano that might erupt at any time".

The same feeling was around in the summer of 1939. Conscription was ordered by Parliament on 26th April and the population in general anticipated another war. Shepard, who fully realised this, continued to go on his travels and to produce his weekly drawings for *Punch*.

During his visits to Devon he had become friendly with the owner of The Castle Hotel at Dartmouth. Some people wanted to pull the building down and build a more modern hotel in its place. The owner said that he could not afford to restore the establishment and Shepard offered to assist financially in order to help save the building. The proprietor also owned a boat at Brixham called 'Gold Seal' and suggested Shepard might like to charter it for £70. The owner could suggest a skipper for whenever it was to be used. Arrangements were duly made for the chartering of the boat that was moored at Kingswear. The skipper was to be Alfred Pitman, the engineer was to be Ted and the veteran deckhand Bill. These would help sail the 'Gold Seal'. For a few summer weeks Ernest, his family and friends enjoyed their short trips around the Devon coast.

The Reluctant Dragon which told of a dragon who had difficulty in breathing fire was illustrated by Shepard and published during the summer.

During the last week in August, Graham telegraphed his father to say that Ann and their baby Minette were going to 'Long Meadow' on the Sunday. Ernest packed, said goodbye to his 'crew' and saw 'Gold Seal' for the last time as it was to be chartered for Admiralty use and was sunk while on active service.

Ernest returned to 'Long Meadow' and waited. Germany invaded Poland. Sunday 3rd September Shepard's diary entry for the day reads "England and France declare war on Germany at 11am. I went to help fill sandbags at the hospital in Seaford".

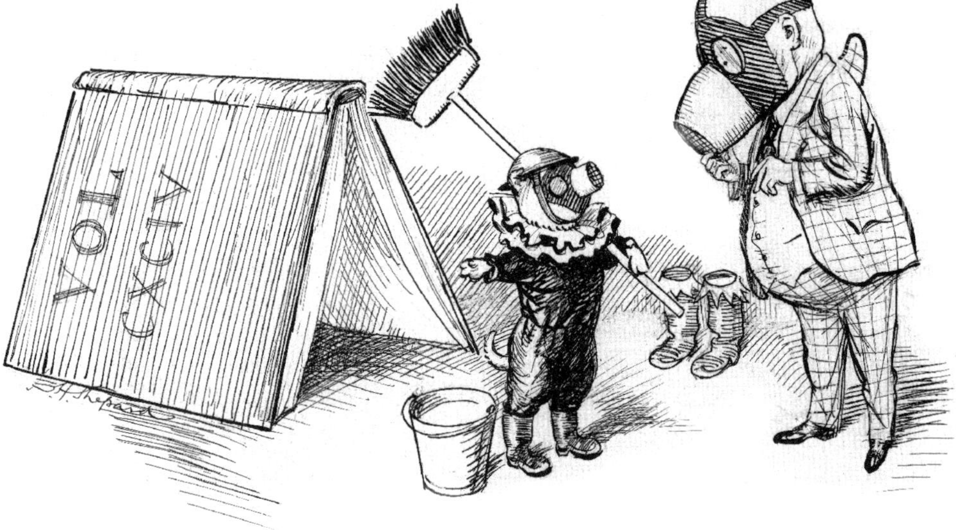

Punch Prepares for War, June 1938 (117)

E.H. Shepard

Chapter 9
The Second World War 1939 - 1945

Punch (117) (119) carried on as usual but on 25th September *The Illustrated London News* moved out to Kings Langley. Things were completely different from 1914. There was less excitement for there were too many memories of twenty years earlier.

Christmas 1939 was not a very festive one. Ernest had a quiet dinner with Mary and Evoe at 'Long Meadow'. Everybody got on with their work. The future looked very bleak. Gardens, parks and common land were turned into vegetable patches and everybody was called upon to "Dig for Victory" (118).

Dig for Victory (118)

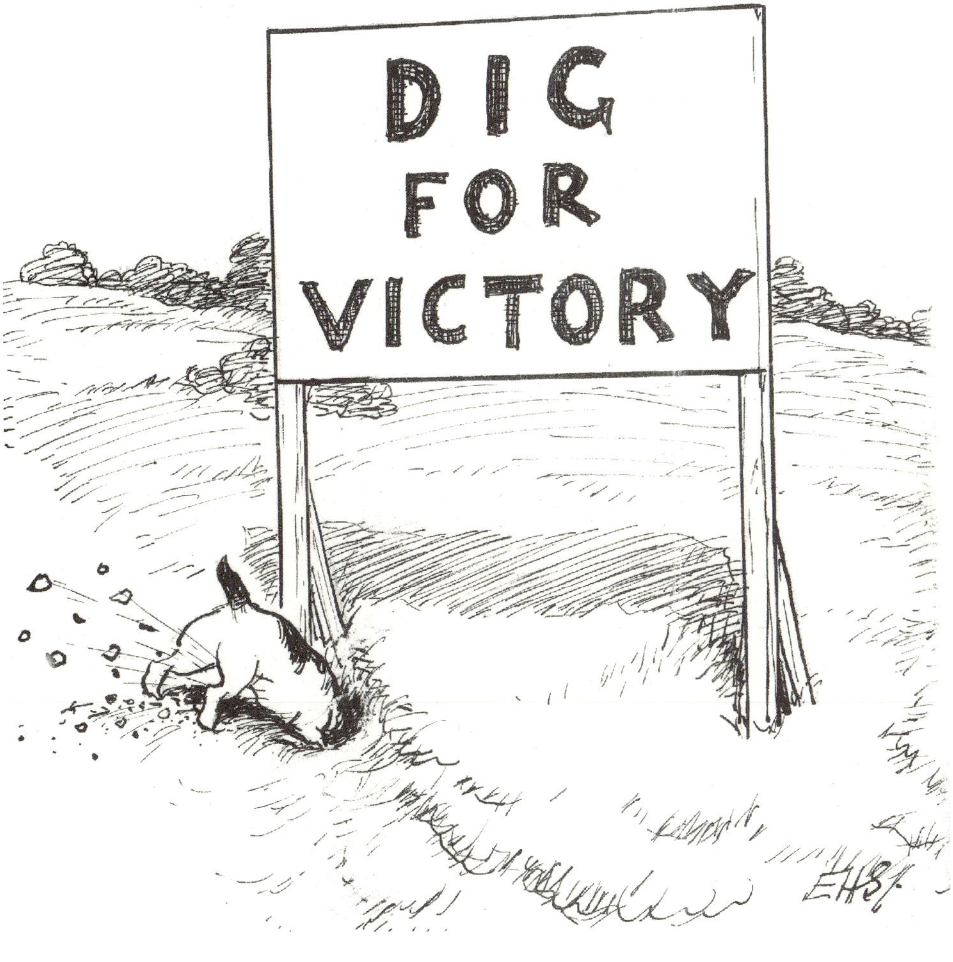

In the late spring of 1940 Colonel Wigan, a near neighbour, paid Shepard a visit specifically to talk about 'Local Defence Volunteers', known at first as the 'LDV'. Every county and town had to recruit from those over military age to join this new Volunteer Force. As most of the men in the local area fell into this age group there was no lack of volunteers. Captain E H Shepard was appointed on 18th May 1940 to command the Local Defence Volunteers which were to become "C" Company, 4th (Guildford) Battalion, Surrey Home Guard.

Very soon it was announced that Belgium had surrendered and the French Army was retreating. The British Expeditionary Force was fighting a rearguard action and falling back on Dunkirk. The local LDV was mobilised and a group, unarmed and without uniforms, patrolled the Downs towards Newlands Corner on their first Sunday evening on duty. After several hours they retired to 'Long Meadow' for refreshments. Within a short time uniforms were issued and a few days later came rifles but these were of the American pattern and did not take English ammunition.

The situation in Europe was frightening. On Sunday 16th June Paris capitulated and Shepard's LDV Company went out on fixed patrol, armed and in uniform for night work on the Downs. The Volunteers title had now been changed to 'Home Guard'.

In late June, Ann and Minette sailed to Canada to join Ann's parents in Montreal for safety and Graham came permanently to 'Long Meadow'. When he had a cable telling of their safe arrival in Canada, he went to the Admiralty for an interview, and received a commission as Sub-Lieutenant in the Royal Naval Volunteer Reserve and was sent to Hove for training.

Ernest's sister Ethel came home from India in poor health and Ernest feared that she would have to go into a home. Eventually a place was found for her in The Home of the Holy Rood which was run by Anglican Nuns at Findon. She died there peacefully on 15th November 1942. While the Blitz was on in London the Home Guard was on a red alert all the time. When the whole of the docks area was alight the red glow could easily be seen from 'Long Meadow'. The Battle for Britain not only kept the Home Guard on duty at night but also throughout the weekends

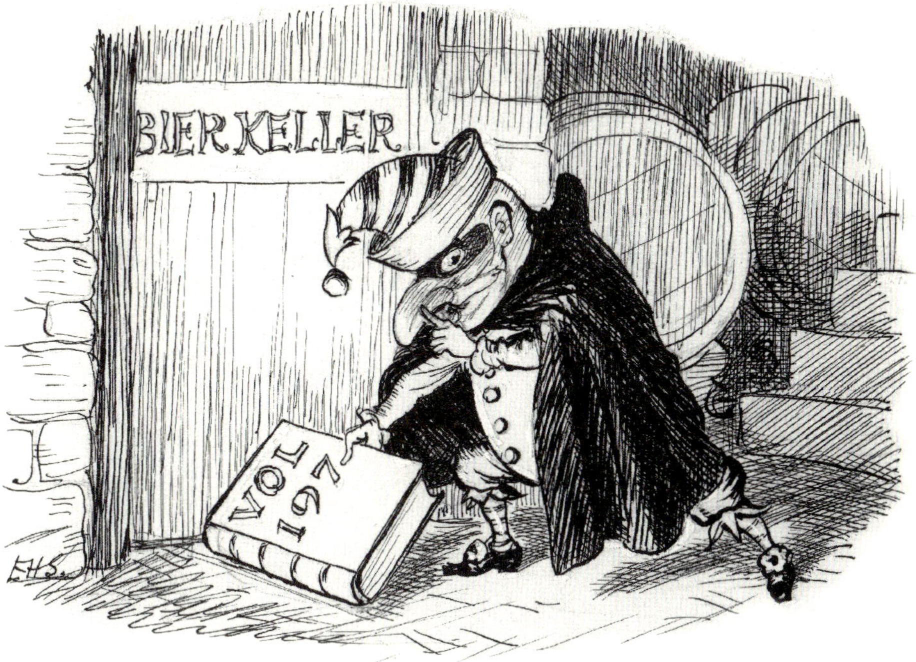

Gunpowder Plot', Punch *(119)*

Every night Shepard's section maintained an all night guard from a house called 'Whiteways' at the end of White Lane where the Home Guard Company had the use of the stables. As in the previous War Shepard was able to use his artistic talent for military purposes. He drew two maps of his immediate area which were used throughout the War. These have been carefully preserved (see end papers of this book). Every weekend he took charge from nightfall to daylight. Armed patrols were constantly on duty but no one was allowed to load a rifle without a special order. Canadian troops who were quartered nearby sent instructions twice a week to Shepard's Company headquarters at Meadow Golf Club.

The Home Guard became another family to him. At Christmas he would send to every member of his Company either a personally drawn card or one of a limited edition just for the Company, friends and members of his family (120). Chris Turnbull, a member of the Company, tells how he used to sit up on top of the Downs watching London burning. Turnbull would smoke, with rifle at the ready, while Shepard would doodle on bits of paper or make complete sketches. Turnbull tells how Shepard on one occasion spent the entire night trying to find ways of satisfactorily drawing, in black and white, a night-time scene so that it was obviously very dark but the viewer could also make out what was happening. Home Guard every night and *Punch* during the day gave Shepard a very heavy load but probably no heavier than other people of his age.

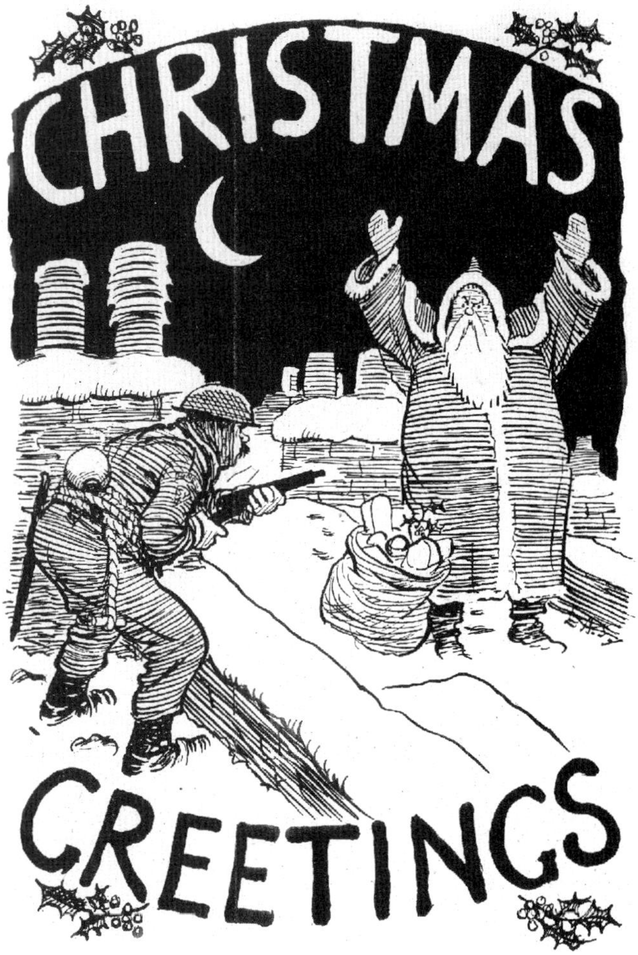

Shepard's Christmas card, 1943 (120)

As soon as Graham left for the Navy he and Mary started to look for a London studio in St John's Wood. They found a small flat in Park Road that served their needs. It was here that he worked on illustrations for *Gracious Majesty* in addition to his contributions to *Punch* (121).

Bernard Partridge was forced to leave London in 1941 owing to bomb damage to his property in Holland Park. He went to live in the country and his position as first cartoonist was given to Shepard. The *Punch* Table had been removed to a 'place of safety' in 1940 and was not returned until peace came. The weekly dinner was abandoned and its place was taken by a ten o'clock meeting on Wednesday mornings at the offices in Bouverie Street.

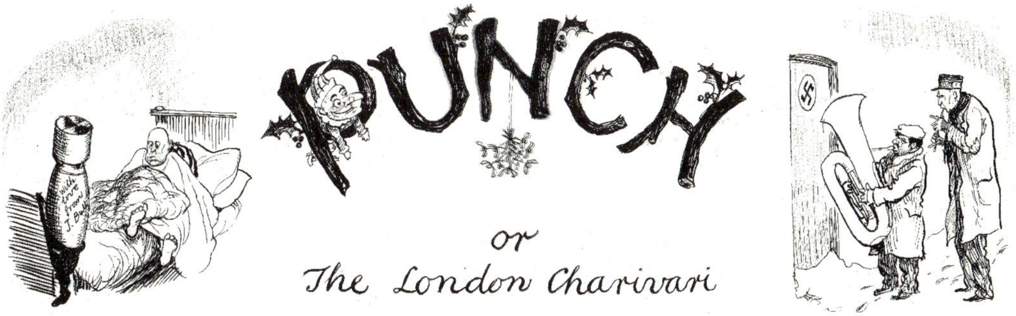

Punch, *Charivari, October 1941*
Showing Mussolini, left, and Marshall Petain, right (121)

On August 6th 1942 Ernest went to the *Punch* meeting in the morning, drew the cartoon in the afternoon, and went to a concert by the Griller Quartet in the evening. There he met Norah Carroll, a nurse at St Mary's Hospital, Paddington. He asked her out to dinner in October and records that "we got on famously".

Another quiet Christmas was held at 'Long Meadow' in 1942 with only his sister-in-law Addie, Mary and Evoe. Immediately after Christmas the weather turned very cold and this lasted throughout January - the cold winter of the War. In mid February 1943 he had dinner with Norah at the Great Western Railway Hotel followed by a concert at St Mary's. It is obvious that they were attracted to each other. In the following months they met whenever nursing duties at St Mary's Hospital and Home Guard duties at Guildford permitted. As with a lot of wartime romances this was not very often.

In February 1943 Ernest was informed that his son was in hospital in Yorkshire on HMS *Polyanthus* which was then moored alongside in Newcastle. Ernest and Mary went to visit Graham in the sick bay and then, somehow, managed to get him to London and then to Guildford on sick leave. There a local doctor saw Graham's injured leg and decided he would completely re-dress and re-plaster it as it was in such a state. In April Graham was fit to go back to the ship which had now been refitted and was ready for its next tour of duty. Ernest drove his son to London Road Station at Guildford to see him on to the train. He was never to see him again.

During the summer he and Norah were both to get leave and travel around the West Country. A week after the end of the holiday, which had been extremely enjoyable, Norah went to 'Long Meadow' for a couple of days, her first visit.

On September 20th a friend from the Admiralty phoned Ernest to inform him that HMS *Polyanthus* had been attacked while on convoy duty in the Atlantic and sunk with all hands. Ernest sent a cable to Ann but she had already been told by the Admiralty. In the first week of October Graham's portrait was published in *The Illustrated London News* as the wartime equivalent of the debutante and engagement picture that had normally graced the inside page.

On 8th November, Ann and Minette arrived back in England. Ernest met them at Euston and they went to Mary Knox's home for the night while Ernest went back to 'Long Meadow' to prepare rooms for them. They were put in the large bedroom with the four-poster bed that had been Mary's. They arrived the next day to the relief of Ernest who felt he had them safely home. The following week Shepard went to London and did his *Punch* work on the Thursday. He then phoned Norah and asked her to meet him for dinner after which they went back to his London flat and he asked her to marry him.

Sarah his housekeeper had been ailing for some time and with the arrival of Ann and her daughter, she found the work too much and went to live with her sister at Shamley Green. The studio was full of the furniture that had once been in the London home of Ann and Graham. It was then left to Ann and Ernest to do the family cleaning and to prepare for Christmas. Norah came on Christmas Eve and everybody helped to prepare the Christmas dinner which was probably a rather sombre gathering. In order to return to duty Norah had to leave Guildford at 2.30pm.

At the end of February the Shepard family appointed Mrs Heath as a live-in housekeeper.

Norah was taken ill in April with a gastric ulcer and had to go to hospital where she remained for 14 days. Shepard went to collect her but before doing so bought an engagement ring. From the hospital Ernest took her to Chalfont St Giles where her father and stepmother lived in Milton's Cottage. Her father was the curator of the Little House Museum.

6th June 1944 was 'D' Day which meant that victory was thought to be in sight. A few nights later the first V1 pilotless plane came across the Channel, and London and parts of the south-east of England were to be bombarded by an entirely new weapon. The small plane was a high explosive bomb. When this plane reached the end of its pre-determined course its engine cut out and it plunged to earth with a devastating effect.

On 9th August Ernest received a telegram from Pie's sister-in-law saying that Lindsay (Pie's brother) had been run over and killed by a train. Personal tragedy had struck again.

Because of the threat of the new V weapons, expectant mothers were being evacuated from St Mary's Hospital in Paddington to 'somewhere in England' where it was thought they would be safe. Norah, with three other nurses, was seconded to accompany a convoy of expectant mothers to Blackpool. Once there the mothers were billeted in various hotels in the town and Norah was left in charge.

The situation in Europe was becoming less threatening for the British Isles and Shepard was able to take some leave in order to visit Norah in Blackpool. The day after his arrival he and Norah went for a long walk. The next morning Norah's staff nurse told Ernest that Norah had mumps and would not go to the hospital to the mothers because of passing on infection. Shepard suggested that Norah pack, meet him at an agreed place, and return to London with him. The only seat for Norah was her suitcase in the corridor. On reaching London they went straight to St Mary's Hospital where she became a patient instead of staff, and Shepard went back to Guildford.

Early in November Norah gave up her work at St Mary's and prepared for their wedding. This took place on 18th November 1944 at St James Church, Bayswater, when Ernest's young grand-daughter was a bridesmaid. Norah wore a long claret coloured dress and was given away by her father (122). The reception was held at a friend's flat and they spent their wedding night at Ernest's studio. They did not go away for a honeymoon but for a few days were able to go to the theatre and had quiet dinners together. Ernest had taken leave from the Home Guard which was on the point of being demobilised and finally ended when there was a stand down parade at Guildford on 3rd December (123).

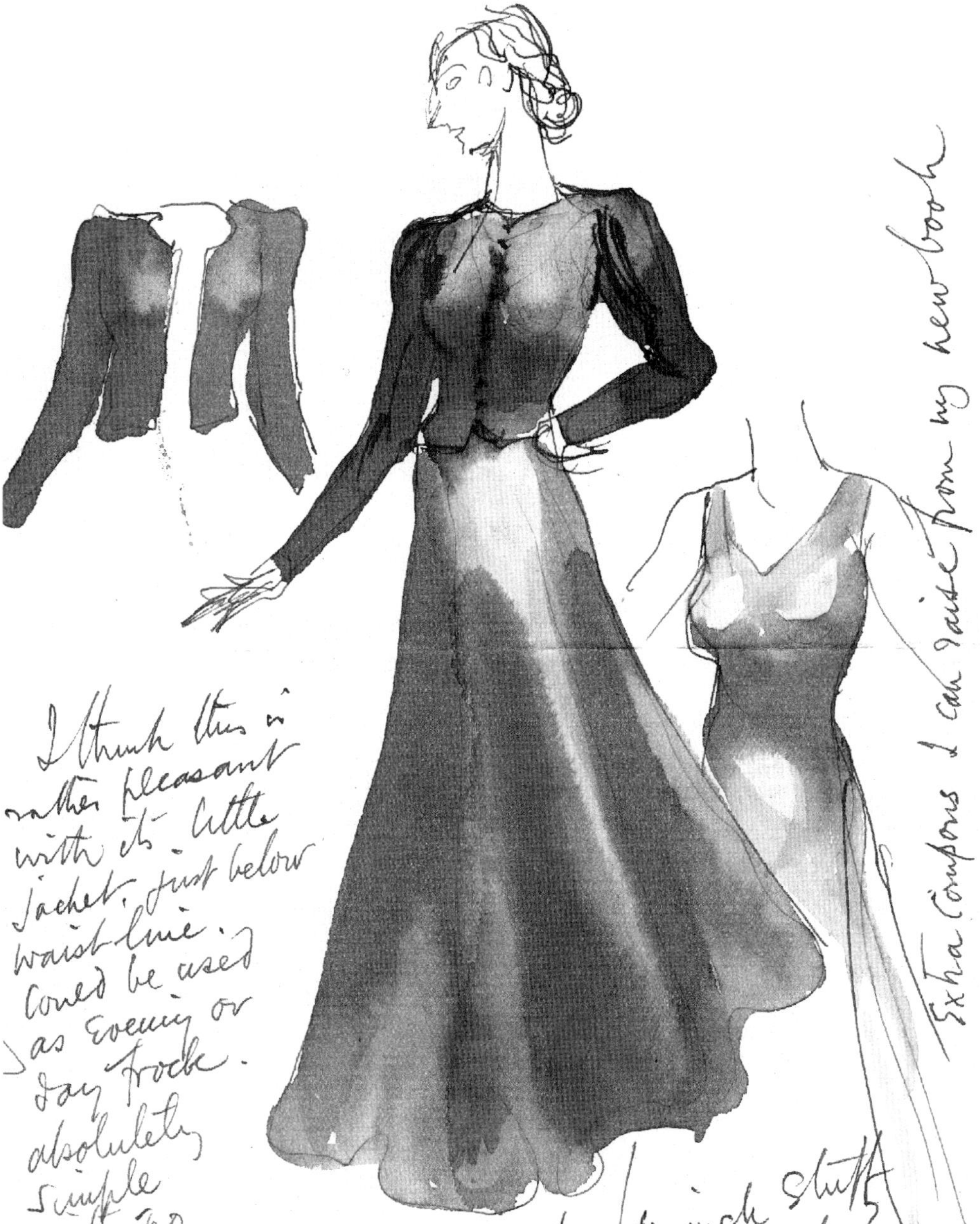

Pen and ink design for Norah's dress (122)

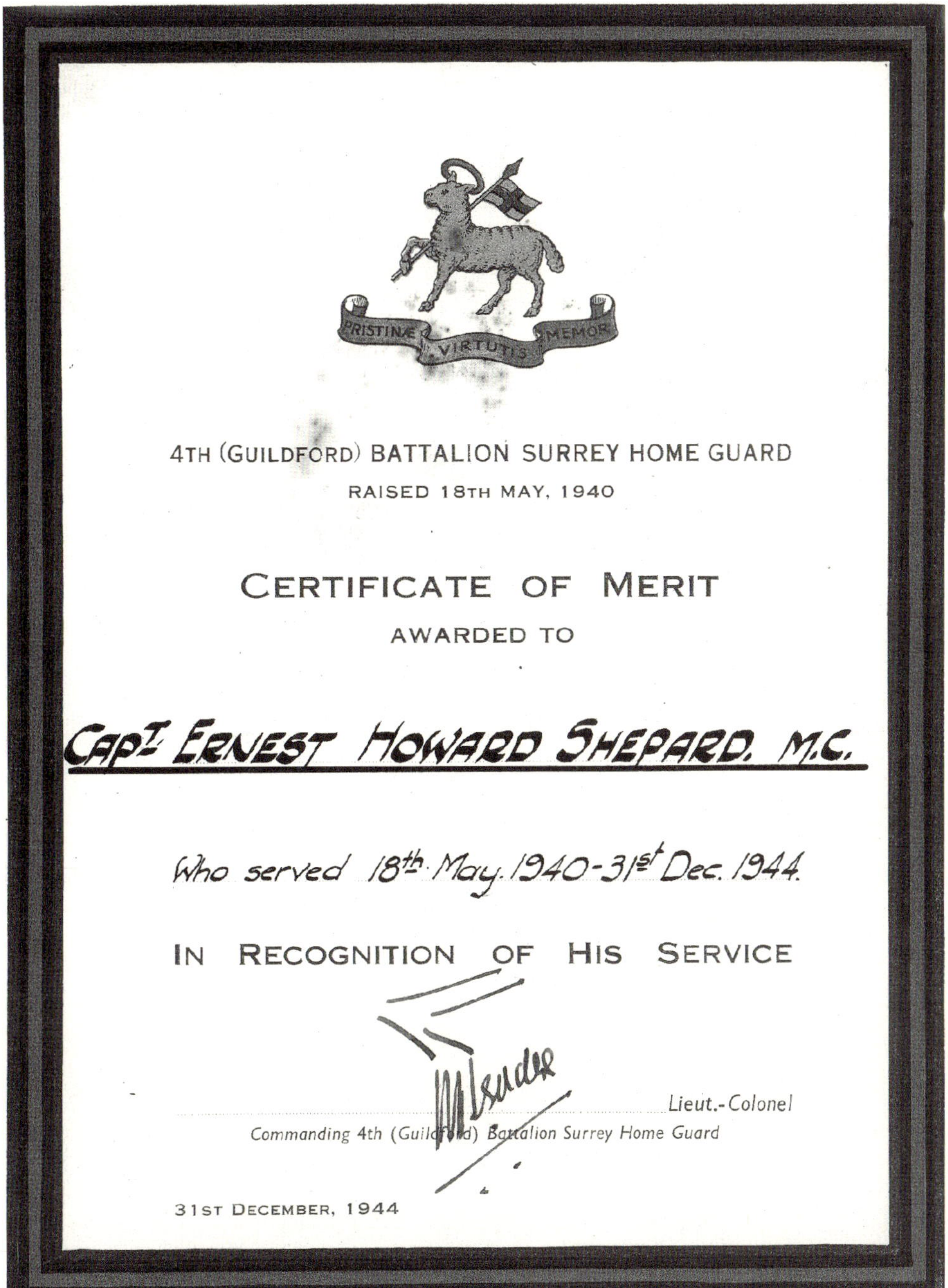
PRISTINÆ VIRTUTIS MEMOR

4TH (GUILDFORD) BATTALION SURREY HOME GUARD

RAISED 18TH MAY, 1940

CERTIFICATE OF MERIT

AWARDED TO

CAPT. ERNEST HOWARD SHEPARD. M.C.

Who served 18th May. 1940 - 31st Dec. 1944.

IN RECOGNITION OF HIS SERVICE

Lieut.-Colonel

Commanding 4th (Guildford) Battalion Surrey Home Guard

31ST DECEMBER, 1944

The Standing Down of the Home Guard (123)

During the second half of 1944 Shepard could concern himself with his family life, as Home Guard responsibilities were reduced. His work for *Punch* however went relentlessly on.

Ann Shepard had never settled down at 'Long Meadow' and was anxious to get back to her people in Montreal. She booked a passage for herself and Minette on December 8th. Ernest and Norah drove them to London where they were met by Mary before they took the boat train. At this stage of the War the seas were considered safe so there needed to be little concern for their safety.

Norah's father became ill on 22nd December and was taken to St Mary's Hospital but he was too ill to recognise visitors and died on 1st January 1945. At the start of the year V2s were arriving. These were rockets that flew over and landed on London without sound and therefore without warning. Although most Londoners took this in their stride there was a small panic evacuation at that time and the Shepards were asked to take in some friends who were living in Clapham. This family brought their cat with them which was not particularly welcome and, although they did not stay very long, it took some time for reminders of the cat to depart!

News of the War improved daily. At the beginning of March threats were made against the lives of both Hitler and Mussolini. (124). On April 29th Mussolini was killed by patriots. Two days later Hitler committed suicide and all the German forces surrendered on 8th May V E (Victory in Europe) Day. Shepard's matter of fact diary records:

Tuesday 8th May 1945, V E Day
Planted potatoes all day
Churchill speaks 3.0, King speaks 9.0
Fireworks & bonfires

In May 1945 Ernest and Norah went by train for a holiday in Devon. Petrol was still rationed. Ernest relaxed and did some painting in addition to his notebook sketches. On 9th August Bernard Partridge died which meant that Shepard returned to being first cartoonist at *Punch*. On 2nd September the Japanese surrendered, V J Day was celebrated and the country knew that the War was really over and it could now look forward to peace.

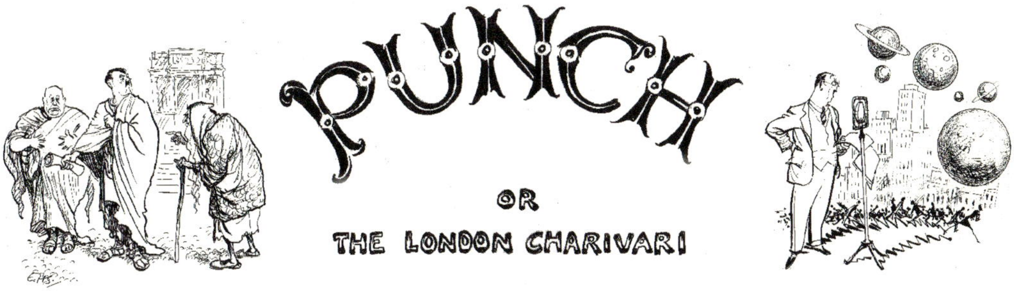

The Ides of March,
Punch, *Charivari, March 1945 (124)*

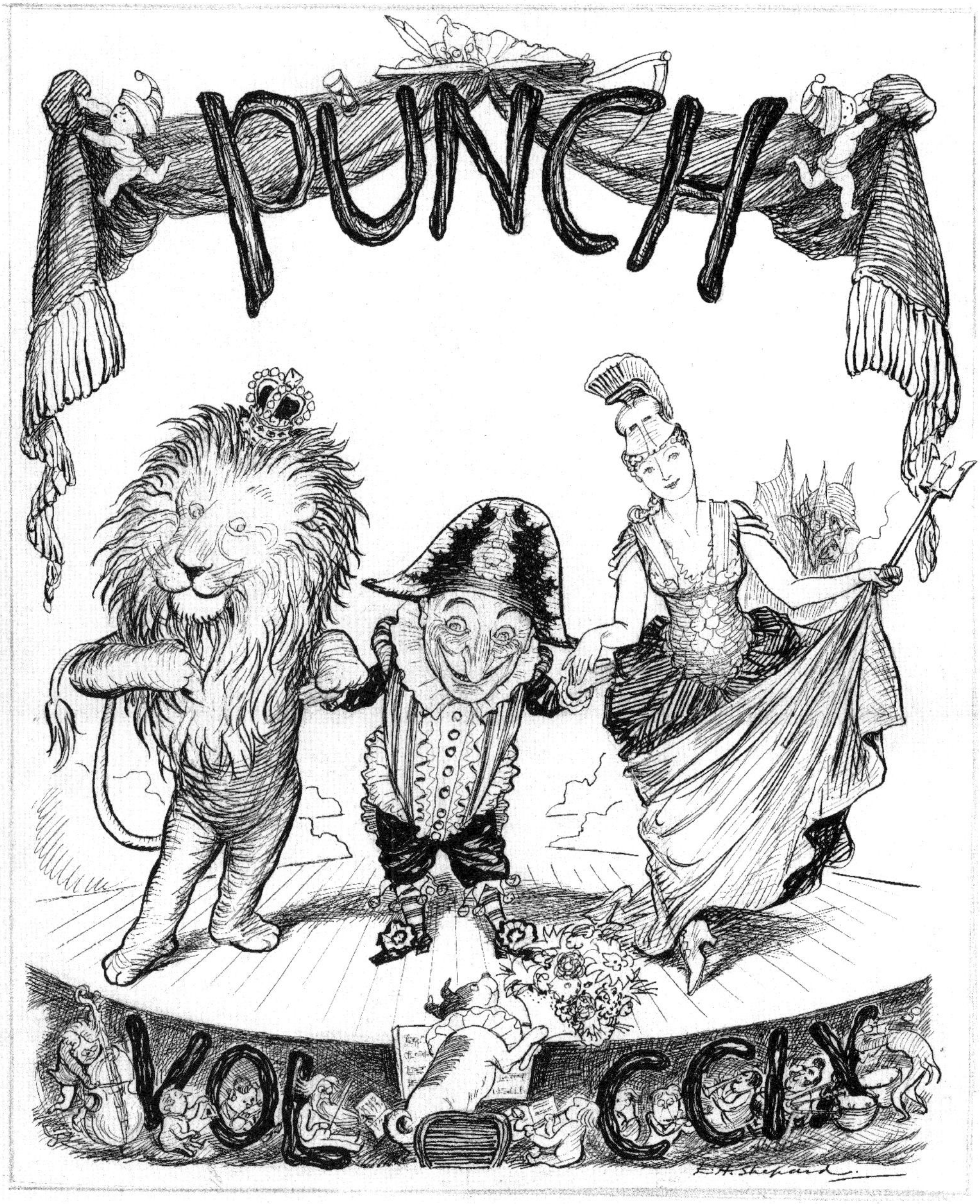

Punch celebrates Peace (125)

E.H. Shepard

Chapter 10
A New Life 1945 - 1955

Peace had come at last and *Punch* celebrated (125).

Ernest and Norah returned to Devon in September, where Ernest again painted and sketched (126) and they visited Alf Pitman, one of the crew of the 'Gold Seal' that Ernest had chartered in 1939 and that had been sunk on active service during the War.

When after the summer break they came back to 'Long Meadow', they planned their new life together and decided that when married they would need a married couple as live-in staff. Mr and Mrs Hogarth moved in as resident housekeeper and chauffeur on 8th October.

Christmas 1945, at 'Long Meadow', was quiet but enjoyable. Their sole houseguest was George Morrow, a member of the *Punch* Table since 1923. Strangely Norah had known Morrow for as long as Ernest had, as he used to teach at an art school where Norah went in the evening to learn drawing.

The next three years saw the establishment of a new way of life, not only for the Shepards but also for the whole of the country. Life was never to be the same as before the war. This was to be a New World with new ideas and new mechanical aids many of which had had their origins in wartime inventions.

During 1947 Shepard had started negotiations for *Golden Age* and *Dream Days* (text by Kenneth Grahame) to be published for the 'Book of the Month Club' in New York. In July a party from *Punch* went to France to see some of the Normandy battlefields and this Shepard commemorated with a painting showing the welcome that they were given by the new Vineyards (*P6*). By the end of the month he was back at *Punch* and looking forward to full resumption of his life of constant professional drawing. In September he was invited to make drawings for the new *Royal Artillery War Book* as he had for the volume on the Great War.

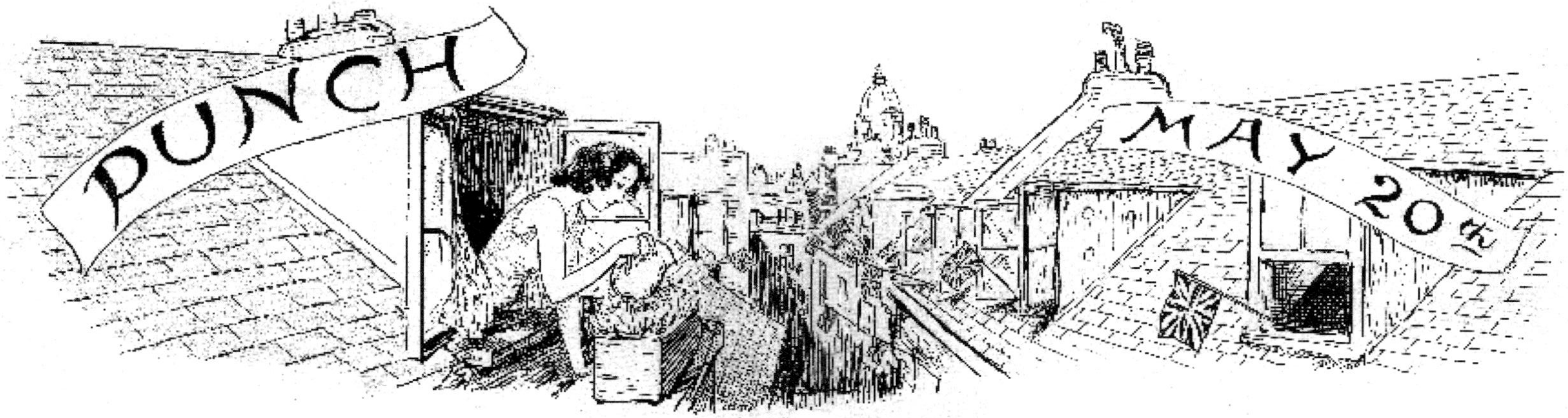

CHARIVARIA

Charivaria, May 1945 (126)

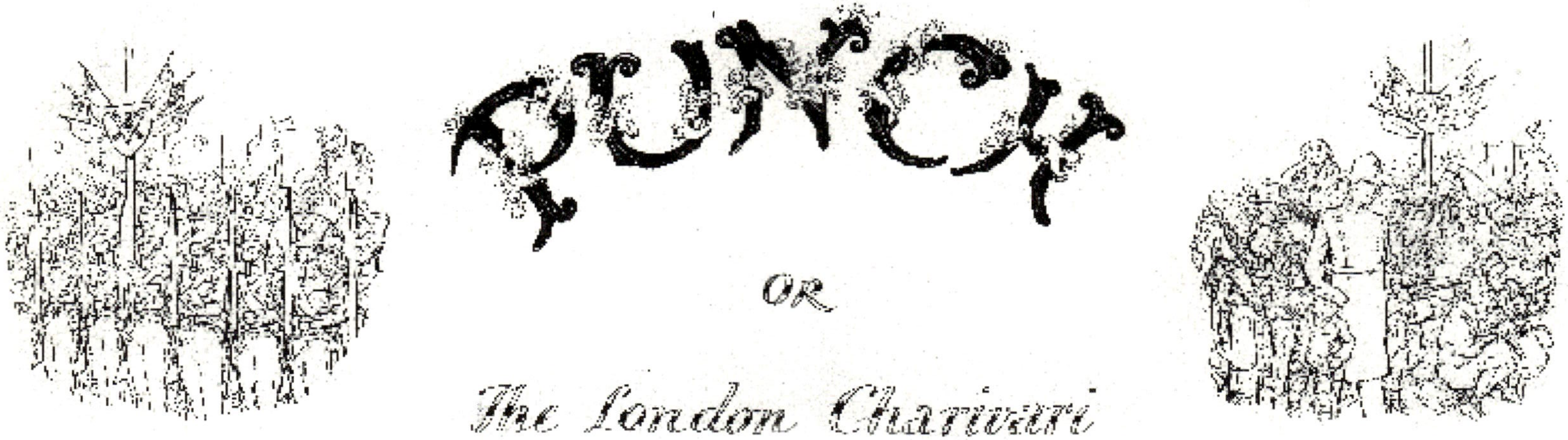

Wedding of the Princess Elizabeth and Lt. Philip Mountbatten, Charivari, drawn October 1947 (127)

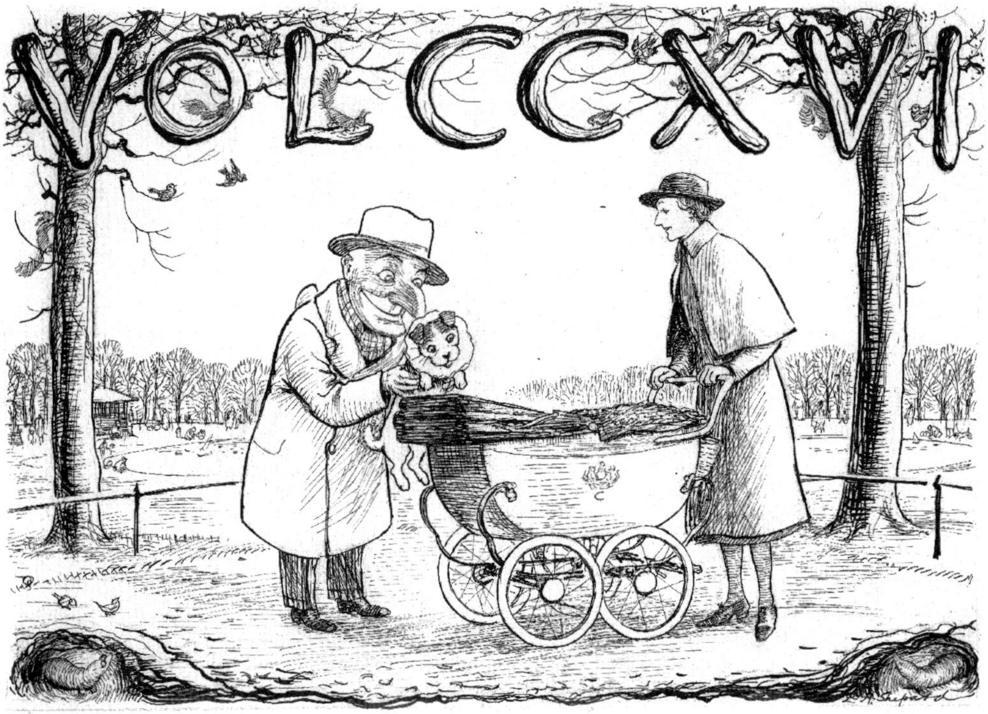

The Return of the Royal Nanny (128)

In October he was working on a double page drawing to commemorate the Royal Wedding of the Princess Elizabeth and Lieutenant Philip Mountbatten, to be created Duke of Edinburgh on his wedding day. He also undertook a special heading for *The London Charivari* which obviously took a great deal of thought and care because it was drawn three weeks before publication instead of the usual two to three days (127).

Three days before the wedding Evoe Knox, Shepard's son-in-law, celebrated fifteen years as Editor of *Punch* but he eventually retired on 30th March 1948. The early part of that year had been bitterly cold. The Thames had frozen over in many places and Evoe had to make the sad decision of closing *Punch* down for a short while until the thaw came.

With his ever caring attention to the life style of his granddaughter and her mother, Ernest purchased a cottage for "Minette and Ann" at Pultingham near Guildford which meant that their future home was secure.

November 1948 saw the birth of Prince Charles and produced Shepard's drawing for Volume CCXVI of *Punch,* 'The Return of the Royal Nanny' (128).

During 1949 Shepard was undertaking various double-page illustrations for *Punch*. These needed research for the detailed work necessary and therefore were taking him considerably longer than his normal cartoons.

In January 1950 milk was de-rationed bringing national life a step nearer to normality whatever that might be.

In addition to the work at Bouverie Street and his illustrations for a small number of books, Shepard took on a regular amount of advertising work for such firms as 'Horlicks, The Malted Milk Drink', and 'Basildon Bond The Notepaper People'.

On holiday with Norah he found great joy in painting rather than sketching. In June when in France his diary states "*I would rather stay in one well chosen place and paint for hours or days*". In September on a cruise he wrote from Genoa "*I painted a harbour scene from our cabin*".

1951, the year of the Festival of Britain, found Shepard illustrating a textbook by Anna B Stewart entitled *Enter David Garrick* which was to be published in the United States of America. This book gave Ernest the opportunity to make special visits to historic sites with Garrick connections in London and elsewhere as he had done previously for Pepys and Johnson.

In May *Punch* gave him a poem by Gibbons Pale about miners in Leicestershire and asked him to provide illustrations. Once more he set out on his travels, this time to Snibstone Mine in Leicestershire in order to obtain accuracy and the right 'atmosphere'.

In July both he and Norah went to Haworth in Yorkshire to draw pictures of the Brontë country. In September they found themselves in Rome where obviously he was in his element making sketches everywhere. In his notes he records "*I drew the Tritone Fountain. I had taken with me from England some Woolworth chalks, these being light and easy to carry, and I found them very useful in colouring my drawings*". He continued to work in chalk for the remainder of the holiday and twenty years later found that they had hardly faded at all.

King George VI died in February 1952 and, while the country was still in mourning, Ernest attended the Memorial Service at Marlborough College on 9th March for the Old Boys who had been killed in the War.

Throughout early summer he was working on drawings for *The Silver Curlew,* text by Eleanor Farjeon. In July he was given a Highland poem to illustrate for *Punch* which presented him with a reason for a holiday in Scotland in order to obtain authentic scenery and background material.

On 19th December he made a very special visit to Middlesex Hospital in order to see AA Milne who was very ill and extremely feeble but seemed pleased to see Shepard.

In 1953 Ernest was commissioned to organise six large cartoons for Guinness and Company. One of these he drew himself, the others were drawn by fellow contemporary cartoonists. These posters were seen throughout Britain during the year of the Coronation of Elizabeth II which event was to provide him with a wealth of opportunities for his artistry. *Punch* produced their special Coronation Number (129) (130).

On 1st June Norah went with a friend to London taking rugs and food so that they could sleep on the kerbside in order to see the Coronation Procession the following day. It rained but they saw everything.

During the summer Shepard worked on *The Cuckoo Clock,* by Mrs Molesworth. He then went to Scotland with the National School Orchestra in order to undertake a commission from *The Illustrated London News* to make large drawings of the orchestra both at rehearsals and in performance. While there he was able to paint a set of watercolours of the scenery.

In the early autumn he had a 'Pictures Show' at Walker's Gallery in Bond Street, London, and did reasonably well financially with sales before it closed on 27th October. On November 8th he attended a memorial service for the fallen at St Martha's-on-the-Hill, on the War Memorial of which Graham's name was inscribed. Ten days later Addie, the last survivor of Pie's sisters, died.

Ernest and Norah now decided that the time had come to look for another house. 'Long Meadow' had become too large for them.

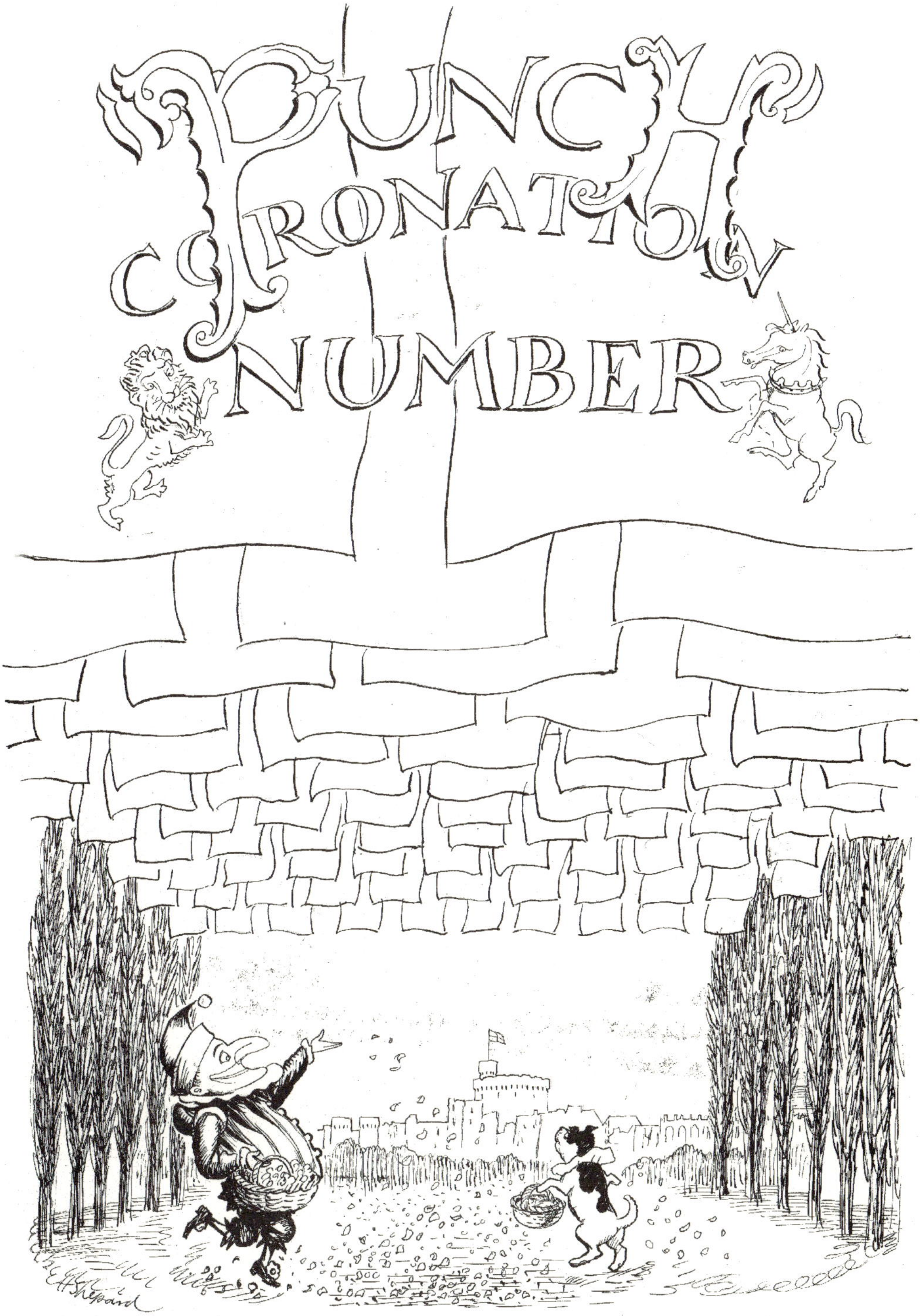

Punch Coronation Number (129)

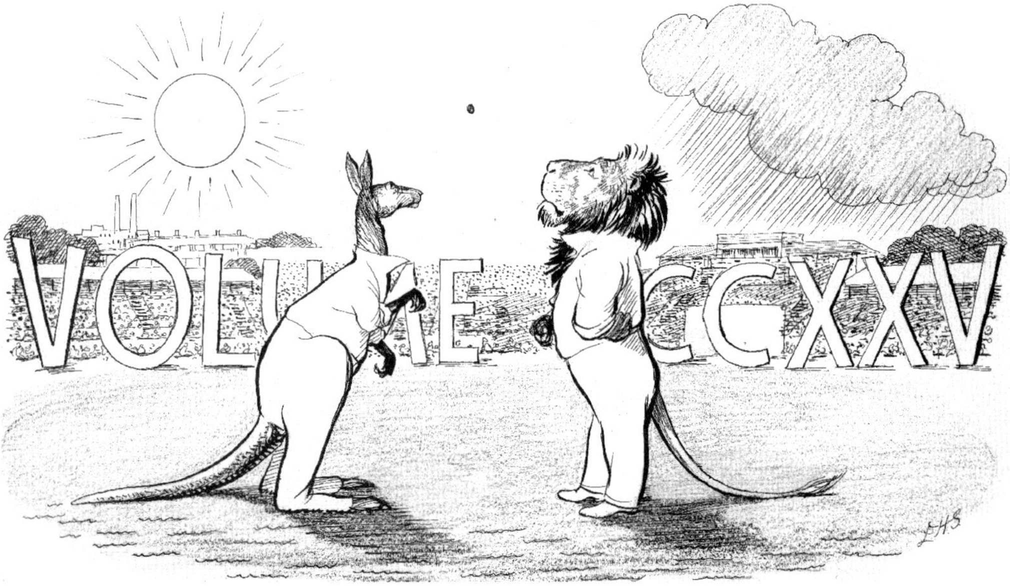

Punch, The Ashes (130)

At the start of 1954 Ernest was at work on illustrations for two books *Daddy Darwin's Dovecote* and *Jackanapes and Other Stories* and his diary records he was "much enjoying it". Unfortunately, no trace of these are in the Archives.

Malcolm Muggeridge had now become Editor of *Punch*. As with all new editors, the time had come for 'changes' and, in March, Shepard became aware that "Muggeridge thought it was time I gave up". He continued to undertake a few topical drawings for *Punch* but no more cartoons.

This did not mean he retired from drawing. He worked on illustrations for *Wild Goose* by Roland Pertwee, *Susan, Bill and the Wolf Dog* and *Susan, Bill and the Ivy Clad Oak* both by Malcolm Saville, and *The Brownies and Other Stories* by Mrs Ewing. Quite a substantial load of work for a gentleman of seventy-five!

In June he went by car to France with Eric Sheaf and upon his return found the text of Eleanor Farjeon's *The Glass Slipper* waiting for him to illustrate.

By the end of the year the Shepards had still not managed to find a suitable house into which they could move. For the whole year they had been house hunting.

In January 1955 they heard of a house in West Sussex at Lodsworth, a small village near Midhurst, only twenty-five miles south of Guildford. It proved to be very suitable and was duly purchased for £5,500. 'Long Meadow' was sold and on 3rd June they moved to 'Woodmancote'.

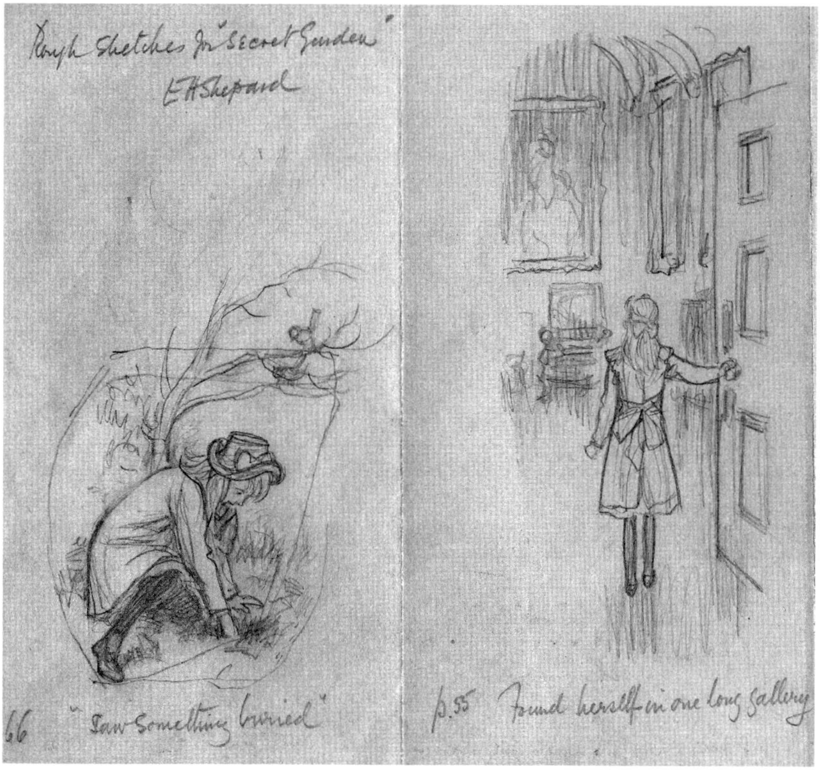

Rough sketches for The Secret Garden *(131)*

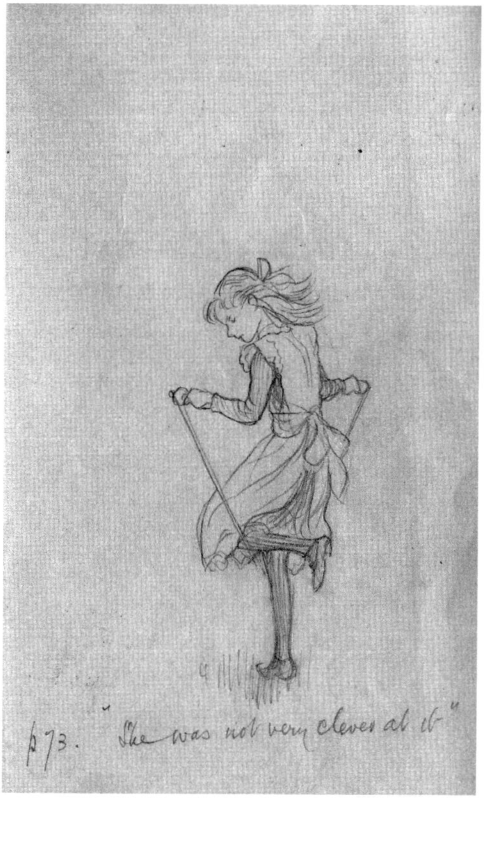

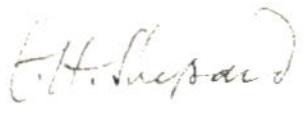

Chapter 11
Woodmancote 1955 - 1976

Norah and Ernest soon settled in at 'Woodmancote' and became part of the community. They went regularly to the church at Lodsworth for matins and he often read the lessons (132) (133).

He completed the illustrations for *The Glass Slipper* which was published soon after the move. He had settled in to his new routine by producing illustrations for *The Cuckoo Clock* by Mrs Molesworth, *Frogmorton* by Susan Colling, *Modern Fairy Tales* edited by R Lancelyn Green and two further books by Malcolm Saville, *Susan, Bill and the Vanishing Boy* and *Susan, Bill and the Vanishing Clock.*

Early in January 1956 Graham Chaplin, Pie's last surviving brother, died. This meant that all Pie's family of her generation had now departed. On the last day of the month A A Milne died. This caused great sadness to Shepard and made him realise not only the great effect that Milne had had on his life but also his own mortality.

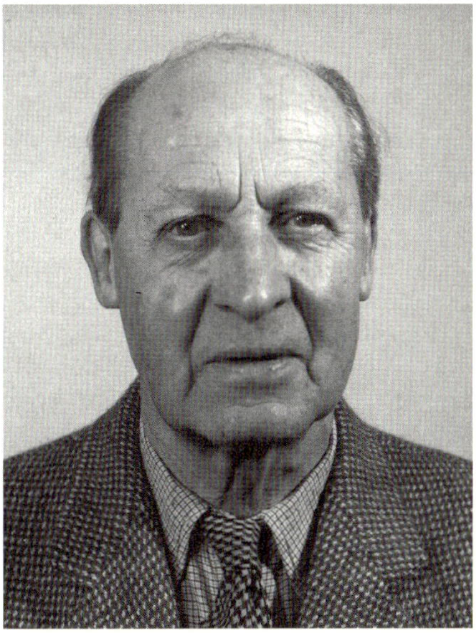

Ernest Shepard (132)

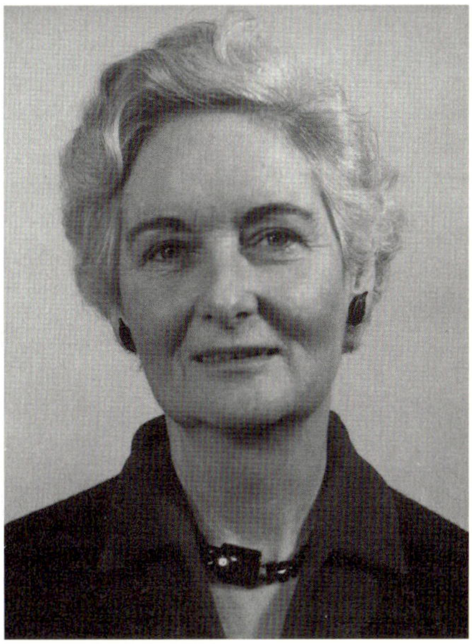

Norah Shepard (133)

Two more *Susan, Bill* books appeared in 1956 - one with the *Saucy Kate* and the other *The Dark Stranger.* Malcolm Saville wrote several interesting children's stories that Shepard loved to bring to life. For *The Secret Garden* by Frances Hodgson-Burnett he produced a series of well-known illustrations (131). *At the Back of the North Wind* by George MacDonald and *The Crystal Mountain* by B D Rugh were published with his illustrations. Going back to the past Shirley Gouldon produced a book called *Royal Reflections* where some of Shepard's beautiful drawings harkened back to his-own childhood with 'in shining ranks' and *Prince Bravo and the Silver Soldiers* (2).

On 14th June Minette, Ernest's only grandchild became engaged to Roger Hunt. Owing to the death of her father during the War Ernest had taken a very special interest in her upbringing and welfare.

It was now a year after settling in at 'Woodmancote' and Ernest realised that now was the time for him to keep his promise, made to Graham before he joined the Royal Navy. This promise haunted Ernest at the time of Graham's death and for years afterwards. He was pleased therefore to start on *Drawn from Memory* which recorded his life in the year 1887. In his hand-written notes about the book he wrote:

"I got on with my illustrations and writing my story. Frequently I made the drawings first, as I had such a vivid picture of the scene in my mind and then proceeded to write the words. I found this a most helpful way, but I had to recast the first three chapters as Norah found so many mistakes in my grammar which she had to correct before typing; she was very good and patient about it all and she typed the whole story herself."

In the first month of 1957 Ernest worked hard at the story and the illustrations while Norah constantly checked his grammar. He produced a coloured jacket, wrote a preface and sorted out a photograph of himself as a young boy in a velveteen suit and lace collar for the frontispiece.

When the manuscript was completed and, with the illustrations, was packed up to send to Methuen, he told Norah that he had dedicated the book to the memory of Graham. Norah had typed the manuscript, corrected grammar mistakes, and proof read it.

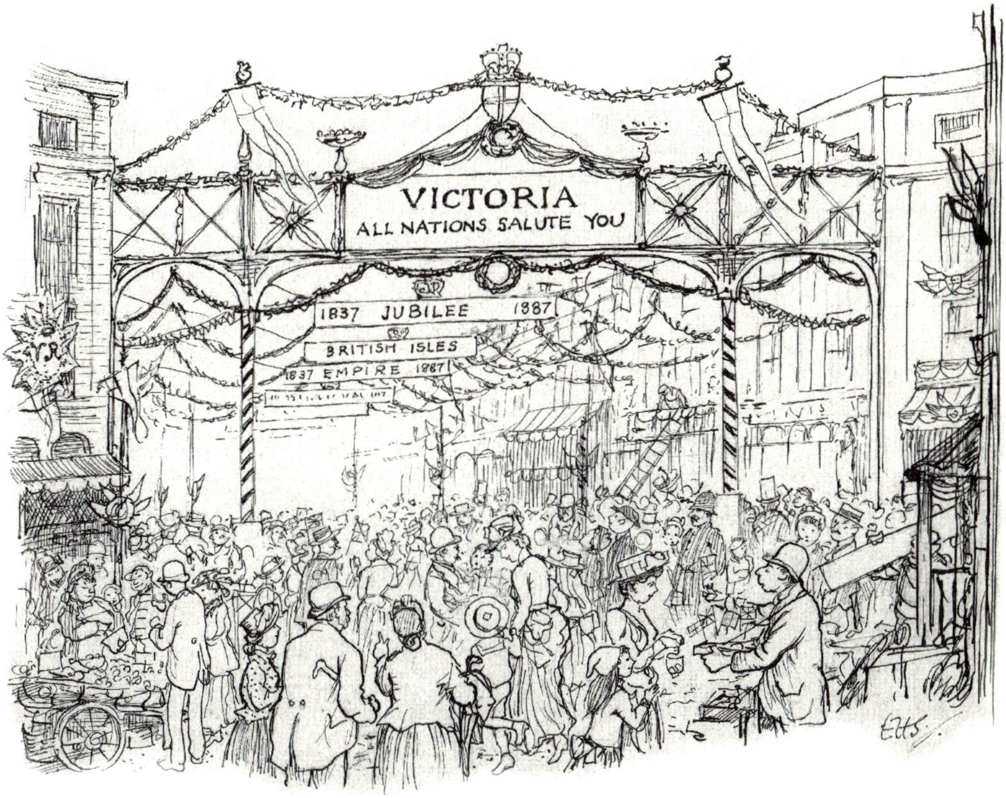

The Triumphal Archway for Queen Victoria's Golden Jubilee
Pen and ink drawing, c.1956 (134)

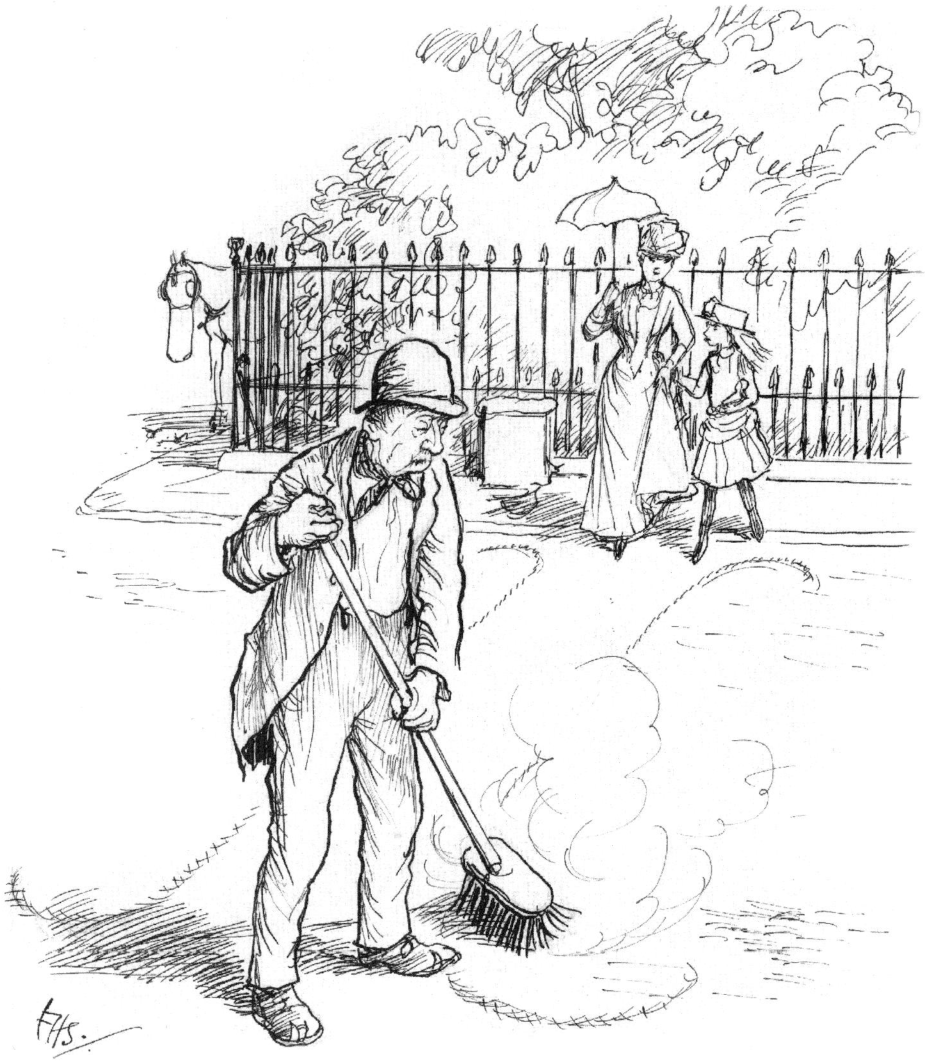

Swept the dust into neat heaps
Pen and ink drawing for Drawn from Memory *(135)*

She was deeply offended about the dedication and there followed a distressing scene at the end of which Norah left the house and did not return for over twenty-four hours. No mention of the situation was made upon her return and they were reconciled.

This event evidently shook Ernest Shepard considerably because he recorded it fully in his writing. He was a man who rarely expressed his personal feelings. He then sent the manuscript to Methuen and when it was published the dedication said "To My Wife Norah and to the Memory of My Son Graham".

He then immediately started work on a reader for Ginns called *Briar Rose*. He also went back to producing a few *Punch* headings for *Charivari* and started to draw pictures for a series of Greek stories.

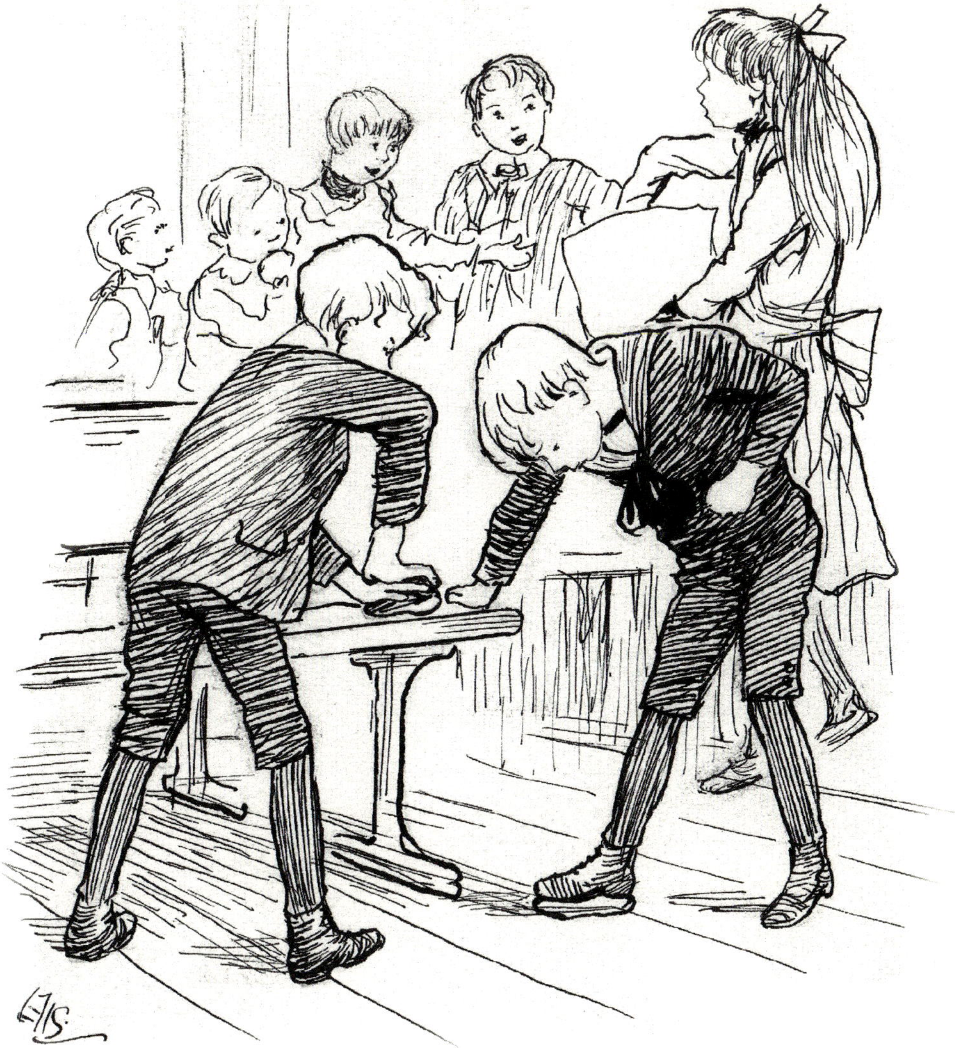

Duly flattened
Pen and ink drawing for Drawn from Memory *(136)*

Shepard was now to turn his attention to illustrating the Milne books in colour. *The World of Pooh,* an anthology, needed eight newly designed colour plates for publication by Dutton in the United States of America in 1957 and by Methuen in the following year.

Excitement was now accelerating in the family as his granddaughter's wedding was quickly approaching. In March Minette, her mother Ann and her future mother-in-law Betty Hunt went to 'Woodmancote' for a special fitting of Minette's wedding dress. In fact, Ernest and Norah went for short holiday to Malta in mid April but came back in time for Minette's marriage to Roger Hunt at Wonersh Church. On 27th April Ernest Shepard led the young bride down the aisle fully realising that she would be the only direct link between him and any future generation, as his daughter, Mary, was childless.

With these personal feelings Ernest returned to Kent Terrace where he had lived with his family until the age of 11 when his mother died and they had to live at Gordon Square with his aunts. He and Norah were accompanied by Gwen Morgan of *The New York Times* as apparently the visit was in connection with the forthcoming publication of *Drawn from Memory,* the first of his autobiographies. He had not seen the place for many years and was sorry to find that it looked extremely shabby. The iron railings around the garden had been replaced by a wire fence. Like most of London's railings they had been a casualty of war in an effort to get a supply of metal for planes and guns. It was a memorable visit for him, he was able to describe it in considerable detail and took photographs in order to record the day - a new approach for Shepard!

In September they went on holiday to Norwich and returned for the 26th, the long awaited publication day of *Drawn from Memory* (134) (135) (136). The book immediately attracted a great deal of attention and made people realise, for the first time, that Shepard was a pen and ink artist of the highest calibre in every subject and was a specialist outside the worlds of Pooh and *Punch.*

In the autumn of 1957 he had a 'Show' of his pictures at the Army and Navy Stores in Victoria. When at home he continued working on drawings including those for *Old Greek Fairy Tales* by R Lancelyn Green and his own Christmas card for the year.

In January 1958 the Shepards went on a voyage to the Amazon. On one journey in a small open bus their "fellow passengers were gay, coloured and friendly. This [friendly] was highly disapproved of by some of our fellow passengers especially Major........who considered we were letting the side down". Never missing an opportunity, Ernest drew a picture of the bus and its passengers. One of the group bought this picture from him at the end of the holiday. He also produced an article on their Amazon travels for *Punch*, the first and last time he ever 'wrote' for them!

He drew a further eight coloured plates for *The World of Christopher Robin,* a second Milne anthology, as a companion volume to the one published the previous year. At the same time he was working on *Drawn from Life,* another autobiographical book. He was determined to undertake more research and take more care with the preparation of this second volume in order to show that he was 'the' master of his art in line drawing. He had been looking for a picture of the Old Canterbury Music Hall and eventually found a print of it in Brixton Library in South London. As this exactly fitted his requirements he sat down and made a pencil copy.

Two afternoon parties were held for friends in July. The first was held at Milne's house on 6th, the second in Shepard's studio when some of his pictures were on show.

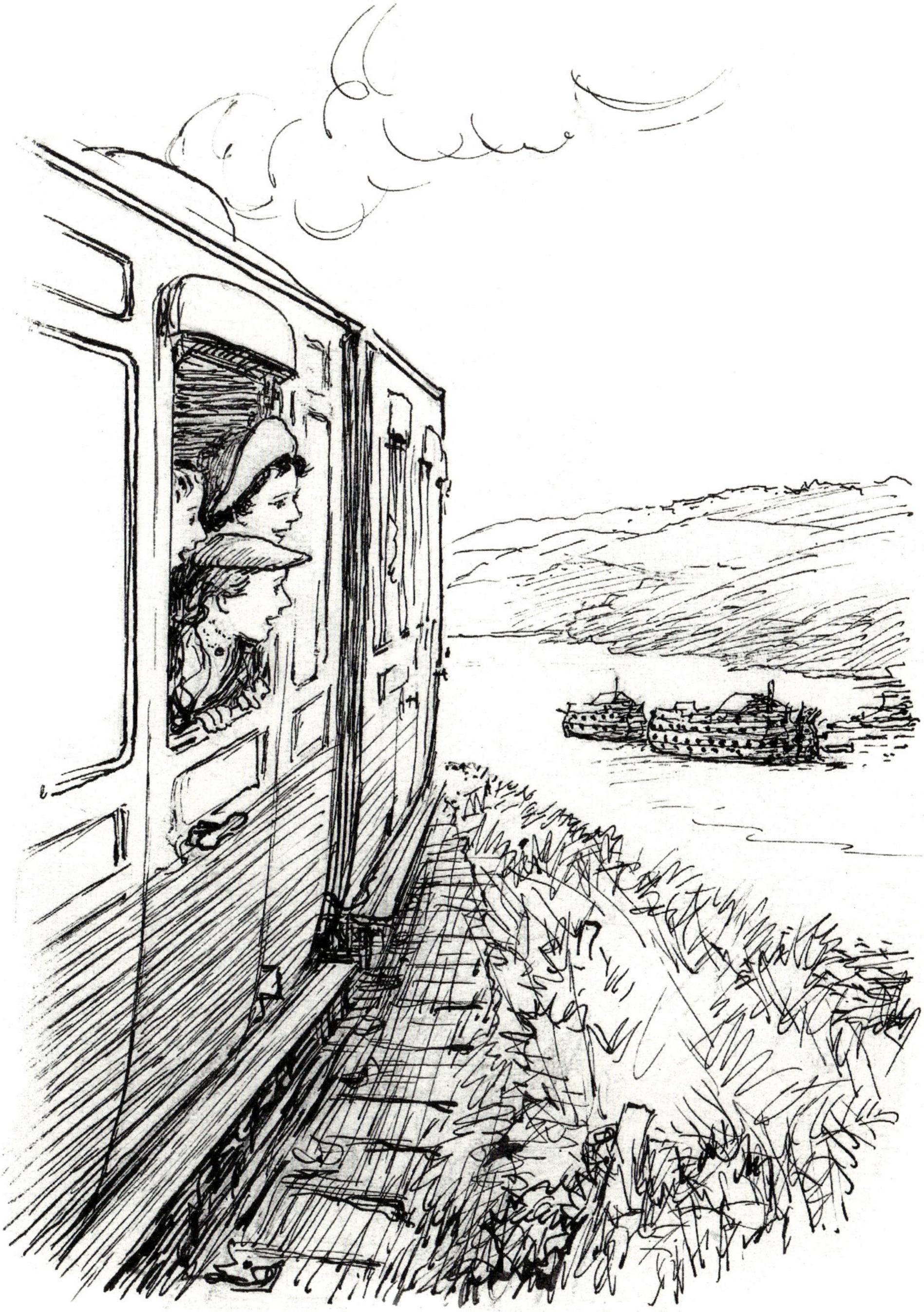

Leant from our carriage window and sang
Pen and ink drawing for Drawn from Life *(137)*

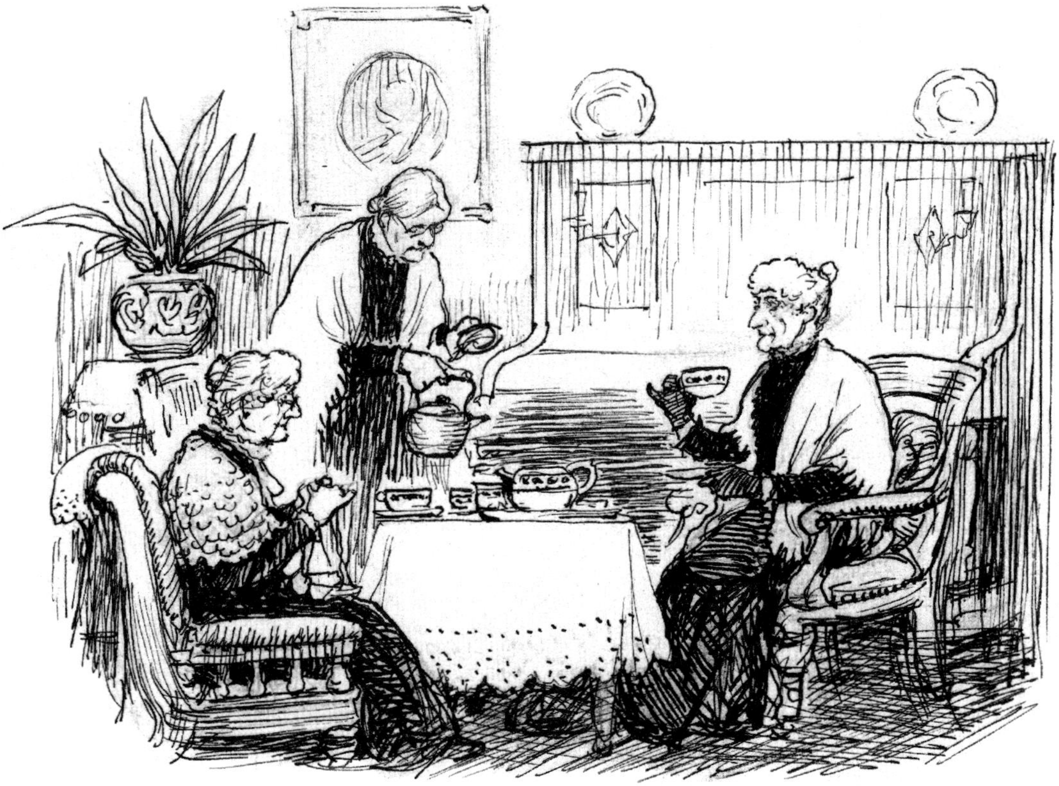

Two pen and ink drawings
from Drawn from Life *(138)*

In September they went to Rugby for a working holiday when Ernest was to complete his drawings for *Tom Brown's Schooldays* which he had recently been invited to illustrate. Upon their return he went to Foyles Gallery where he had arranged a 'Picture Show' of thirty of his drawings for the month of October. A further eight colour plates were then required for a new edition of *The Wind in the Willows*. Colour pictures were quickly becoming an essential element in the production of children's books.

Although there are now many translations in existence of *Winnie the Pooh* the first was in 1958 when Dr Alexander Leonard had a Latin version printed in Brazil for private distribution. Two years later Methuen agreed to publish it with the title *Winnie Ille Pu* and asked Shepard to create a specially designed dust jacket with Pooh dressed as a Roman Centurion and Piglet as a Legion Standard Bearer. This first was on sale in England in 1961 and later followed by *Domus Anguli Puensis (The House at Pooh Corner).* These two volumes are now a 'must' for many sixth form classics students.

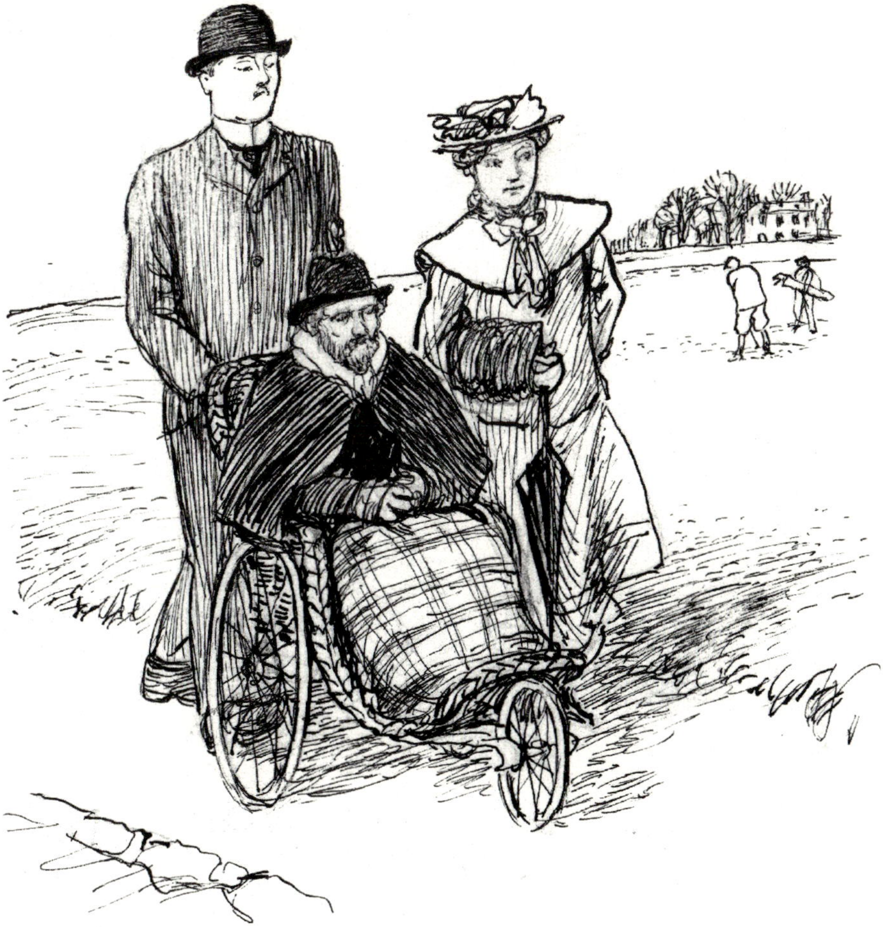

The Shepards made two interesting overseas trips in 1960. The first was in April to Greece where Ernest made numerous chalk sketches of the ancient sites including the Acropolis and Olympia. It was during this holiday that they went to Treviso airport from which, forty-three years previously, Ernest had had his first flight on duty during the Great War.

The second trip during September was to Denmark where he sketched for a new edition of *Hans Andersen's Fairy Tales* which had been commissioned by the Oxford University Press two months before.

The contract for *Drawn from Life* was signed with Methuen on 8th March 1961 after which Ernest and Norah had another holiday in Amsterdam to complete the work for the *Hans Andersen* book.

The summer months found Ernest drawing for *The Tatler*, illustrating another school reader, *A Noble Company,* for Ginn and various revision sketches of Pooh. He took great pains to paint a large map of Seven Acre Wood for a special presentation to the Philadelphia Library.

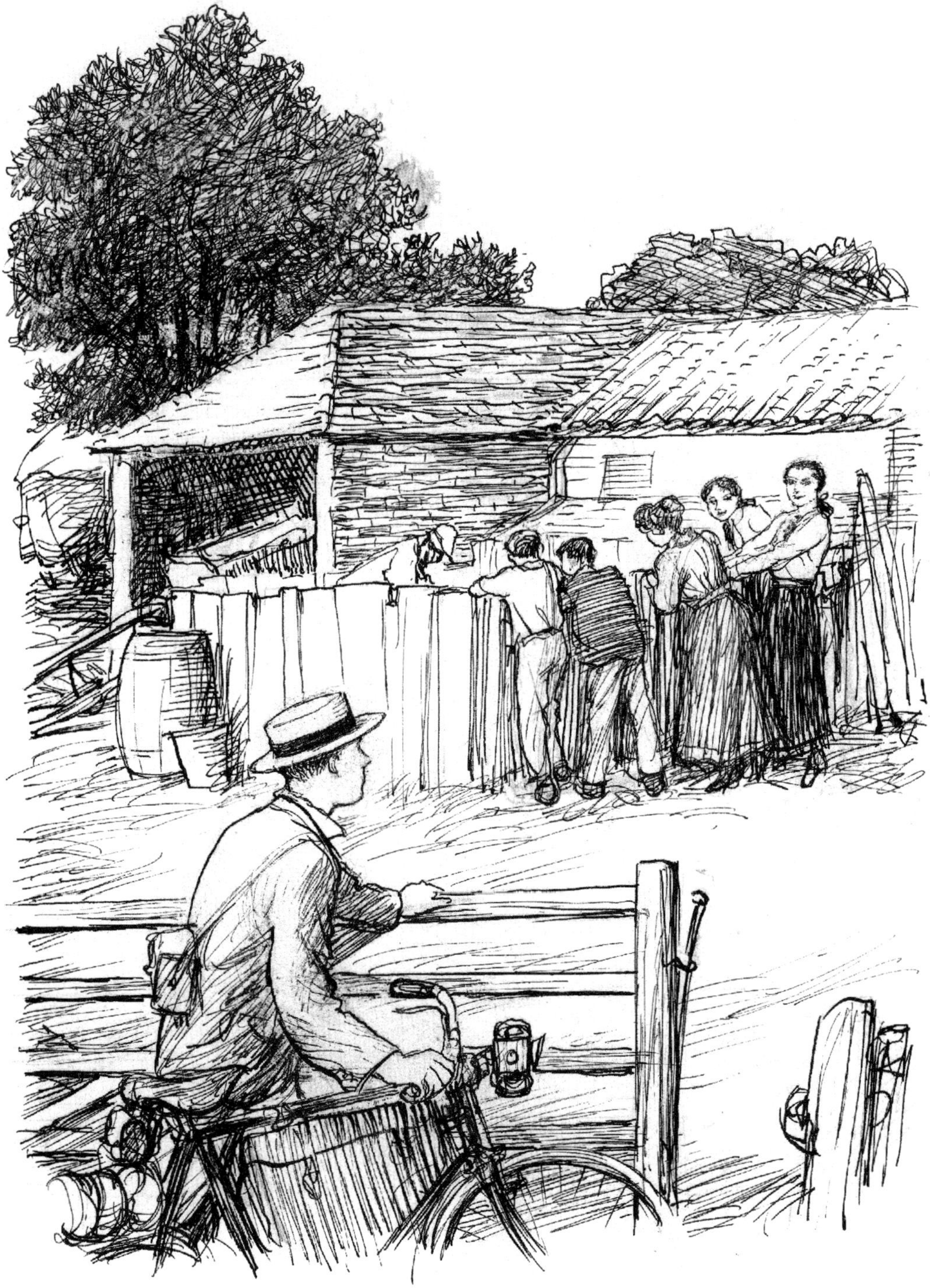

A litter of pigs
Pen and ink drawing for Drawn from Life *(139)*

Within his personal life he looked to the past and to the future. In May he visited Pie's grave at Shamley Green and on it planted a picotee carnation. In June he started a portrait of Norah of which he wrote "it is very bad but she is difficult to paint".

On 26th October *Drawn from Life* was published. This book covers the period from the death of his mother in 1890, when he was only eleven years old, until his marriage to Pie in 1904. The extra care taken during the four-year preparation of this volume proved worthwhile. The standard of the drawings is faultless and the words not only tell of Shepard's private life but also act as a textbook for the social life at the turn of the last century (137) (138) (139).

At the same time *Hans Andersen's Fairy Tales* was also published and brought to life the traditional Danish stories with line illustrations that had been executed in locations where Andersen had told the stories.

The pace of Ernest's life was slowing down. In 1962 he made a broadcast for the BBC, created a cover design for *Our Parish Magazine* and produced sketches for *The Flattered Flying Fish* by E V Rieu. His private life went from elation to despair. Elation is shown in his diary at the birth of his great-granddaughter Arabella on 26th July with her christening on 6th October. Despair is recorded with such entries as "very painful knee - in bed" and, on 21st December, "birthday [83rd]. Knee treated at Guildford Hospital".

Norah travelled to Tasmania to see her brother and his family in January 1963. Remaining at home, Ernest declined a book commission from Elliat Macrae mainly because of his bad knee which was extremely painful in spite of treatment. His right hand was also causing trouble and giving him some pain. He did, however, partly to cheer himself up, agree to undertake some sketches for *The Pooh Birthday Book* and revised drawings for *The Wind in the Willows*. At one stage, before Norah came home on 1st March, his housekeeper was unwell so he arranged to stay at 'The Angel' in Midhurst.

Once Norah had returned they settled into a quiet life at 'Woodmancote', but Ernest's health meant that they had many visits to the hospital for a cardiograph and other tests. Eventually in October he was given an encouraging verdict and put on tablets for the rest of his life, that is for a further thirteen years.

With this diagnosis behind him Ernest organised a studio exhibition for local church funds in November and he and Norah went to Israel in December where they painted by the Sea of Galilee and sketched in Capernaum.

During the following year Shepard had been working on coloured drawings for Duttons, jacket designs for paperbacks to be issued by Methuen, and had accepted the Macrae commission for twenty drawings for a new *Pooh* series that he had declined previously. He had always wanted to write stories as well as illustrate them and now found the time to work on two ideas that he had had in mind for some years.

In October, with posterity in mind, he donated his Charles Keane easel to the Haslemere Museum. He had a tablet fixed to the easel. He also gave them the throne which he had used for his models. After the presentation he arranged for an exhibition of his work at the Museum in May of the following year.

On 9th March 1965 he and Norah drove to Alfriston which Ernest knew so well. It was there that his father had found the partly ruined church house. His father had caused this to be restored and handed over as the first building to be owned by the National Trust which previously had taken only land under its wing (140).

In May the weekly Wednesday lunch at the *Punch* Table, since the foundation of the magazine, was changed to once a month. In the other weeks morning coffee would be served in the offices at 11am when the cartoons would be discussed.

In the mid-sixties the copyright on all the Pooh characters was sold to the Disney Corporation and thus the merchandise which can now be purchased in various forms all over the world bears the Disney copyright as an imprint.

The first of his 'own' stories, *Ben and Brock,* was published in 1965. This was the story of a young boy, Ben, and his friend, Brock the badger. The badger family have other animal friends and the reader follows their underground and above ground life. Children love to read about animals in 'human situations', they can equate themselves to the subjects. The line drawings are all in black and white and, at the time of publication, it was a great success (141) (142) (143) (144).

In 1966 the second of his own stories *Betsy and Joe* was published. Betsy is a squirrel and Joe is a tramp. This tells how they shared meals and adventures together. The tramp, as recorded in Shepard's book, was a dying breed when the book was written and therefore the pull on the child readers in the mid sixties was less meaningful. The drawings of the countryside and the portrayal of the villages and fields are a historic record of the time (145) (146) (147).

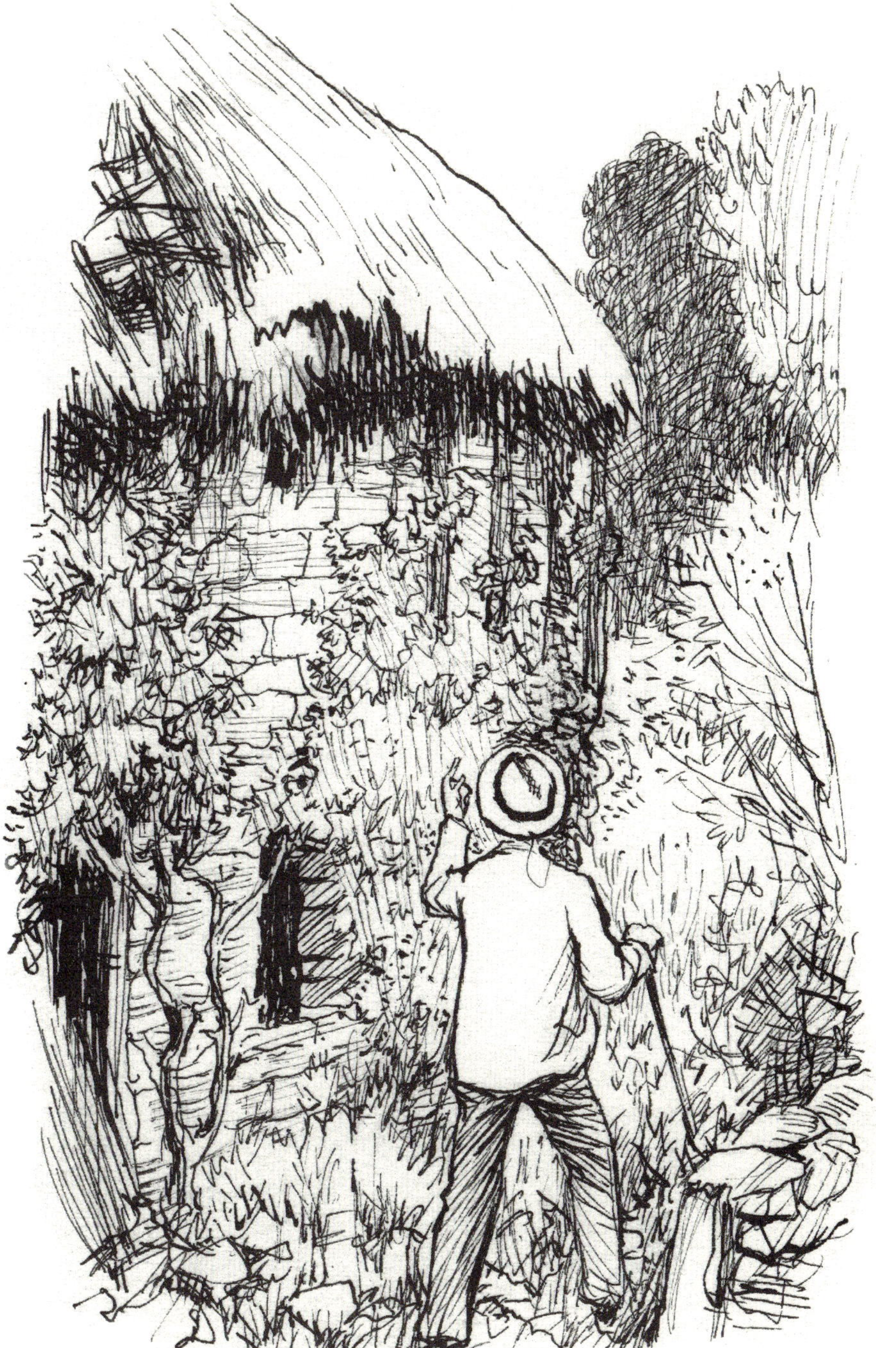

Ruined church house, Alfriston
Pen and ink drawing for Drawn from Life *(140)*

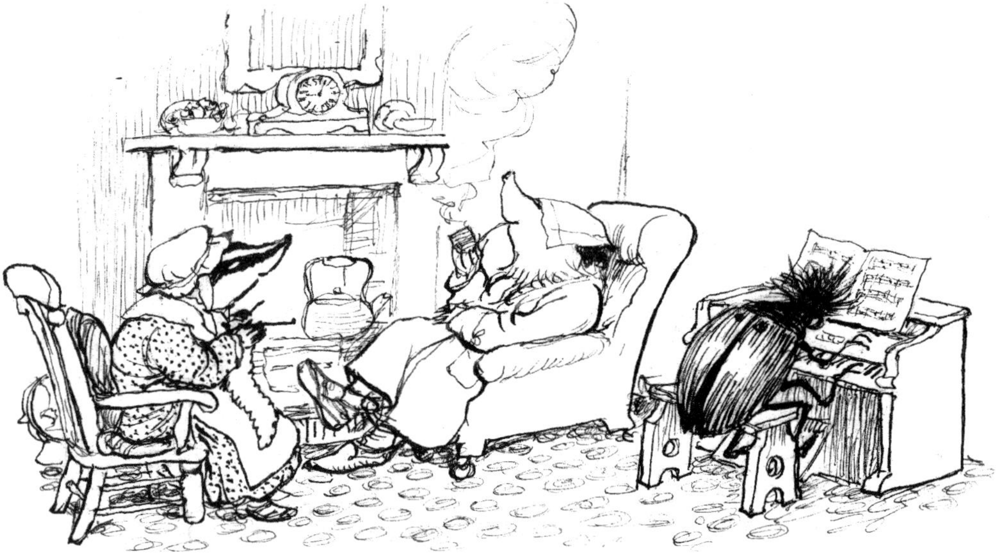

A new house and a harmonium (141)

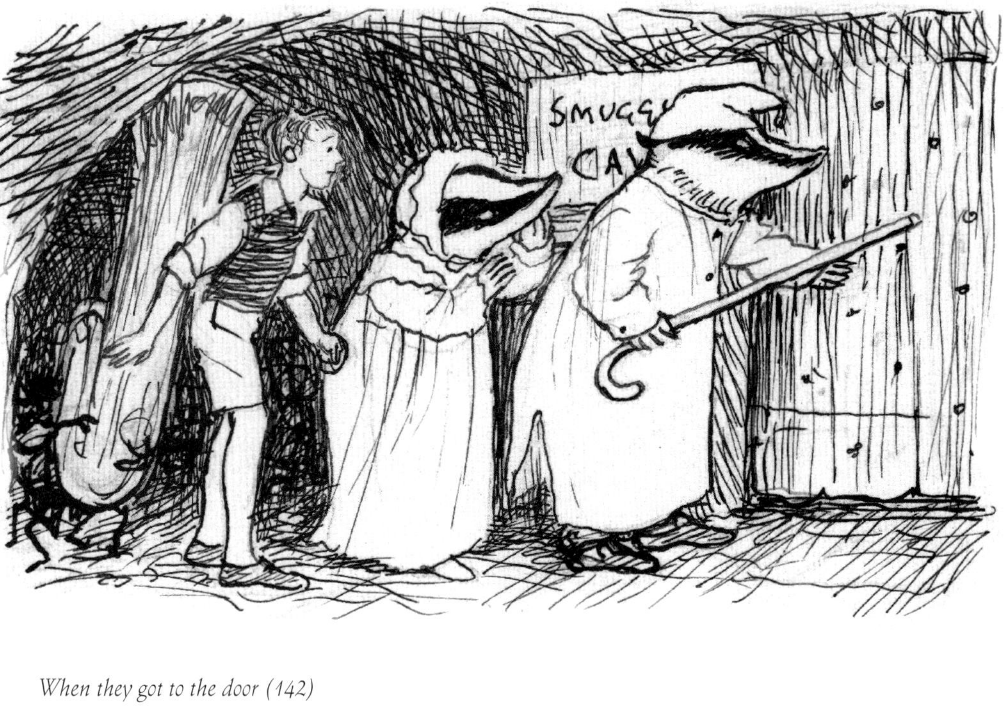

When they got to the door (142)

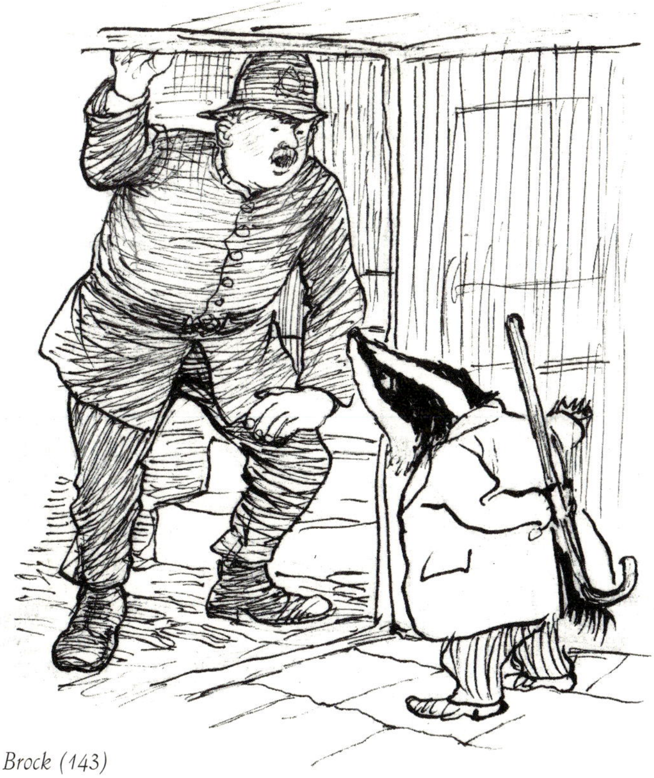

Good morning Mr Brock (143)

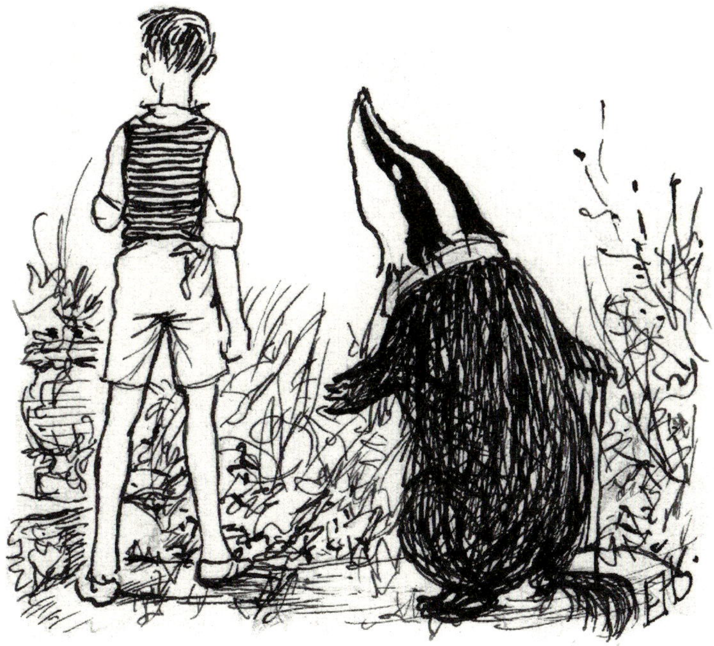

Now alas, I can't afford to keep up the place (144)

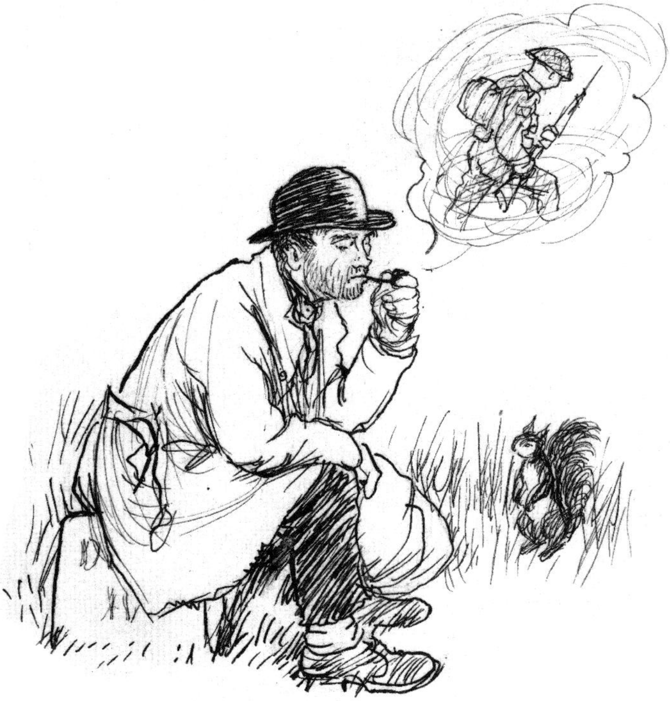

Took to the road, and 'ere I am (145)

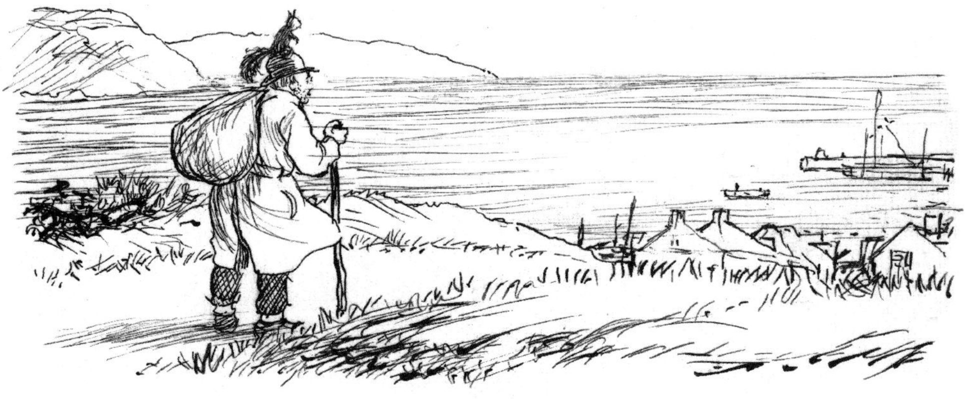

Climbed on his hat (146)

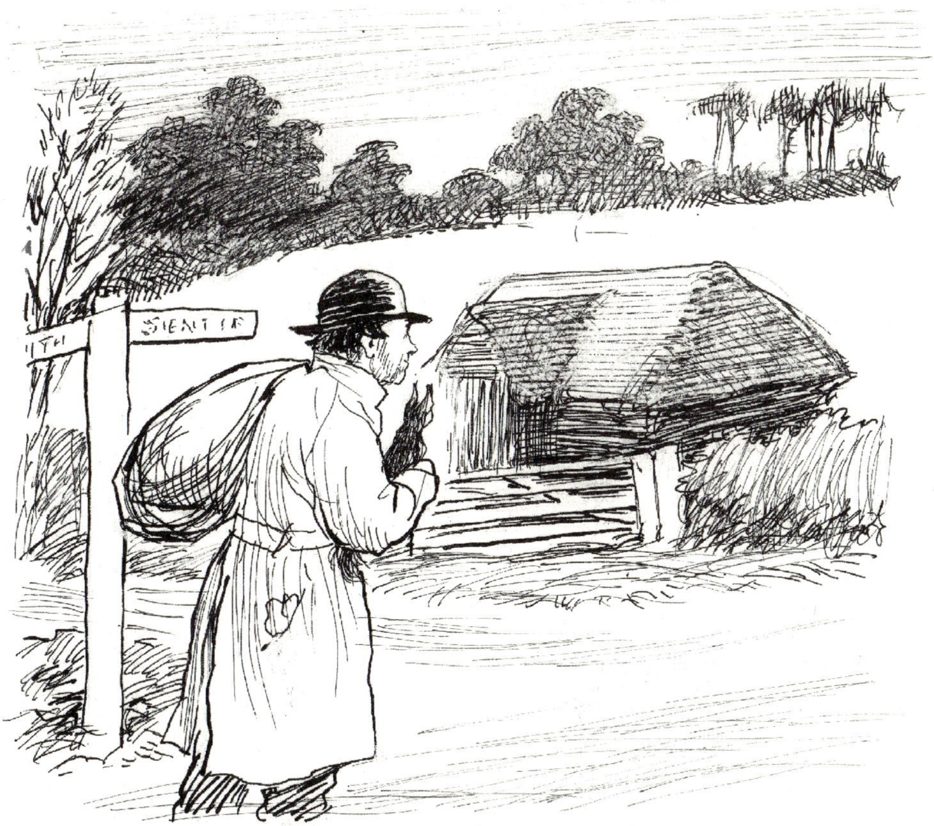

Came to a crossroads (147)

Giles Hunt, Minette's son and Ernest's great-grandson, was christened in March 1966.

During the year Ernest had coloured some of the sketches for the Milne poems and produced a cover for *The Pooh Cook Book* (P.7). He said "it was rather fun doing it for Duttons gave me a free hand". Duttons were the American publishers for the Pooh books. On 4th September Pooh's fortieth birthday was celebrated.

Locally, Ernest became very involved in church affairs. He read the lesson at most of the services, sat on church committees and was involved in hospitality for visitors to the parish. In July of the following year he was detailed to receive Lynda Bird Johnson, daughter of the American President, accompanied by Lady Bessborough and two security guards when they came to see his drawings at Lodsworth. He gave each of them a Pooh sketch. Two years later Lady Bird Johnson, the President's wife, came for what was described locally as 'a royal visit'. Shepard presented the First Lady of America with an original drawing.

Such a gift was not just special for this occasion. Throughout his life he enjoyed visitors especially children and it seems that they never left without a sketch that he had specially drawn or one that he would say was "no longer wanted". These drawings became investments for the young children and it is often their grandchildren who send these 'investments' to the London auction houses to realise their assets.

From December 1967 until April the following year they went on a voyage to Tasmania where at Devonport they were greeted at the boat by Norah's family and local reporters. He sketched and painted while there and also throughout his return journey on board.

Once home he went straight to work on drawings for Dents, the publisher, although in June it was decided he would no longer drive.

At about this time Ernest and Norah discussed whether the Pooh pencil drawings should be offered to the Victoria and Albert Museum. This offer was made and accepted by the Museum in April 1969. In the previous month Methuen had informed him that they would like a full colour edition of *The Wind in the Willows*. He worked on this daily and by June the work was almost complete and, in fact, was published later in the year. At the same time Methuen told him they wanted the same treatment for *Winnie the Pooh*!

On 10th December 1969 a luncheon was given at the Garrick Club by the Directors of Methuen to celebrate his 90th birthday. The menu contained drawings of many of his wonderful characters from *The Wind in the Willows, Winnie the Pooh* and *The House at Pooh Corner.* Norah was present at the celebration and signed the menu card as did other guests present (148) (149).

In March 1970 he auctioned some of his original drawings and made five thousand pounds after which he went to Ireland where he relaxed and spent many days just painting by the sea. When he came home again in May it was decided to install a new security system at the house, presumably following the publicity of the value of the drawings that had been sold at the auction.

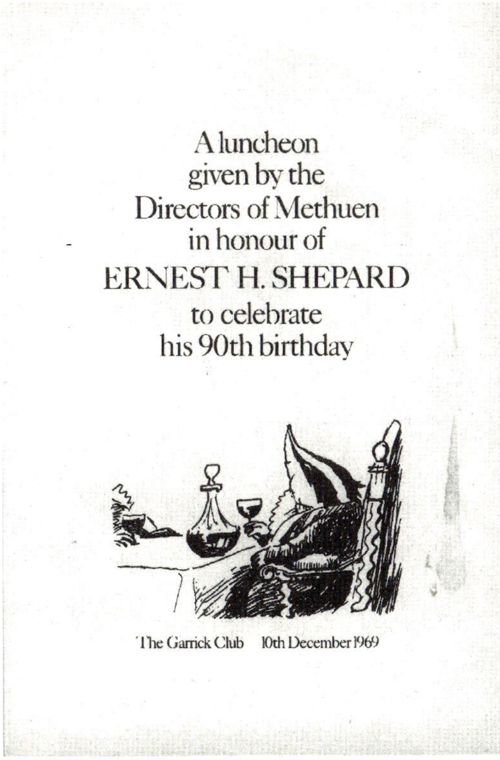
A luncheon
given by the
Directors of Methuen
in honour of
ERNEST H. SHEPARD
to celebrate
his 90th birthday

The Garrick Club 10th December 1969

Luncheon menu cover (148)

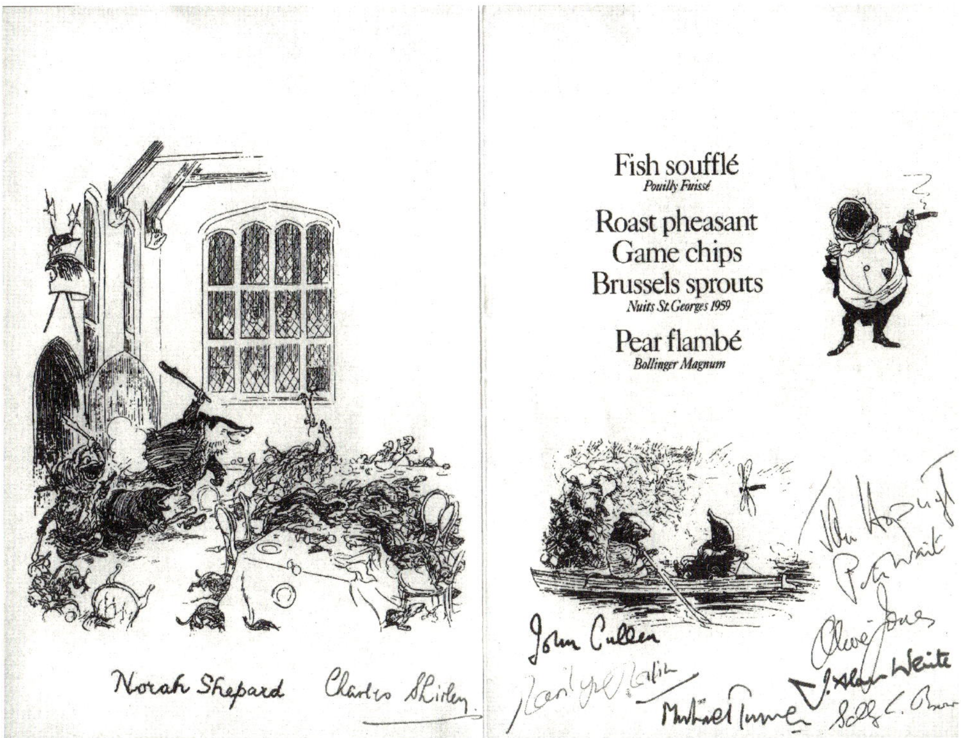
Fish soufflé
Pouilly Fuissé
Roast pheasant
Game chips
Brussels sprouts
Nuits St. Georges 1959
Pear flambé
Bollinger Magnum

Menu and signatures (149)

On two consecutive pages of the notebook that he was using in 1970 Shepard drew two sketches of a 'Pooh Orchestra'. They were drawn in ink and painted in watercolour. The first page shows Piglet playing the timpani, a triangle and a double base. The second page shows Eeyore with a euphonium. These two paintings were signed and dated in ink and then 'Ernest H Shepard, November 1970'. This means that he was still painting eighty-three years after his watercolour of Whiteleys Fire painted in 1887. These paintings were unknown until August 1997 when they were found by one of the archivists on a routine check of the contents of the notebooks (P.8).

In December he signed an agreement with Methuen to reprint *Drawn from Memory* the following year. In the Queen's Birthday Honours List of 1972 he was appointed an officer of 'The Most Excellent Order of the British Empire'. In April 1974 E H Shepard visited Surrey University and gave to the Vice Chancellor the residue of his drawings, his manuscripts (including *Drawn from Memory* and *Drawn from Life),* his diaries, memorabilia and all his papers.

On 24th March 1976 Ernest Howard Shepard died at Midhurst in Sussex, aged 96 years, fifty years after the first publication of *Winnie the Pooh.*

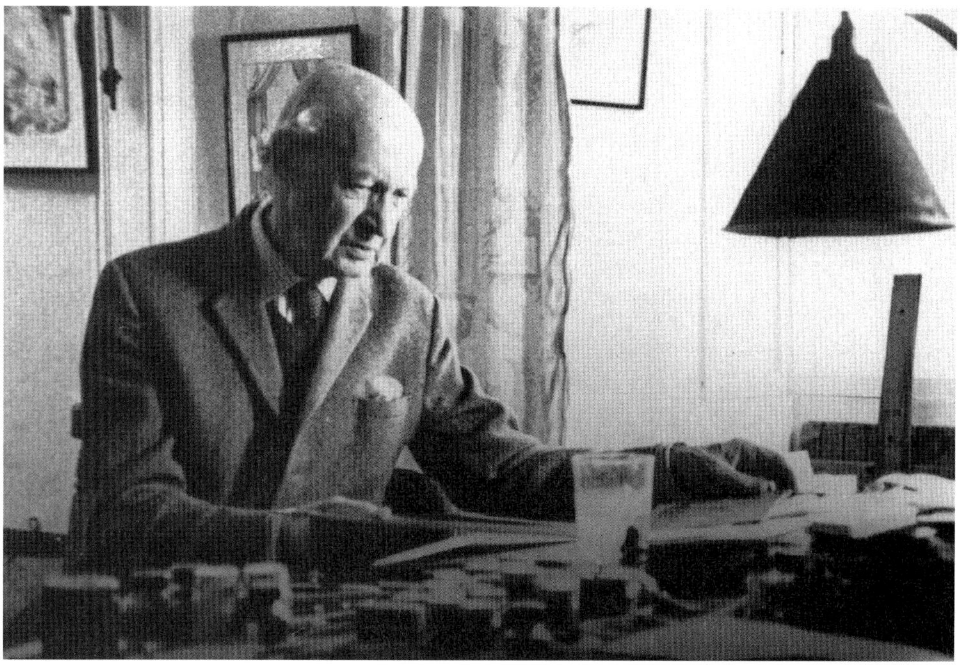

Ernest Shepard in his study at Woodmancote (150)

E.H. Shepard

LIST OF COLOUR PLATES

End papers are a copy of a map painted by E H Shepard for the use of his Home Guard Company in 1940

E.H. Shepard

LIST OF BLACK AND WHITE ILLUSTRATIONS

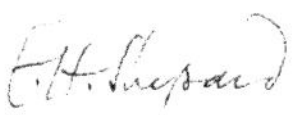

CHRONOLOGY OF SHEPARD'S LIFE

from The Shepard Archive at The University of Surrey

1879 E.H.S. born in St John's Wood
Educated at St Paul's School

1894 Family spent the summer at Shalford, south of Guildford, in a rented Vicarage. 50 years previously E.H.S's grandfather had built his family seat at Guildown.

1897 Studied at Heatherleys and Royal Academy Schools

1901 First picture exhibited at Royal Academy.
Studio at Glebe Place, Chelsea, until 1903

1904 Married Florence Chaplin
Moved to Arden Cottage, Shamley Green (later known as Rose Cottage)

1906 First drawing accepted for *Punch*

1907 Son, Graham, born

1909 Daughter, Mary, born
E.H.S. and family move to Red Cottage, Hulbrook Lane, Shamley Green. Studio remains there

1915 E.H.S. commissioned in Royal Artillery.
Served at Battles of the Somme, Arras, and 3rd Ypres Awarded M.C.

1916 Served in Italy, Montello and Asiago

1919 Finished service as a Major

1921 Joined staff of *Punch*

1924 Commissioned to illustrate:
When We Were Very Young (published same year)
Winnie the Pooh
Now We Are Six
The House at Pooh Corner

1925 *Playtime and Company*
Holly Tree, etc

1926 *Winnie the Pooh*
Everybody's Pepys

1927 E.H.S's wife Florence died
Jeremy
Little One's Log
Let's Pretend
Now We Are Six
Fun and Fantasy

1928 Shepard family moved to Long Meadow at Longdown
The House at Pooh Corner
The Golden Age

1930 *Everybody's Boswell*
Dream Days

1931 *Wind in the Willows (*Kenneth Grahame)
Christmas Poems (Drinkwater)
Bevis

1932 Son Graham married Ann Gibbon
Sycamore Square

1933 *Everybody's Lamb*
The Cricket in the Cage

1934 *Victoria Regina* (Laurence Housman)

1935 *Perfume from Provence* (Lady Fortescue)

1936 *Modern Struwelpeter*

1937 Daughter Mary married E V Knox, editor of *Punch*
Graham and Ann Shepard's daughter, Minette, born
Golden Sovereign (Laurence Housman)
Cheddar Gorge
As The Bee Sucks (E V Lucas)

1939 Captain of Home Guard outside Guildford
The Reluctant Dragon

1941 *Gracious Majesty* (Laurence Housman)

1943 Graham Shepard died at sea

1944 E.H.S. married second wife Norah Carroll

1948 *Golden Age* and *Dream Days* (Kenneth Grahame) published for Book of the Month Club in New York
Bertie's Escapade (Kenneth Grahame)

1951 *Enter David Garrick* (Anna B Stewart) published in U.S.A.

1953 *Silver Curlew* (Eleanor Farjeon)

1954 *Cuckoo Clock* (Mrs Molesworth)
Susan, Bill and the Wolf-dog (Malcolm Saville)

1955 Moved to 'Woodmancote', Lodsworth, West Sussex
Glass Slipper (Eleanor Farjeon)
Operation Wild Goose (Roland Pertwee)
Crystal Mountain (B. D. Rugh) published in U.S.A.
Frogmorton (Susan Colling)
The Brownies (Mrs Ewing)

1956 *The Islanders* (Roland Pertwee)
The Pancake (Child?s Reader)

1957 *Drawn from Memory* (Autobiography of early boyhood)
Briar Rose (Child's Reader)

1958 *Old Greek Fairy Tales*

1959 *Tom Brown's School Days* (Thomas Hughes)

1960 *Noble Company* (Child's Reader)

1961 *Drawn from Life* (A further autobiography)
Hans Andersen's Fairy Tales

1965 *Ben and Brock*

1966 *Betsy and Joe*

1969 Illustrations in colour for new edition of:
The Wind in the Willows
Coloured cover for *The Pooh Cook Book* (U.S.A.)

1970 Illustrations in colour for new editions of:
Winnie the Pooh
House at Pooh Corner

1971 Coloured cover for *The Pooh Party Book* (U.S.A.)

1972 Appointed O.B.E.

1974 In April E.H.S. visited Surrey University and gave to the Vice Chancellor the residue of his drawings, his diaries, manuscripts, memorabilia and other papers

1976 Died 24 March at Midhurst, Sussex, aged 96 years, fifty years after the first publication of *Winnie the Pooh.*

E.H. Shepard

SHEPARD ARCHIVE, UNIVERSITY OF SURREY

List of books known to have been written and/or illustrated by E.H.S.
*We knowingly hold illustrations for items marked ***
*Where we have very few it is marked **
There are many drawings for which we have not yet been able to allocate to a known publication.
We believe we have material from publications marked #.

1906 onwards - *Punch***

1915 *The Chartered Company* (Nelson)

1924 *When We Were Very Young**

1925 *Playtime and Company#*
Holly Tree, etc

1926 *Winnie the Pooh**
*Everybody's Pepys**

1927 *Jeremy*
*Little One's Log***
*Let's Pretend**
*Now We Are Six**
*Fun and Fantasy**

1928 *The House at Pooh Corner **
The Golden Age

1930 *Everybody's Boswell **
Dream Days#

1931 *The Wind in the Willows* (Kenneth Grahame)
Christmas Poems
Bevis
Mother Goose

1932 *Sycamore Square* (Jan Struther)

1933 *Everybody's Lamb **
The Cricket in the Cage

1934	*Victoria Regina* (Laurence Housman)
1936	*Modern Struwelpeter*
1937	*Golden Sovereign* (Laurence Housman) *Cheddar Gorge*
1937	*As the Bee Sucks* (E V Lucas) *Extra Perfume from Provence* (Lady Fortescue)
1939	*The Reluctant Dragon*
1941	*Gracious Majesty* (Laurence Housman)
1948	*Golden Age* and *Dream Days* (Kenneth Grahame) published for Book of the Month Club in New York *Bertie's Escapade* (Kenneth Grahame)
1949	*York*
1950	*Drover's Tale*
1951	*Enter David Garrick* (Anna B Stewart) published in U.S.A.
1953	*Silver Curlew* (Eleanor Farjeon)*
1954	*Cuckoo Clock* (Mrs Molesworth) *Susan, Bill and the Wolf-dog* (Malcolm Saville)
1955	*Glass Slipper* (Eleanor Farjeon) # *Operation Wild Goose* (Roland Pertwee) *Crystal Mountain* (B. D. Rugh) published in U.S.A. *Frogmorton* (Susan Colling) *The Brownies* (Mrs Ewing)
1956	*The Islanders* (Roland Pertwee) *The Pancake* (Child's Reader)
1957	*Drawn from Memory* (Autobiography of early boyhood)** *Briar Rose* (Child's Reader)#
1958	*Old Greek Fairy Tales*

1959 *Tom Brown's School Days* (Thomas Hughes) #

1960 *Noble Company* (Child's Reader)

1961 *Drawn from Life* (A further autobiography)**
Hans Andersen's Fairy Tales

1965 *Ben and Brock***

1966 *Betsy and Joe***

1969 Illustrations in colour for new edition of:
Wind in the Willows

1969 Coloured cover for:
The Pooh Cook Book published in U.S.A.**

1970 Illustrations in colour for new editions of:
Winnie the Pooh
House at Pooh Corner

1971 Coloured cover for:
The Pooh Party Book published in U.S.A.

We believe that the following books were written and/or illustrated by E.H.S. (Dates unknown)

David Copperfield (Nelson edition)

*Prince Bravo and the Silver Soldiers***

*Silver Rose**

Roman Road *

*Two Million Bananas**

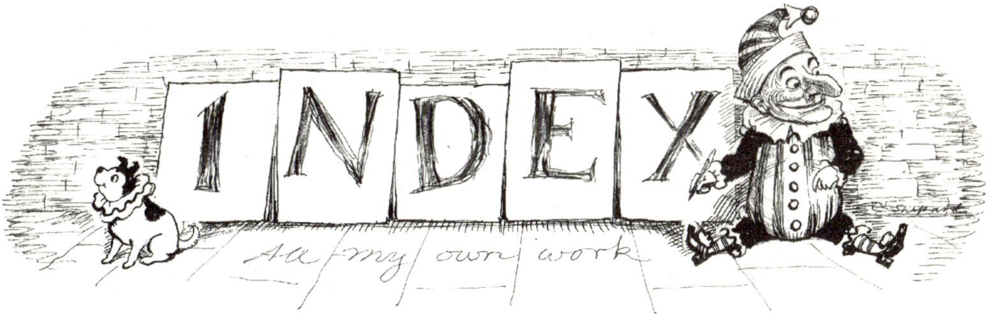

E H SHEPARD INDEX
compiled by Valerie Lewis Chandler

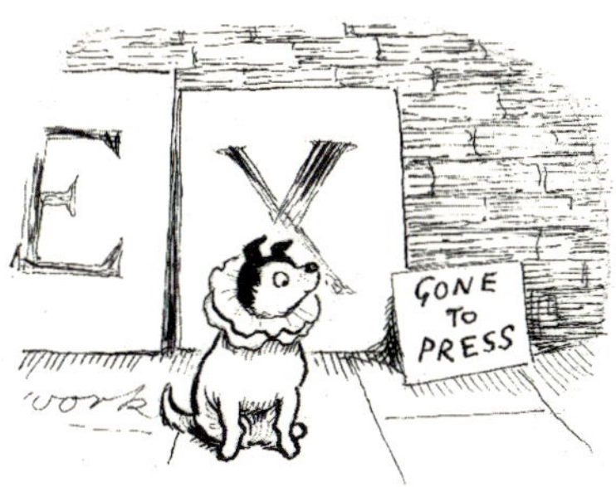
GONE TO PRESS

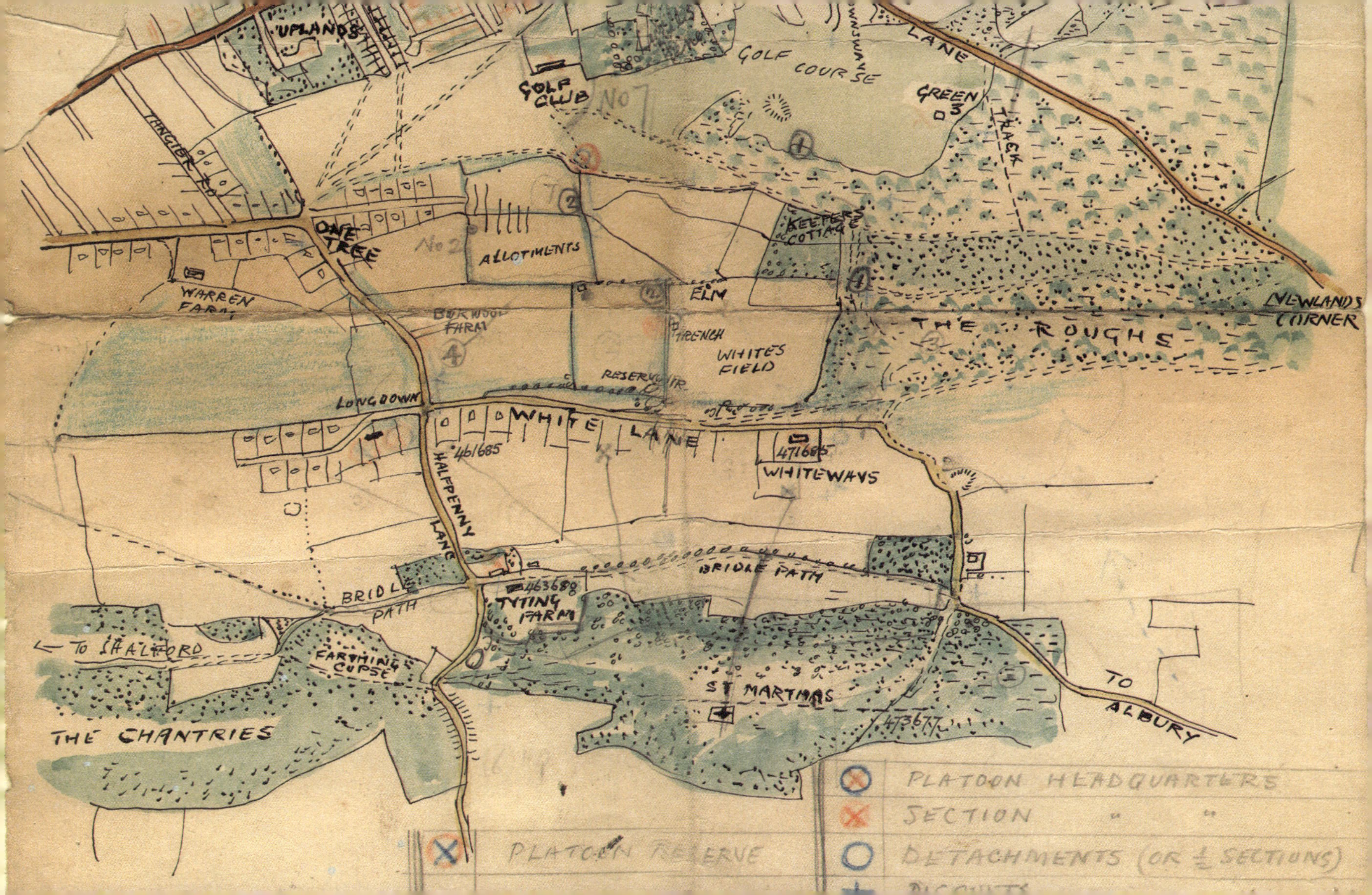
UPLANDS
GOLF CLUB
No 7
GOLF COURSE
LANE
GREEN 3
TRACK
TANGIER RD
ONE TREE
No 2
ALLOTMENTS
KEEPERS COTTAGE
WARREN FARM
ELM
NEWLANDS CORNER
BERWOOD FARM
TRENCH
WHITES FIELD
THE ROUGHS
RESERVOIR
LONGDOWN
WHITE LANE
461685
471685
WHITEWAYS
HALFPENNY LANE
BRIDLE PATH
463688
TYTING FARM
← TO SHALFORD
FARTHING COPSE
ST MARTHAS
TO ALBURY
THE CHANTRIES
473677
PLATOON HEADQUARTERS
SECTION " "
PLATOON RESERVE
DETACHMENTS (OR ½ SECTIONS)